Environmental, Social, and Governance Investment: Opportunities and Risks for Asia

ASIAN DEVELOPMENT BANK INSTITUTE

ISBN 978-4-89974-205-0 (Print)
ISBN 978-4-89974-206-7 (PDF)

The views in this publication do not necessarily reflect the views and policies of the Asian Development Bank Institute (ADBI), its Advisory Council, ADB's Board or Governors, or the governments of ADB members.

ADBI does not guarantee the accuracy of the data included in this publication and accepts no responsibility for any consequence of their use. ADBI uses proper ADB member names and abbreviations throughout and any variation or inaccuracy, including in citations and references, should be read as referring to the correct name.

By making any designation of or reference to a particular territory or geographic area, or by using the term "recognize," "country," or other geographical names in this publication, ADBI does not intend to make any judgments as to the legal or other status of any territory or area.

Users are restricted from reselling, redistributing, or creating derivative works without the express, written consent of ADBI.

The Asian Development Bank recognizes "China" as the People's Republic of China, "Korea" as the Republic of Korea, and "Vietnam" as Viet Nam.

Note: In this publication, "$" refers to US dollars.

Asian Development Bank Institute
Kasumigaseki Building 8F
3-2-5, Kasumigaseki, Chiyoda-ku
Tokyo 100-6008, Japan
www.adbi.org

Contents

Tables and Figures

Figures

List of Contributors

Abdul Aziz is a researcher at the Fiscal Policy Agency, Ministry of Finance of the Republic of Indonesia.

Toshikazu Hayashi is a chief analyst at Nissay Asset Management, Japan.

Yasuyuki Kato is director of the Money Design Research Institute, a research professor at Tokyo Metropolitan University, and visiting professor at Kyoto University, Japan.

Upalat Korwatanasakul is an assistant professor at the School of Social Sciences, Waseda University, Japan.

Lian Liu is a research associate at the Asian Development Bank Institute, Japan.

Muhammad Ayub Mehar is a professor at Iqra University in Karachi, Pakistan.

Peter J. Morgan is a senior consulting economist and vice chair for research at the Asian Development Bank Institute, Japan.

Naoko Nemoto is a financial economist at the Asian Development Bank Institute, Japan.

Miyu Otsuka is a graduate of the Graduate School of Economics, Keio University, Japan.

Kiyotaka Sasaki is a visiting professor at Hitotsubashi University, and former Director-General of the Strategy Development and Management Bureau, Financial Services Agency, Japan.

Falendra Kumar Sudan is a professor in the Department of Economics, the University of Jammu, India.

Farhad Taghizadeh-Hesary is an associate professor at Tokai University, Japan. He is also a visiting professor at Keio University, Japan, and a distinguished research fellow and external scientific member of the University of Economics Ho Chi Minh City, Viet Nam.

Diane-Gabrielle Tremblay is a professor, Université du Québec, Téluq, Montreal, Canada.

Mahinda Wijesiri is a postdoctoral fellow, Université du Québec, Téluq, Montreal, Canada.

Naoyuki Yoshino is a former dean of the Asian Development Bank Institute. He is also professor emeritus, Keio University; director, Financial Research Center, Financial Services Agency, Japan; visiting professor, National Graduate Institute for Policy Studies, Japan; and a visiting lecturer, University of Tokyo.

Foreword

Kiyotaka Sasaki[1]

Why Sustainable Development Goals and Environmental, Social, and Governance Investment Matter for Financial Regulators: Japan Financial Services Agency's Policies

Why the Japan Financial Services Agency is committed to the Sustainable Development Goals and environmental, social, and governance investment

Since 2017, the JFSA has been fundamentally reforming its business and organization. The JFSA reaffirmed its goal to contribute to sustainable economic growth and to improve people's welfare, including through more active investment, which is the agency's highest mission. The JFSA has, therefore, changed its supervisory approaches:

- **From compliance with minimum standards to employing best practices.** The JFSA used to require financial institutions to comply with only the minimum standards of laws and regulations. The minimum requirement, however, is no longer adequate. The JFSA now encourages best practices in business, compliance, and risk management.
- **From backward looking to forward looking.** Conventional supervision is backward looking, critical of what has happened. The JFSA learned from the 2008 global financial crisis and understands that financial supervision must be forward looking.

---

[1]   Kiyotaka Sasaki, visiting professor at Hitotsubashi University and former director general of the Strategy Development and Management Department of the Japan Financial Services Agency (JFSA), delivered the keynote speech at the conference, Environmental, Social and Governance Investment: Opportunities and Risks, on 13 November 2019. He covered two topics: why the JFSA is committed to the Sustainable Development Goals (SDGs) and environmental, social, and governance (ESG) investment; and the alignment of the JFSA's policies and measures with the SDGs and ESG, especially in relation to investment.

- **From rule based to principle based.** Rules and laws are the base of financial regulation. An overly rule-based approach, however, is not effective. Like European agencies, the JFSA is shifting from a rule-based to a principle-based approach.
- **From focusing on micro and/or individual issues to more holistic and root-cause analysis.** The JFSA needs to be more holistic and identify the root causes behind any wrongdoing or risk it happening again.

The JFSA has aligned its policies with the SDGs and ESG based on the supervisory approaches above. The JFSA expects more from financial firms:

- **Sustainability of business model and governance of regulated entities.** Without a sustainable business model, financial firms take on too much risk or are too profit-oriented, which may hurt the interests of investors or individual consumers. Without a sustainable business model and governance, no private entity could long survive.
- **Role of stakeholders: investors, consumers, communities, societies.** The banks provide money to borrowers and borrowers use money to invest, which could help develop the economy and society.
- **Risk management.** Risk management is a relatively new and undefined idea but it is being used more and more in Japan. Conventional compliance is designed to compel compliance with laws and regulations. Risk management, however, also covers reputational risk and compliance with ESG and SDGs. Even though ESG and SDGs are not legal requirements or legally binding, the JFSA encourages firms to be in line with them.

The Japan Financial Services Agency's measures for the Sustainable Development Goals and environmental, social, and governance investment

As part of its reform, the JFSA developed a strategy in June 2018 to achieve the SDGs. The JFSA started by mapping its SDG policies and redesigning its financial regulatory policies to be in line with global SDGs. The exercise was highly effective for three reasons:

- The JFSA became more accountable globally. Many of its measures and policies are well understood in the Japanese context and some are unique to Japan and not easily understood by other countries. Once the JFSA aligned these measures with the SDGs, however, they were much easier to explain to international communities.

- Even in Japan, the existing measures became better understood in the context of the SDGs.
- The exercise changed the JFSA mindset, encouraging thinking from different angles, which helped in formulating new financial policies and measures.

The following are concrete measures for achieving the SDGs:

- **The JFSA encourages private sector voluntary initiatives,** not just compliance with laws and regulations. Without ownership by firms, the SDGs and ESG investment would be ineffective. The JFSA decided, therefore, not to take a conventional compliance approach.
- **Principle-based approach.** The JFSA avoids making the SDGs a compliance issue based on rules or ticking boxes.
- **Sharing best practices through disclosure.** The JFSA encourages private banks to disclose what they are doing, which could pave the way for greater competition among market participants.
- **Easing interaction in the private sector.** The JFSA reaches out to and interacts with publicly listed companies to raise awareness.
- **Developing public–private ecosystems for SDGs and ESG.**

The following are examples of promoting the SDGs and ESG investment in Japan:

Corporate governance code and stewardship code. These codes apply to issuers and investors. The corporate governance code was created by the Tokyo Stock Exchange and the Japan Stock Exchange in 2014 for self-regulation by publicly listed companies and is not legally binding. But the code encourages listed public issuers to comply with it or explain the reasons for noncompliance. The stewardship code is for institutional investors. Both codes have principles regarding environmental, social, and corporate governance. The codes started to be implemented 5 years ago and the JFSA notes that corporate governance among Japanese issuers has become progressively more effective, among boards of directors, for example, and in increasing disclosures.

Climate change and the Financial Stability Board Taskforce on Climate-related Financial Disclosures (TCFD). An increasing number of Japanese companies comply with the TCFD principles. Disclosure is voluntary and not legally binding. In May 2019, the JFSA and the Government of Japan hosted a TCFD consortium, the private sector forum for the TCFD supported by the government. The JFSA shared examples of the TCFD.

Financial literacy education for youth, students, and older people, with an ESG investment perspective. Such education is necessary to improve the quality of life and to promote sustainable economic growth. Japan is an aging country. The aged have a huge amount of financial assets but are unable to invest wisely because they lack financial literacy. Education will enable them to enjoy a good quality of life after retirement.

The goal of the JFSA is to ensure sustainable economic growth and improve people's welfare, a goal compatible with the SDGs.

Abbreviations

ADB	Asian Development Bank
AJC	ASEAN–Japan Centre
ASEAN	Association of Southeast Asian Nations
BCA	Bank Central Asia
BNI	Bank Nasional Indonesia
BRI	Bank Rakyat Indonesia
CBOE	Chicago Board Options Exchange
CDS	credit default swap
CDSB	Climate Disclosure Standards Board
CO2	carbon dioxide
CSR	corporate social responsibility
DCF	discounted cash flow
DEA	data envelopment analysis
DEP	deposit regression equation
DEQ	debt-to-equity ratio
ESG	environmental, social, and governance
EU	European Union
FDI	foreign direct investment
FEM	fixed effect method
FTSE	Financial Times Stock Exchange
GDP	gross domestic product
GHG	greenhouse gas
GMM	generalized method of moments
GRI	Global Reporting Initiative
GSIA	Global Sustainable Investment Alliance
GSP+	Generalised System of Preferences Plus
GW	gigawatts
International <IR> Framework	International Integrated Reporting Framework
IRENA	International Renewable Energy Agency
ISO	International Organization for Standardization
JFSA	Japan Financial Services Agency
Lao PDR	Lao People's Democratic Republic

MFI	microfinance institution
MIX	Microfinance Information Exchange
MSCI	Morgan Stanley Capital International
MSMEs	micro, small, and medium-sized enterprises
NBFI	nonbank financial institution
NOx	nitrogen oxide
NRI	Nomura Research Institute
NSBM	network slacks-based measures
OLS	ordinary least square
PLS	pooled least square
PRC	People's Republic of China
PRI	Principles for Responsible Investment
QE	quantitative easing
REM	random effect method
SASB	Sustainability Accounting Standards Board
SCP	state capital participation
SDG	Sustainable Development Goal
SET	Stock Exchange of Thailand
STC	stock/share price regression equation
SRI	socially responsible investment
TCFD	Task Force on Climate-related Financial Disclosures
UN	United Nations
VIX	volatility index
WASTE	combustible renewables and waste as percentage of total energy
WHO	World Health Organization

1

Environmental, Social, and Governance Investment: Concepts, Prospects, and the Policy Landscape

Upalat Korwatanasakul

1.1 Introduction

1.1.1 Conceptualization of Environmental, Social, and Governance Investment

Environmental, social, and governance (ESG) factors have become an important part of global investment decisions. ESG investment encompasses a broad array of measures and is receiving increasingly widespread attention and recognition from policy makers, investors, and the public for promoting sustainable working practices and company operations. In particular, investors have begun to realize that ESG factors contribute to efficiency, productivity, long-term risk management, and operational enhancement. ESG investment represents an approach through which companies can act sustainably by taking action in certain areas and also provide value to their investors, going beyond simple profit. ESG investment signals that a company is sustainable and that it operates responsibly, in turn adding value to society and all stakeholders.

This study defines ESG investment as any investment that considers ESG factors. The investment can encompass responsible investment as well as corporate social responsibility (CSR). ESG investment is distinct as a desirable approach even for investors who only consider financial returns because ESG factors can increase not only social and but also financial value. ESG investing does not focus on specific areas or themes but is holistic.

ESG can play a strong role in achieving the United Nations (UN) Sustainable Development Goals (SDGs). The 17 SDGs were agreed upon by countries in 2015 as part of the UN's 2030 Agenda for Sustainable Development. The goals relate to a range of important social and economic issues identified as the main priorities for sustainable development in the coming decades. Many of the goals and the methods for achieving them are interrelated with the activities and business decisions of investors. ESG investment can improve sustainability, boost economic growth, and strengthen risk management. ESG investment and the SDGs can reinforce each other.

ESG factors are traditionally nonfinancial or nonmaterial, usually qualitative, and often difficult to measure quantitatively. They generally have a medium-to-long-term horizon and are subject to changing regulations and policies. The scope of ESG factors can vary greatly depending on the industry. Industries that rely heavily on resources may, for example, have differing ESG factors or place greater significance on certain factors than do service industries. The scope of ESG investment includes three main aspects:

Environmental factors. Through their production and output activities, companies can cause negative externalities through pollution and the depletion of natural resources, with associated detrimental impacts on ecosystems, the climate, and human health, among others. Environmental factors comprise measures to protect and minimize the risks to the environment and efforts to conserve resources. Examples include reducing greenhouse gas emissions, complying with government regulations on pollution, and conserving and managing resources through water and waste management and energy-saving practices.

Social factors. The social scope of ESG investment relates to the positive impacts and opportunities that a company may provide for society as well as the management of any social risks. These factors can apply generally to society, affecting how companies use their corporate influence to benefit society and how society in turn views the company and its reputation. The factors may also apply more specifically to social aspects within a company, such as the relations between the company and its workers and the implementation of safe working practices and standards, with impacts on company values. Social factors include social and policy impact evaluation, health and safety measures, and employee relations.

Governance factors. These are related to the structure and management practices of companies and can be viewed as a commitment to business ethics and proper business conduct. Companies can attract long-term investment by showing their willingness to align with the interests of shareholders and management. Examples of governance factors include transparency measures and corporate governance.

1.1.2 Drivers of Environmental, Social, and Governance Investment

Entrepreneurs have strong incentives for considering ESG investment for their core business strategies. Yet, many are unclear about how ESG factors relate to business performance and the associated benefits. The main draw of ESG factors is that they can benefit companies and society simultaneously. Several contributing factors have driven the rise in interest in ESG investment. It now plays a large role in mainstream investment, reflecting the financial market origin of the concept of ESG factors, and investors are increasingly demanding ESG-related indicators from companies.

The first driver is that investors increasingly prefer long-term investment because short-term investment is often associated with higher risks. Long-term investment decisions benefit from investors having more information about companies, and ESG factors can comprise a large part of this information. Investments now take place on a global scale and helping investors be more educated and aware of companies' operating practices, reputation, and commitments can play a vital role assessing companies, wherever they are.

Providing an insight into the intangible assets of a company is the second driver of ESG investment. Evaluating the expected performance of a company goes beyond simply assessing its financial assets. Investors should rely on an overall evaluation of a company to determine its market value. A company's efforts to invest in human capital through employee training, its cooperation with product standards and safety regulations, and its reputation for fair working practices—among many other previously mentioned ESG factors—can contribute to establishing the viability of an investment decision.

Lastly, entrepreneurs, governments, the media, and the public have become strong supporters of ESG investment, fueling its rapid growth. Growing demand from environmentally and socially conscious consumers and business clients around the world has spurred companies to be more accountable for their working practices and the impacts of their activities on society and the environment. As a result, companies are placing greater focus on ESG factors and indicators and improving transparency and reporting to demonstrate their commitment and to remain competitive with other companies.

1.1.3 How Environmental, Social, and Governance Investment Can Lead to Outperformance

While awareness of the benefits of ESG investment is increasing, many entrepreneurs remain unclear on the relationship between ESG investment and financial performance or on how they can include ESG investment in their core business strategies. This may lead to doubts about whether ESG investment can raise profits and lead to companies' "outperformance." However, ESG investment does not result in a trade-off with profit but is in line with business incentives and creates value for firms. ESG investment can, therefore, lead to outperformance through a variety of mechanisms.

First, ESG investment helps firms lower costs and boost revenues and profits. ESG firms are, on average, more profitable than non-ESG firms (Korwatanasakul and Majoe, 2019). ESG factors are highly unlikely to have a detrimental effect on firms' financial performance. The reason is that measures to boost ESG performance generally do not oppose or hinder companies' profit-generating activities. Promoting ESG factors need not sacrifice profit; they instead add value for companies, leading to a win–win situation. Companies and investors, as well as society and the government, serve to gain from an emphasis on ESG performance.

The second mechanism is that ESG factors directly and indirectly contribute to increasing the sustainability of companies and can enable firms to outperform their rivals. Firms that do not realize that they could gain from incorporating ESG investment into their business strategies fail to consider the signaled benefits to business performance as well as the governance, societal, corporate, and other beneficial attributes.

Furthermore, ESG is linked to lower volatility in company performance as ESG factors can lead to better risk management through increased brand awareness and, hence, decreased reputational risk and volatility. Nonfinancial indicators such as information on management practices allow investors to form more thorough risk assessments that would not otherwise be possible using financial information alone. This medium-to-long-term stability is important for firms when considering risk management, and investors tend to be averse to investing in companies with poor sustainability as it can signal weak working practices and low engagement with communities and society.

Lastly, ESG investment can help build and encourage collaboration within companies. This may be brought about through working collectively toward ESG-led goals, which often requires cross-functional cooperation. ESG factors can directly heighten collaboration through increased productivity and efficiency from better management and improved staff retention and employee satisfaction, among others.

Since it originated from the financial market, ESG investment is commonly perceived as only for financial investors. However, ESG factors should be a priority for all kinds of investors, including those in the real sector or enterprises. ESG factors are important as an indicator of a company's long-term commitments and, therefore, a signal to investors. As ESG factors promote business objectives, incorporating ESG-related objectives into company strategies can help add value to companies and allow them to differentiate themselves from their rivals. ESG can be crucial to maximize profit for all companies. ESG can even help new companies and micro, small, and medium-sized enterprises (MSMEs) become more productive and competitive by boosting their reputation. Therefore, all companies, regardless of their size or whether they are listed on a stock market, should integrate ESG investment into their core business strategies and consider it an essential part of their growth strategies.

1.2 Environmental, Social, and Governance Investment

1.2.1 Trends and Prospects

In recent decades, ESG investment has gained global momentum and is now regarded as one of the fastest-growing investment areas in the world (Figure 1.1, Figure 1.2). Behind this rapid growth has been the knowledge that ESG factors can increase companies' financial performance, in contrast with previous beliefs that intangible, environmental, or sustainable performance could only be improved by sacrificing financial gain and profit.

The largest sustainable investment strategy globally is negative and exclusionary screening ($19.8 trillion), followed by ESG integration ($17.5 trillion) (Figure 1.2). ESG integration is the primary sustainable investment strategy in the United States (US), Canada, Australia and New Zealand, and Asia excluding Japan, while corporate engagement and shareholder action are the largest investment strategy in Japan. ESG integration continued to grow in 2014–2018 (Figure 1.2). The annual growth rate of ESG integration was about 24%, to which Europe and the US were the largest contributors. In Asia, including Japan, ESG integration investment strategies are still in their early stages, with high potential for growth. This trend is apparent in Table 1.1, which shows the impressive growth rates of sustainable investing assets for Asia excluding Japan (16%) and Japan (6,690% or 67 times larger) in 2014–2016.

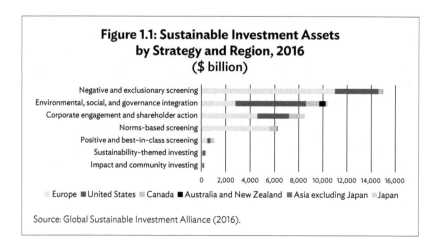

Figure 1.1: Sustainable Investment Assets by Strategy and Region, 2016 ($ billion)

Source: Global Sustainable Investment Alliance (2016).

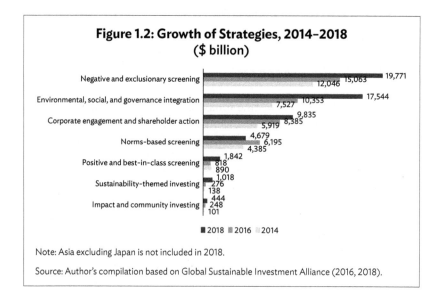

Figure 1.2: Growth of Strategies, 2014–2018 ($ billion)

Note: Asia excluding Japan is not included in 2018.

Source: Author's compilation based on Global Sustainable Investment Alliance (2016, 2018).

Malaysia is the largest market (30%) for sustainable investing in Asia excluding Japan and among Association of Southeast Asian Nations (ASEAN) Member States. In 2012–2014, however, sustainable investing grew fastest in Singapore and Indonesia, and Singapore is considered a center for technology and sustainable investment products while Indonesia is positioned as a hub of Islamic funds (GSIA, 2016).

Table 1.1: Growth of Sustainable Investing Assets by Country or Region, 2014–2016

Country or Region	SRI Assets in 2014 ($ billion)	SRI Assets in 2016 ($ billion)	Growth Over Period (%)	Compound Annual Growth Rate (%)
Europe	10,775	12,040	11.7	5.7
United States	6,572	8,723	32.7	15.2
Canada	729	1,086	49.0	22.0
Australia and New Zealand	148	516	247.5	86.4
Asia excluding Japan	45	52	15.7	7.6
Japan	7	474	6,689.6	724.0
Total	18,276	22,890	25.2	11.9

SRI = sustainable investing.
Source: Global Sustainable Investment Alliance (2016).

1.2.2 Current Initiatives and the Policy Landscape

Global Context

ESG investment has received strong support from governments and international organizations, such as the UN, and many ESG-related aspects are emphasized in the SDGs, which similarly promote inclusive and sustainable economic growth and sustainable consumption and production patterns. A plethora of ESG-related initiatives has arisen in recent years to promote awareness and actions covering a range of thematic areas across countries and regions and targeting all levels of stakeholders. Table 1.2 lists some of the active initiatives that incorporate ESG-related elements.

Table 1.2: Key Global Initiatives Covering Elements of Environmental, Social, and Governance Investment

Organization or Economy	Initiative
United Nations (UN)	UN-supported Principles for Responsible Investment
	UN Environment Programme
	UN Framework Convention on Climate Change

continued on next page

Table 1.2 *continued*

Organization or Economy	Initiative
	UN Green Climate Fund
	UN Global Compact
	Principles for Responsible Agricultural Investment[a]
G20	G20 Green Finance Study Group
	Global Infrastructure Hub
Organisation for Economic Co-operation and Development	High-Level Principles on Long-Term Investment
	Work stream on Governance and Fiduciary Duty
Financial Stability Board	Task Force on Climate-Related Financial Risks
European Union (EU)	EU Energy Union
	EU Capital Markets Union
	European Fund for Strategic Investments
	EU Non-Financial Reporting Directive
	ESG and fiduciary duty initiatives
	Product disclosure initiatives
Belgium	Vandenbroucke Law (2003)
	Laws against financing of landmines and cluster munitions (2007)
Denmark	Amendment to the Danish Financial Statements Act
France	Grenelle Law II, Articles 224 and 225
	Energy Transitions for Green Growth Law, Article 173
Germany	The Renewable Energy Act
	Amendment in regulations concerning pensions funds
Italy	Mandatory disclosure of ESG for pension funds
	New measure on pension funds' investment policy
Netherlands	Green Investment Directive
Norway	Norwegian Act on Annual Accounting
Spain	Sustainable Economy Law—Mandatory Disclosure of ESG
	Law modernizing Spain's Social Security System
Sweden	Mandatory Disclosure of ESG for Pension Funds
	Public Pension Funds Act
United Kingdom	Amendments to 1995 Pensions Act: Pension Disclosure Regulation
Hong Kong, China	Social Innovation and Entrepreneurship Development Fund

continued on next page

Table 1.2 *continued*

Organization or Economy	Initiative
India	Ministry of Corporate Affairs' new Corporate and Social Responsibility Policy under the Companies Act 2013
Indonesia	National Centre for Sustainability Reporting
Japan	Principles for Financial Action for the 21st Century
Malaysia	Business Sustainability Program
Philippines	National Renewable Energy Program 2011–2013
Singapore	Sustainable Singapore Blueprint
Thailand	Feed-in Premium Program
Viet Nam	Climate Investment Funds' Clean Technology Fund

ESG = environmental, social, and governance.

[a] Jointly developed by the United Nations Conference on Trade and Development, the Food and Agriculture Organization of the United Nations, the International Fund for Agricultural Development, and the World Bank.

Source: Korwatanasakul and Majoe (2019).

Several standalone initiatives are increasing knowledge of ESG investment and the importance of ESG factors for investment (Table 1.2).

Principles for Responsible Investment (PRI). The PRI aim to promote responsible investment mainly among institutional investors by increasing understanding of how ESG can be applied to investment. The PRI were launched in 2006 in partnership with the UN and are an investor-sponsored initiative. The PRI advocate the benefits of increased returns and minimized risks from responsible investment through a set of six principles:[1]

    (i)   Incorporate ESG issues into investment analysis and decision-making processes.

    (ii) Be active owners and incorporate ESG issues into ownership policies and practices.

  (iii) Seek appropriate disclosure on ESG issues by entities.

  (iv) Promote the acceptance and implementation of the principles within the investment industry.

   (v) Implement the principles more effectively.

  (vi) Report on the activities and progress in implementing the principles.

---

[1]   Adapted from the Principles for Responsible Investment. https://www.unpri.org/about-the-pri

The initiative increases awareness of the importance of ESG issues and has received over 1,500 signatories and widespread acceptance by market participants. As of December 2016, the combined value of the assets managed by the signatories had exceeded $60 trillion.

Global Reporting Initiative (GRI). An independent organization founded in 1997, based in Amsterdam, Netherlands, the GRI increases awareness and understanding of sustainability through effective communication and reporting on issues such as climate change and governance. The initiative's Sustainability Reporting Standards comprise widely used global standards for sustainability reporting and include over 400 indicators of corporate sustainability performance.

The GRI has four priority areas: (i) lead in creating standards and guidelines for sustainable development, (ii) harmonize the sustainability field by providing a central hub for sustainability-related frameworks and engaging in collaborative and partnership opportunities, (iii) lead efficient and effective sustainability reporting and elevate and streamline the reporting process, and (iv) encourage the use of sustainability information to boost performance and transparency.

Sustainable Stock Exchanges Initiative. Launched in 2009, the initiative is a UN partnership program of the United Nations Conference on Trade and Development, the UN Global Compact, the United Nations Environment Programme Finance Initiative, and the PRI. The initiative's goal is to work with stock exchanges, market regulators, and companies to improve ESG performance and further sustainable investment through research, consensus building, and technical assistance.

The initiative includes most exchanges worldwide and provides a platform for collaboration, information sharing, and support among all stakeholders. As a UN-partnered initiative, it contributes to four SDGs: goal 5, gender equality; goal 8, decent work and economic growth; goal 12, responsible consumption and production; and goal 13, climate action. The initiative focuses on areas that are of particular importance for stock exchanges—including guidance and encouragement of companies to implement ESG reporting, promotion of green finance, gender equality, and small and medium-sized enterprise growth—and takes a variety of measures such as publication of guidelines and action plans and recommendation of indicators.

Table 1.3 shows the prevalence of ESG issues in the financial markets of selected ASEAN and non-ASEAN economies. While ESG mechanisms have not been adopted across the board, the stock exchanges of several ASEAN Member States require ESG reporting as a listing requirement, offer guidance on ESG reporting, and provide ESG training, among other measures. ESG investment has improved since 2018 in Indonesia, the Philippines, Japan, and the Republic of Korea. Recently, the Japan

Table 1.3: Sustainable Stock Exchanges Initiative in Selected Asian Economies, 2019

Economy	Stock Exchange	Number of Listed Companies	Market Capitalization ($ million)	SSE Partner Exchange	Has Annual Sustainability Report	Requires ESG Reporting as a Listing Rule	Has Written Guidance on ESG Reporting	Offers ESG-Related Training	Has Sustainability-Related Indexes
ASEAN									
Indonesia	Indonesia Stock Exchange	626	516,000	Yes	Yes	Yes	Yes	Yes	Yes
Malaysia	Bursa Malaysia	904	455,773	Yes	Yes	Yes	Yes	Yes	Yes
Philippines	Philippine Stock Exchange	266	290,339	Yes	Yes	Yes	Yes	Yes	No
Singapore	Singapore Exchange	749	1,100,000	Yes	Yes	Yes	Yes	Yes	Yes
Thailand	Stock Exchange of Thailand	688	595,373	Yes	Yes	Yes	Yes	Yes	Yes
Viet Nam	Ho Chi Minh Stock Exchange	344	116,657	Yes	Yes	Yes	Yes	Yes	Yes
Viet Nam	Hanoi Stock Exchange	366	49,000	Yes	No	Yes	Yes	Yes	No
Selected economies									
Australia	Australia Securities Exchange	2,275	1,507,050	Yes	No	No	Yes	No	No
China, People's Republic of	Shanghai Stock Exchange	1,403	5,568,909	Yes	Yes	No	Yes	Yes	Yes

continued on next page

Table 1.3 *continued*

Economy	Stock Exchange	Number of Listed Companies	Market Capitalization ($ million)	SSE Partner Exchange	Has Annual Sustainability Report	Requires ESG Reporting as a Listing Rule	Has Written Guidance on ESG Reporting	Offers ESG-Related Training	Has Sustainability-Related Indexes
China, People's Republic of	Shenzhen Stock Exchange	2,170	3,030,000	Yes	No	No	Yes	Yes	Yes
Hong Kong, China	Hong Kong Exchanges and Clearing	2,186	4,443,082	Yes	Yes	Yes	Yes	Yes	Yes
India	National Stock Exchange of India	1,878	2,379,901	Yes	Yes	Yes	Yes	Yes	Yes
India	Bombay Stock Exchange	5,616	2,373,884	Yes	Yes	Yes	Yes	Yes	Yes
Japan	Japan Exchange Group	3,604	6,222,825	Yes	Yes	No	Yes	Yes	Yes
Korea, Republic of	Korea Exchange	2,138	1,869,629	Yes	No	No	No	Yes	Yes
New Zealand	New Zealand Stock Exchange	176	98,685	Yes	No	No	Yes	No	No

ASEAN = Association of Southeast Asian Nations; ESG = environmental, social, and governance; SSE = Sustainable Stock Exchanges.

Note: For more details, see http://www.sseinitiative.org/. The underlined numbers indicate the change from 2018.

Source: Author's compilation based on the Sustainable Stock Exchanges Initiative's database (2019); Korwatanasakul and Majoe (2019).

Exchange Group adopted a written guidance on ESG reporting, while the Korea Exchange started providing ESG-related training. These initiatives indicate a growing trend and progressive support for ESG investment among stock exchanges in ASEAN economies and their neighbors. However, progress is slow and more efforts are needed to stimulate ESG investment in East Asia.

East Asian Context

Japan.[2] ESG investment has and will continue to have an important role in capital markets. Japan's Stewardship Code was established in 2014 by the Japan Financial Services Agency to help companies achieve sustainable growth through investment and dialogue. The code provides an important example of the possible relationship between ESG factors and long-term value creation. The code aims to guide institutional investors on factors relating to the medium- and long-term evaluation of companies, such as through considering a company's management strategies and operating policies. The code refers to risk monitoring through consideration of risks related to environmental and social matters.

The Ministry of Economy, Trade and Industry published the Ito Review in 2014. It stresses that in addition to financial information, investors should focus on nonfinancial factors such as ESG issues and connect them with costs and investment returns. The document highlights the need to incorporate the level of trust of stakeholders into corporate valuations and evaluations of company performance.

The Corporate Governance Code was released in 2015, signaling that Japan supported ESG performance indicators for investors. The code states that companies should aim for maximum transparency and go beyond the legally required reporting and compliance requirements for both financial and nonfinancial information. The code encompasses ESG issues such as reporting on governance mechanisms, risks, and strategies.

Following these developments, the Government Pension Investment Fund signed the PRI, and the Working Group on Incorporating Issues Regarding Sustainability into Investment (ESG Working Group) was established. It produces guidelines to promote ESG investment and organizes meetings and symposiums, among other activities, to increase awareness and dialogue on ESG matters.

As a result of a number of developments in 2016–2018, sustainable investing assets in Japan grew from 3% to 18%, of which ESG investment accounted for ¥122 trillion and was regarded as a leading sustainable investing strategy (GSIA, 2018).

---

2   For more details, see the ESG Working Group Report by the Ministry of Environment, Japan (2017).

Republic of Korea. While sustainable management is increasingly recognized as good for business, only a few companies have fully formulated long-term strategies that fully integrate ESG factors. There are some positive changes, including the movement of big corporates such as Hyundai and Samsung in adjusting their corporate governance structures as well as the engagement efforts of public pensions, institutional investors, and the Korea Exchange. The National Pension Service joined the PRI in 2009 and formed a benchmark indicator (NPS-FnGuide) and ESG evaluation system in 2015 (Lee 2018). The Korea Exchange helped promote ESG investment by developing an ESG indicator—KRX ESG Leaders 150—and offering ESG-related training in 2019.

Despite the positive changes, however, ESG investment has been limited and there are few public pensions and institutional investors in this area (Table 1.4). The lack of ESG investment demand is partly the result of investors' skepticism that such investment would be profitable. Insufficient support and guidelines from the Korea Exchange also contribute to low ESG investment. An annual sustainability report and written guidance on ESG reporting are required but not yet implemented (Table 1.3). In 2017, ESG domestic institutional investment amounted to W7.2 trillion, or 0.9% of all assets under management, while ESG investment funds among public offering funds are worth W397 billion, or 0.2% of all public offering funds (Table 1.4).

Table 1.4: Environmental, Social, and Governance Investment of Domestic Pension Funds and Public Offering Funds in the Republic of Korea, 2016–2017
(W billion)

	2016		2017	
	Amount	Share (%)	Amount	Share (%)
National Pension Service	6,370	1.1	6,880	1.1
Teachers Pension	212	1.5	102	0.6
Government Employees Pension Service	40	0.6	74	1.0
Korea Post	132	0.1	151	0.1
The Korean Teachers' Credit Union	0	0.0	40	0.2
Total	6,754	0.9	7,247	0.9
Public offering funds	261	0.1	397	0.2

Source: Lee (2018).

People's Republic of China (PRC). ESG investment in the PRC is still limited and the ESG concept has not been fully integrated into most domestic companies' core business strategies and investment philosophies. The PRC was ranked 23rd (out of 25 countries) in Bloomberg's ESG disclosure scores. As in ASEAN countries, however, the trend of ESG investment is positive (Korwatanasakul and Majoe, 2019).

The development of ESG investment began with environment-related products such as green bonds, sustainable bonds, green thematic mutual funds, among others. The PRC developed a green bond market in 2015 and, after 1 year, became the world's largest issuer of green bonds in 2016. Its green bonds account for 26% of sustainable bond issuance globally (Funds Global Asia 2018). The PRC has been investing intensively in renewable energy (30% of global investment) and energy efficiency (27%) (Funds Global Asia 2018).

The domestic and international trend of thematic environmental investment coupled with stricter government regulations on company disclosure, especially environmental issues, are the main drivers of ESG investment in the PRC. With recent economic and social development, awareness of social responsibility has been increasing. PRC companies and investors are reactive and open to new investment opportunities from both domestic and international demand for ESG investment. Such demand encourages companies and investors to adopt ESG investment. The government and stock exchanges also accelerate ESG investment. The Shanghai and the Shenzhen stock exchanges joined the Sustainable Stock Exchanges Initiative with a strong commitment to support the development of sustainable markets in the PRC (Table 1.3), while the China Securities Regulatory Commission and the Ministry of the Environment have been promoting environmental information disclosure by listed companies. An annual sustainability report and ESG reporting are not required for companies to list on a stock exchange (Table 1.3), but the commission requires all listed companies and bond issuers to report ESG risks annually by 2020. PRC companies, investors, the government, and the exchanges are developing ESG investment, which aligns with the PRC's national priorities of high-quality and green development.

Like other Asian economies, the PRC, and even Hong Kong, China, face fundamental challenges such as misperceptions about ESG investment, limited capacity to fully integrate ESG investment, and insufficient guidelines and support from exchanges and the government. A limited understanding of ESG integration and ESG issues is the top barrier to ESG integration in both economies. The issues of partial ESG investment with a significant bias toward the "E" factor and lack of transparency are common in the PRC.

ASEAN Context

ASEAN Member States have varying levels of ESG investment development and policy implementation. While awareness of ESG investment has been increasing substantially in recent years, much progress still has to be made in moving beyond awareness building to the practical development and implementation of ESG frameworks. ESG disclosure and transparency have been improving. This is more apparent in ASEAN Member States where changes in policies, regulation, and guidelines have been actively promoted and driven by stakeholders in the private and public sectors, such as civil society or government-led initiatives. Examples include nongovernment organizations and professional organizations in Indonesia, such as the National Centre for Sustainability Reporting, which are working to highlight the importance of disclosure for ESG investors. Malaysia's Business Sustainability Program encourages and educates companies to incorporate sustainability into their business strategies.

Business incentives have prompted companies to make strategic choices to explore ESG-related disclosure. The growing market for sustainable investment means that increasing transparency and reporting can provide companies with an entry point into the market and give them a competitive edge over their rivals, signaling to investors a company's commitment to innovative and profit-enhancing business decisions and development.

Governments and the private sector can promote ESG development. At the government level, targeted policies and regulations on ESG are still lacking. In this respect, further national measures are key to unlock the potential of firms in the ASEAN region by accelerating the uptake of support for ESG investment. It has mostly been carried out in the financial sector and markets. Stock exchanges have been the drivers behind it, helping raise awareness among larger enterprises. This has established a trend and standards within the industry and can have positive spillover effects for MSMEs across all industries.

ASEAN stock exchanges have seen strong and sustained progression in their global rankings for disclosure (Table 1.5). The Stock Exchange of Thailand (SET) rose from 40th place in 2013 to 10th in 2017, marking a continual year-on-year progression. Behind this strong performance has been increasing disclosure rates, growth, and timeliness among large firms, encouraged by the voluntary reporting guidelines published by the stock exchange in 2012 and the subsequent mandatory requirements issued by the securities regulator in 2014.

Table 1.5: Sustainability Disclosure Rankings of Stock Exchanges in ASEAN and Selected Economies, 2013–2017

Ranking						Score (%)			
2013	2014	2015	2016	2017	Exchange Name	Disclosure	Disclosure Growth	Timeliness	Overall
40	27	17	13	10	SET	73.8	62.5	69.0	70.1
24	23	19	17	15	Bursa Malaysia	51.1	62.6	80.9	62.4
18	22	15	18	16	SGX	53.1	53.9	78.5	60.9
37	38	31	34	25	IDX	39.3	34.4	66.6	46.5
26	18	14	15	27	SSE	25.8	35.3	85.7	45.7
39	33	28	32	29	PSE	43.9	33.9	42.8	41.6
16	31	35	–	32	KRX	42.8	27.9	45.2	40.5
3	12	21	28	36	TSE	53.6	33.3	19.0	39.2
38	26	20	43	37	SZSE	20.2	15.5	83.3	38.2
–	–	–	–	53	HOSE	12.1	3.6	–	9.6

HOSE = Ho Chi Minh City Stock Exchange, IDX = Indonesia Stock Exchange, KRX = Korea Exchange, PSE = Philippine Stock Exchange, SET = Stock Exchange of Thailand, SGX = Singapore Exchange, SSE = Shanghai Stock Exchange, SZSE = Shenzhen Stock Exchange, TSE = Tokyo Stock Exchange.
Note: The 2017 ranking covers 55 economies.
Source: Korwatanasakul and Majoe (2019).

Responsible investment is gaining ground in Asia, and its vulnerability to environment and climate change–related risks has spurred interest and uptake in ESG investing. This is evident from Table 1.6, which compares ESG milestones among some ASEAN Member States. The stock exchanges have largely been successful in offering ESG-related training, but Indonesia and the Philippines have yet to introduce mandatory ESG reporting or publish written guidance on ESG reporting. Many countries have developed sustainability indexes, although room for improvement remains in this area. Figure 1.3 shows that governance-related disclosure is the most comprehensive form of ESG reporting, while the social and environmental aspects are lagging in disclosure quality. The following section will discuss the state of ESG investment and disclosure in more detail for individual ASEAN Member States.

Table 1.6: ASEAN's Sustainability Landscape

Country	Stock Exchange	Requires ESG Reporting	Written Guidance on ESG Reporting	ESG-Related Training	Sustainability-Related Indices
Brunei Darussalam	–	No	No	No	No
Cambodia	CSX	No	No	No	No
Indonesia	IDX	Yes	Yes	Yes	Yes
Lao PDR	LSX	No	No	No	No
Malaysia	BURSA	Yes	Yes	Yes	Yes
Myanmar	YSX	No	No	No	No
Philippines	PSE	Yes	Yes	Yes	No
Singapore	SGX	Yes	Yes	Yes	Yes
Thailand	SET	Yes	Yes	Yes	Yes
Viet Nam	HOSE	Yes	Yes	Yes	Yes
Viet Nam	HNX	Yes	Yes	Yes	No

ASEAN = Association of Southeast Asian Nations, CSX = Cambodia Securities Exchange, ESG = environmental, social, and governance, HNX = Hanoi Stock Exchange, HOSE = Ho Chi Minh City Stock Exchange, IDX = Indonesia Stock Exchange, Lao PDR = Lao People's Democratic Republic, LSX = Lao Securities Exchange, PSE = Philippine Stock Exchange, SET = Stock Exchange of Thailand, SGX = Singapore Exchange, YSX = Yangon Stock Exchange.

Note: The underlined numbers indicate the change from 2018.

Source: Adapted by the author from Korwatanasakul and Majoe (2019).

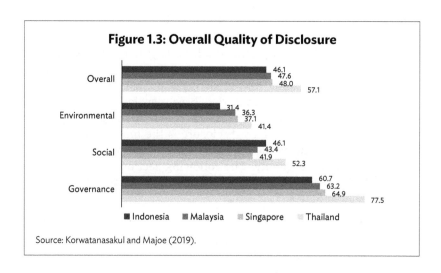

Figure 1.3: Overall Quality of Disclosure

Overall
- 46.1
- 47.6
- 48.0
- 57.1

Environmental
- 31.4
- 36.3
- 37.1
- 41.4

Social
- 46.1
- 43.4
- 41.9
- 52.3

Governance
- 60.7
- 63.2
- 64.9
- 77.5

■ Indonesia   ■ Malaysia   ▨ Singapore   ▨ Thailand

Source: Korwatanasakul and Majoe (2019).

In **Brunei Darussalam,** awareness of ESG is still in its early stages and no independent nongovernment organizations are promoting ESG-related monitoring or practices. However, some laws focus on labor-related issues that are consistent with some ESG factors. Laws to protect wildlife similarly signal Brunei's efforts in line with the environmental aspect of ESG. Because the country has limited ESG commitments, the Business Environment Council (2015) estimates suggest that the government is not likely to issue ESG reporting requirements in the medium term.

As in Brunei Darussalam, awareness of ESG in **Cambodia** is limited. However, in 2019, a movement of independent nongovernment organizations, including Oxfam, CSR Asia, among others, promoted the importance of ESG investment. Although ESG practices barely exist in the country, a few firms, including Cambodian Mango Farms and NagaCorp, started incorporating ESG factors into their business philosophy and strategies. With increasing international pressure to promote sustainable development, Cambodia needs to do more or risk being left behind. Financial institutions and the banking sector may pioneer ESG investment and raise awareness of its importance.

Indonesia is among the least active of the ASEAN-6 members on ESG issues.[3] However, it is a hub for Islamic funds, demonstrating the fast-growing demand for sustainable investment in ASEAN. Indonesia has strong potential gains from increased ESG awareness because the country is highly vulnerable to natural disasters and climate change. Indonesia does, however, face many ESG challenges. Environmental challenges include pollution, environmental degradation, and resource conservation. Social challenges include unemployment, income inequality, health and safety issues, and discrimination. Governance challenges include lack of corporate transparency, risk and volatility, and corruption.

The government has taken steps to improve ESG disclosure by requiring all listed companies to include in their annual reports information on discharging their social and environmental responsibilities. The market regulator also requires such companies to report on their CSR.

Several regulations are related to ESG, including laws on labor inspections and occupational safety, regulations that require state-owned enterprises to report on their partnership and community developments, and legislation requiring enterprises to report on their environment-related developments.

An index created by the Indonesia Stock Exchange and KEHATI (an Indonesian biodiversity foundation) scores private companies based

---

[3]   ASEAN-6 comprises Brunei Darussalam, Indonesia, Malaysia, the Philippines, Singapore, and Thailand.

on their CSR efforts, to promote and recognize those with a strong focus on sustainable development.

The Lao People's Democratic Republic (Lao PDR) is one of the most active countries outside ASEAN-6 in promoting responsible investment, especially in agriculture. The Ministry of Planning and Investment's Quality Investment Promotion initiative encourages environmental and social responsibility among investors. Firms such as Lao Tobacco Limited, Stora Enso Lao PDR, and Lao Banana Company have focused on the "S" element of ESG, aiming to contribute to community development and maintain good relationships with their workers.[4]

The Lao PDR has no CSR, ESG, or sustainability policies relating to disclosure. The government will need to play a key role in implementing and encouraging such measures and increase targeted coordination.

Malaysia has continually shown strong ESG progress and its listed companies rank among the highest in the ASEAN Corporate Governance Scorecard Country Report and Assessments. The country is expected to further develop its corporate governance disclosure and ESG frameworks through the Securities Commission's Corporate Governance Blueprint.

Bursa Malaysia, the country's stock exchange, has been a strong proponent of sustainability and ESG for long-term value creation. Bursa Malaysia requires CSR disclosures from its listed companies. Companies must detail their CSR activities in their annual reports or otherwise explain why they did not engage in such activities. ESG disclosure requirements are similarly imposed in the country's Main Market Listing Requirements and the Malaysian Code on Corporate Governance. Together with the Financial Times Stock Exchange (FTSE), Bursa Malaysia launched the FTSE4Good Bursa Malaysia in 2014, an ESG index that aims to highlight companies with strong ESG performance, help investors with their investment-related decisions, promote sustainability, and encourage efficient and transparent ESG reporting. The index comprises the top 200 companies based on defined and transparent ESG criteria.

Other initiatives to enhance ESG investment include the Sustainable and Responsible Investment Sukuk framework, introduced in 2014, and the Environmental Quality Act, which tackles environmental emissions and pollution.

Myanmar has no obligatory CSR initiatives and disclosure by companies is still voluntary. The Myanmar Forest Policy focuses on the sustainable use and development of forests and the Environmental

---

[4]   For more details see ASEAN Secretariat (2017).

Conservation Law covers environmental quality standards. Myanmar has much potential for significant ESG development and it is hoped that sustainability and CSR practices will continue to grow significantly in the medium term.

The Philippines is the least active member of ASEAN-6. Corporate governance has improved in the decades since the Asian financial crisis, but much progress still must be made. The Institute of Corporate Directors was set up in 1999 to increase the standard of corporate governance. The institute's corporate governance health checks allow companies to compare their governance practices with those recommended in the ASEAN Corporate Governance Scorecard. Only 5% of publicly listed companies do so, however, highlighting the need for companies to go beyond national legislative requirements and increase transparent communications with their stakeholders. There is much room for improvement in household goods, mining, and transportation companies, which face corruption and bribery, poor labor conditions, and environmental risks.

The Philippines Stock Exchange requires listed companies to report on their governance aspects of sustainability, although no requirements pertain to the "E" or "S" elements of ESG. The Corporate Social Responsibility Act is intended to make companies account for and disclose their CSR-related activities. However, many companies have avoided fully incorporating CSR into their company management strategies.

The Clean Water Act and Clean Air Act have promoted environmental change and increased companies' responsibilities, while the Philippine Securities and Exchange Commission has encouraged ESG disclosure and reporting on environmental factors in addition to activities related to corporate governance. Further disclosure requirements may be introduced in the medium term.

Singapore places strong emphasis on sustainable investment and aims to be a source of growth in ASEAN. The Singapore Stock Exchange encourages its listed companies to be more sustainable through two initiatives. First, it requires all listed companies to publish sustainability reports on their ESG performance at least annually on a "comply or explain" basis. These reports are intended to allow investors to make more informed investment decisions and supplement the traditional reports that consist only of financial performance. Second, the stock exchange has launched four sustainability indexes. The indexes are in response to increasing demand for measurements of ESG factors amid climate change, labor, and governance issues, and the indexes give investors the ability to identify which companies lead in ESG performance.

Several detailed regulations and legislation on ESG issues have strong potential for the further development of ESG. The Energy Conservation Act, for example, pushes large operators to report on energy use conservation and submit reports to the government on energy management. The Environmental Public Health Act requires large companies to report on waste data and waste reduction plans. The Employment Act and Workplace Safety and Health Act include regulations on social and labor aspects. Companies should continue to report on their ESG activities following the Ministry of the Environment and Water Resources' Sustainable Singapore Blueprint.

Thailand has emerged as a forerunner of ESG in ASEAN, and Thai companies comprise the highest share among ASEAN members in the Dow Jones Sustainability Indices. The country has among the highest levels of ESG disclosure in ASEAN and makes reporting mandatory. The SET requires annual reporting on ESG disclosure by its listed companies. The SET established the Corporate Social Responsibility Institute in 2007, signaling increasing awareness of CSR and ESG. Regulations related to specific ESG elements include the Occupational Safety, Health and Environment Act; the Enhancement and Conservation of National Environmental Quality Act; and the Environmental Quality Standard. More listed Thai companies are being chosen for inclusion in the Dow Jones Sustainability Indices, confirming their high performance. The SET is producing a sustainability index for ESG reporting.

Viet Nam is broadly committed to promoting ESG, and it engages in a range of ESG initiatives at the stock exchanges in Ho Chi Minh and Ha Noi (Table 1.3), which list a total of more than 700 companies. The Ho Chi Minh Stock Exchange, in particular, has comprehensive measures to promote ESG measures and factors, including the use of annual sustainability reports and the reporting requirement to ensure company accountability. The exchange supports companies by providing training on ESG-related issues, written guidance on reporting, and indexes to monitor progress, targets, and achievements. A 2015 circular requires listed companies to report on their impacts on society and the environment. The Environmental Protection Law relates to environmental protection, environmental impact and climate change assessments, and resource conservation. The Labour Code aims to protect workers through legislation on working hours, workers' rights, health and safety, and minimum wages. Viet Nam shows good potential and the introduction of the Sustainability Reporting Awards shows increasing awareness of and priority given to ESG issues. Further disclosure requirements can be expected in the medium term.

1.3 Environmental, Social, and Governance Investment Performance: A Case Study of ASEAN Enterprises

In 2018, the ASEAN–Japan Centre (AJC) conducted a survey of ASEAN firms on ESG investment to show its direct impact on firms' economic performance. Based on a purposive sampling method, the survey included 143 firms from 10 industries and 10 ASEAN Member States, which is representative of a broad picture of investment in ASEAN. To focus on real rather than financial investment, the sample excludes the financial sector, e.g., banks, investment funds, insurance companies, and real estate. The survey reviewed multiple years of each firm's annual reports and sustainability reports and explored firms' awareness of ESG investment and ESG adoption. The survey sought to gain insights into firms' strategic approach, practical ESG investment, performance measures, and challenges.[5]

The result shows that ESG investment is associated with greater profitability (Figure 1.4): ESG firms are, on average, more profitable than non-ESG firms, confirming the growing trends and prospects for ASEAN ESG investment presented in section 2. Second, the adoption of ESG investment and SDG-related strategies is gaining momentum. ASEAN-5 shows a promising trend for ESG investment, while greater efforts are necessary for the rest of the ASEAN Member States. Third, ESG investment varies by industry: ESG firms are mainly in the food, beverage, and tobacco industry; the industrial machinery and materials industry; and the transportation industry, while adoption of ESG investment has been slow in the hotel, restaurant, and leisure industries and the retail and trading industry. Lastly, ESG investment has been implicitly and unsystematically implemented among ASEAN firms, implying potential for ESG investment growth. The main challenge is that even though ESG factors are found in firms' sustainability and governance strategies, the firms still face difficulties in fully integrating ESG investment into their core business strategies. Therefore, further efforts should be spent on the explicit and systematic integration of ESG investment.

The best practices of ESG initiatives among ASEAN firms presented in the survey support and further explain the findings, especially the higher profitability of ESG firms. In general, ESG investment helps

---

[5]   For more details see Korwatanasakul and Majoe (2019).

firms raise profitability through two mechanisms—cost reduction and revenue generation. Firms with best practices comprehensively report concrete statistics on either cost reduction or income generation or both. ASEAN ESG firms are creative and innovative in integrating ESG investment in their business strategies. They offer new business solutions and products to their clients while utilizing new technology and innovation in production to improve efficiency. Most of the firms focus on the "E" factor because demand from environmentally conscious clients is growing and because "E" is easier than other factors to quantify. However, some firms also focus on the "S" factor as they believe improving the working environment and stakeholder involvement, especially for workers and suppliers, can result in higher operational efficiency and lower operational and transactional costs. Regarding the "G" factor, all firms report on corporate governance but only a few show concrete statistics related to cost and revenue benefits or attempt to estimate the costs of governance-related risks.

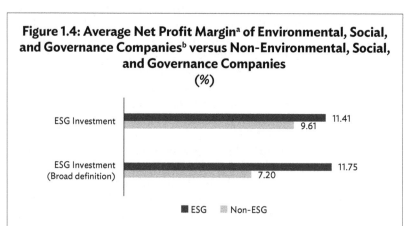

Figure 1.4: Average Net Profit Margin[a] of Environmental, Social, and Governance Companies[b] versus Non-Environmental, Social, and Governance Companies
(%)

ESG = environmental, social, and governance.

[a] The net profit margin is calculated from the net profit divided by the total revenue. The net profit margin is averaged over time (1990–2018) and across companies to obtain average profit margins for both ESG and non-ESG companies.

[b] ESG companies are companies that either incorporate ESG factors into their strategies or have a section for ESG investment in their annual reports, sustainability reports, or their homepages. ESG investment includes ESG companies and companies that report activities related to sustainability but do not explicitly include ESG perspectives in their strategies or have a section on ESG investment in their annual reports, sustainability reports, or homepages.

Source: Korwatanasakul and Majoe (2019).

1.4 Challenges and the Way Forward

1.4.1 Existing Issues and Challenges

While the trends of and efforts to promote ESG investment are significant and encouraging, challenges remain for Asian entrepreneurs. Many Asian firms have not fully integrated ESG investment into their core business strategies and suffer from inadequate support from the public sector. The link between ESG investment and achievement of the SDGs is still weak. Further progress by firms, exchanges, and policy makers is particularly important. These challenges should be tackled urgently to take advantage of the growth potential of ESG investment.

Misperceptions about Environmental, Social, and Governance Investment

As ESG investment is generally in its early stages in Asia, some firms still consider ESG investment unnecessary or even burdensome. Many investors and even policy makers do not understand the importance of ESG investment. Despite increasing demand for sustainable and impact investment solutions and a growing body of evidence to support the effectiveness of ESG investment, particularly from a financial perspective, many investors are still unclear about the relationship between ESG investment and economic or real performance.

The first misperception is that ESG investment is costly and unprofitable. Some firms believe that ESG investment is relevant only when considering investment in the financial market. ESG investment, however, creates financial value for investors, correlates with lower volatility, and does not lower investor financial returns. The AJC survey shows that ESG investment is associated with greater economic or real performance, including lower costs, higher revenue, and greater profit. Therefore, ESG investment is profitable and relevant to all investors and entrepreneurs, whether they invest in the financial or the real sector. All companies, regardless of whether they are listed on a stock market, should integrate ESG investment into their core business strategies and consider ESG investment as an essential part of their growth strategies.

Finally, firms embrace the belief that consumers and investors care little about ESG factors. The survey showed that few firms develop a robust story or framework for their ESG investment. Since they do not realize that communicating their ESG initiatives and performance to consumers, business clients, and investors is important, many firms report on sustainability performance in an implicit, unintegrated, and unsystematic manner. Nevertheless, demand for ESG investment is growing around the world and gradually in Asia, especially in ASEAN. Consumers and investors are becoming more conscious of ESG factors. Recently, global and domestic demand from environmentally and socially conscious consumers and business clients has been growing. Firms should, therefore, consciously integrate ESG investment into their business strategies to respond to these customers.

Limited Capacity to Fully Integrate Environmental, Social, and Governance Investment

The main challenge to the development of ESG investment is that Asian firms, even those in developed economies such as Japan and the Republic of Korea, still do not have the capacity to fully integrate ESG factors into their core business strategies.

Lack of know-how. The concept of ESG investment is new and broad. ESG factors are traditionally nonfinancial and, therefore, difficult to measure quantitatively. Depending on the industry, the scope of ESG investment can vary greatly. Even within the same industry, ESG investment can be broad-based as it includes multiple aspects, such as cost reduction, supply chain management, and technology development; and several stakeholders, such as consumers, communities, and regulators. Therefore, there is no one-size-fits-all solution for firms to fully integrate ESG investment. The lack of a standardized and objective method for implementing ESG investment and measuring its results poses a daunting prospect to many firms. However, this challenge also offers an opportunity to implement ESG initiatives and incorporate them into core business strategies by allowing firms to become creative, innovative, and flexible.

Lack of resources. MSMEs lack not just know-how, which even large firms lack, but also financial and human resources, which poses a greater hurdle to integrating ESG investment. The key to overcoming these challenges is creativity and innovation.

Insufficient Guidelines and Support from Exchanges and Government

Guidelines from exchanges in many countries are generally insufficient. Although the exchanges have been promoting ESG among listed companies, greater support from the exchanges is still needed. The survey showed that only one-third of the surveyed companies are implementing ESG investment. Some firms probably have not recognized the benefits of ESG investment, while others may be aware of ESG investment but do not know where to start, which is related to their misperceptions of ESG investment and limited capacity to integrate ESG factors. National policies and regulations on ESG investment are still lacking. ESG investment has mostly been carried out in the financial sector and financial markets. Unlisted firms, especially MSMEs, have been left behind.

1.4.2 Policy Recommendations

ESG investment offers substantial benefits for both investors and companies. This section identifies some practical steps that companies can take to incorporate ESG investment and recommends ways for policy makers and regulators to further promote it.

Entrepreneurs

Companies can gain a competitive advantage from prioritizing ESG performance and sustainability. Executives should place this at the core of their companies' values and identity to increase awareness within the company as well as among stakeholders and investors. By incorporating ESG investment into the overall corporate strategy, related initiatives can collaborate to produce synergies and drive corporate growth. This will have direct and positive effects on the value and future growth paths of companies. The following are some practical steps to achieve fully integrated ESG investment.

Change perceptions of ESG investment. As ESG investment is associated with higher profitability and lower risk whether or not companies are listed on a stock market, companies should recognize the increasing importance of ESG investment and respond with appropriate business strategies. Demand is growing from consumers, investors, and business clients for ESG-related products and solutions. A perception and corporate culture in favor of ESG investment can be achieved by a top-down approach in which ESG information and initiatives are delivered directly by executives and management teams. Internal education and communication will allow change to come from within the organization.

Plan for an effective ESG strategy. To ensure that ESG initiatives are sustainable and effective, companies should invest in and pursue quantifiable targets for sustainability rather than focus on rankings. Companies can do this by proving their commitment to increasing their ESG performance and sustainability and strengthening the relationship between *financial* and *economic* outcomes and ESG activities. Appropriate reporting is indispensable to set and affirm their commitment to ESG-related outcomes and targets. Targeting transparent and objective goals will provide the most efficient use of resources for working toward long-term and sustainable measures. It is important to understand that different businesses and industries are facing a range of sustainability issues and ESG strategies must, therefore, be designed accordingly. Once these tangible sustainability measures are in place, a long-term ESG strategy can be implemented that is suited to the company and aligned with the expectations and objectives of all stakeholders.

Take action. Fully integrating ESG investment into core business strategies demands time, knowledge, and resources. The scope of ESG investment can be broad and indefinite. This means that there are also indefinite opportunities waiting for firms to explore. Firms that are more creative, flexible, and innovative will find themselves at an advantage. The AJC survey shows that firms with product innovation and creativity in incorporating ESG factors into their business ideas can reduce costs and generate revenue. Firms with limited financial and human resources, such as MSMEs, can start ESG investment by incorporating ESG factors into their existing products or activities and analyze their existing initiatives and discover the ESG factors they might have already incorporated.

Work with peers and involve all stakeholders. Overcoming challenges, such as lack of know-how and resources, will require entrepreneurs, especially those running MSMEs, to make full use of their combined knowledge and economies of scale. By working together, entrepreneurs can share information, e.g., best practices and common problems and solutions, among others. Involving other stakeholders, such as employees, consumers, distributors, regulators, and policy makers, in the design and implementation of ESG initiatives through dialogues and consultations will help entrepreneurs understand ESG issues even better and deliver the right mix of ESG initiatives. These efforts will create an investment environment that promotes fully integrated ESG investment among entrepreneurs and sustainable development in society.

Regulators and Policy Makers

Stock exchanges and the government can implement policies and regulations that promote rigorous ESG investment by companies listed on the domestic stock exchange, as well as unlisted companies together with investment promotion agencies and ministries.

Communicate the benefits of ESG investment. While the survey results show the benefits of ESG investment, many entrepreneurs are still skeptical that it can contribute to a firm's financial and economic performance. The most pressing agenda for policy makers is to change entrepreneurs' perceptions of ESG investment by conveying its benefits to them and society.

Implement mandatory sustainability disclosure regulations. Policy makers can make sustainability disclosure mandatory for listed and unlisted entities. Policy makers must create a clear set of key ESG performance indicators and indexes that meet international standards and tackle current domestic ESG issues. A key ESG performance index can be divided into a general index that applies to all firms and industry-specific indexes that apply differently to firms by industry. Policy makers should provide a standard format for sustainability reports that is simple and easy to understand by stakeholders to involve them in monitoring.

Provide specific guidelines and support. Policy makers should provide a clear set of guidelines on ESG investment. They must be tailored to specific industries as they have different ESG priorities. Stock exchanges and governments may provide individual consultation sessions for entrepreneurs interested in ESG investment but unfamiliar with the concept. Policy makers can act as a medium to establish a framework or dialogue that enables all stakeholders to develop detailed ESG standards and best-practice guidelines.

Evaluate firms' ESG performance periodically. Regulators and policy makers are recommended to keep track of and evaluate firms' ESG investment performance. The evaluation result should be disclosed to the public to create competitive pressure among firms and involve all stakeholders in monitoring. Through the evaluation process, regulators and policy makers can come to understand the situation of ESG investment and learn about the problems and issues of ESG factor integration faced by firms. This will further help policy makers improve policies and regulations and better design new policy instruments to help firms implement ESG investment.

Policy makers are also recommended to compile an ESG database of evaluation results. It will help policy makers analyze the trends and progression of ESG investment and its long-term impacts on firms' financial and economic performance and on society.

Take advantage of the digital age. Regulators and policy makers can utilize information technology and big data to implement policies and regulations, by promoting ESG investment, assimilating ESG investment information, evaluating ESG performance, and compiling ESG data, among others. By taking advantage of technology, regulators and policy makers can reduce transaction costs, improve work efficiency, and connect all stakeholders to help monitor firms' ESG performance and design proper policies and regulations that meet society's needs.

Emphasize the links between ESG investment and the SDGs. ESG investment can play a strong role in achieving the SDGs. However, the link between the two concepts is still weak. Therefore, governments should communicate the importance of SDGs to the business sector and show how ESG investment can help promote the SDGs. Governments should provide technical support and guidelines to all firms to help them align their ESG initiatives with the SDGs.

1.5 Concluding Remarks

The importance and benefits of ESG investment are evident in the growing demand for it around the world, including Asia, and the finding that it is associated with greater profitability, both in *financial* and *economic* performance. All firms, regardless of their size and whether they are listed on a stock market, should, therefore, integrate ESG investment into their core business strategies and implement it as an essential part of their growth strategies.

Asia, especially ASEAN, has made strong and encouraging progress in increasing the uptake of ESG investment and the adoption of strategies that consider the SDGs. ASEAN ESG firms have innovative and creative strategies for incorporating ESG investment into business strategies and objectives. Such firms utilize the latest technologies and offer new business solutions and products along with concerted consideration of ESG factors. Although significant progress is still needed for the "S" and "G" factors of ESG, the "E" factor now plays a strong role in the strategies of many firms.

Challenges remain. Asian firms have not fully integrated ESG investment into their core business strategies, and inadequate support from governments may aggravate the current ESG situation. Although firms, regulators, and policy makers are the main players in ESG investment, involving other stakeholders through frameworks and dialogue can help accelerate progress. All stakeholders can work together to design well-rounded and comprehensive ESG initiatives at the firm level and shape better ESG-related policy instruments at the national level. Through these efforts, it is hoped that ESG issues will be reflected in an increasing number of initiatives, policies, and regulations, resulting in a better ESG investment environment and sustainable development.

References

ASEAN Secretariat. 2017. *ASEAN at 50: A Historic Milestone for FDI and MNEs in ASEAN*. Jakarta: ASEAN Secretariat.

Business Environment Council. 2015. https://www.bec.org.hk (accessed 31 October 2019).

Funds Global Asia. 2018. *ESG: China Gets Serious about ESG.* http://fundsglobalasia.com/June-2018/esg-china-gets-serious-about-esg (accessed 31 October 2019).

Global Sustainable Investment Alliance (GSIA). 2016. *Global Sustainable Investment Review 2016*. Brussels: GSIA.

Global Sustainable Investment Alliance (GSIA). 2018. *Global Sustainable Investment Review 2018*. Brussels: GSIA.

Korwatanasakul, U., and A. Majoe. 2019. *ESG Investment: Towards Sustainable Development in ASEAN and Japan*. Tokyo: ASEAN–Japan Centre.

Lee, J. 2018. Improving the Efficiency of Environment, Social, and Governance Investments. *Development Asia*. https://development.asia/insight/improving-efficiency-environment-social-and-governance-investments (accessed 31 October 2019).

Ministry of Environment, Japan. 2017. *ESG Working Group Report*. Tokyo: Ministry of Environment.

Principles for Responsible Investment (PRI). About the PRI. https://www.unpri.org/about-the-pri (accessed 31 October 2019).

Sustainable Stock Exchanges Initiative. 2019. Stock Exchange Database. http://www.sseinitiative.org/ (accessed 31 October 2019).

2

Competition in Extra-Financial Information Disclosure Frameworks and Standards: Significance and Challenges for Effective Convergence

Toshikazu Hayashi

2.1 Introduction

In recent years, an increasing number of frameworks and standards for corporate extra-financial (or sustainability) information disclosure have been developed globally, such as the Global Reporting Initiative (GRI) Standards, the International Integrated Reporting Framework (International <IR> Framework), the Sustainability Accounting Standards Board (SASB) Standards, the Task Force on Climate-related Financial Disclosures (TCFD) Recommendations Report, among others (Figure 2.1). Thanks to them, corporate extra-financial disclosures have progressed substantially. The first extra-financial report was issued in 1989 (Kolk, 2004) and since then an increasing number of companies have embarked on voluntary disclosure of their extra-financial information. The KPMG Survey of Corporate Responsibility Reporting—one of the most comprehensive surveys conducted globally—found that 72% of 4,900 companies (the top 100 companies by revenue in each of the 49 countries surveyed) issued extra-financial reports in 2017, up from 12% in 1993 (KPMG, 2017). More than 10,000 extra-financial reports are published every year, according to the Corporate Register Ltd, which provides an online directory of extra-financial reports.

Many practitioners and scholars have raised concerns about the inconsistency among extra-financial information disclosure

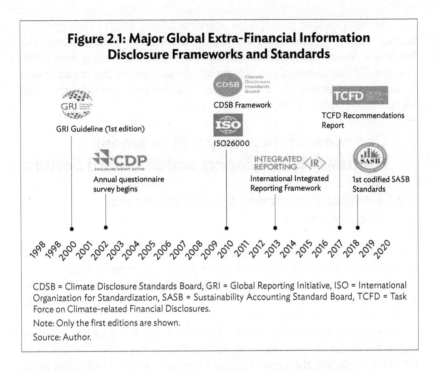

**Figure 2.1: Major Global Extra-Financial Information
Disclosure Frameworks and Standards**

CDSB = Climate Disclosure Standards Board, GRI = Global Reporting Initiative, ISO = International
Organization for Standardization, SASB = Sustainability Accounting Standard Board, TCFD = Task
Force on Climate-related Financial Disclosures.
Note: Only the first editions are shown.
Source: Author.

frameworks and standards caused by the increase in their number and lack of communication or coordination among them, which reduces the comparability of reporting data (Douma and Dallas, 2018; Barker and Eccles, 2018, 2019; WEF, 2019; GPIF, 2019a, 2019b; Cambourg, 2019; Bernow et al., 2019). The inconsistency makes navigating frameworks and standards complex and preparing reporting material burdensome, bringing about "reporting fatigue." The above literature discusses the need for more coordination among frameworks and standards to make them more consistent or even to converge.

Major global framework developers and standard setters are mostly competing nongovernment organizations (Table 2.1). Competition would benefit e-commerce privacy protection standards (Jamal, Maier, and Sunder 2003, 2005) and telephony standards (Jamal and Sunder 2014), but is this true for extra-financial information disclosure frameworks and standards? Too many inconsistent frameworks and standards might result in less efficient and less effective corporate reporting practices. What challenges need to be met to enjoy the benefits of competition among extra-financial information disclosure frameworks and standards?

The next section presents an overview of the status of competition among major global frameworks and standards, then reviews the literature about competition among financial accounting standards. Section 2.3 discusses three potential challenges in the competition among extra-financial information disclosure frameworks and standards. Section 2.4 presents conclusions.

2.2 Overview of the Competition among Framework Developers and Standard Setters

2.2.1 Competitive Landscape of Frameworks and Standards

Table 2.1 shows the overview of major global framework developers and standard setters, scope of disclosure, and company penetration.

The seven organizations are all nongovernment organizations. The TCFD is a less formal entity than others. Adoption of frameworks and standards by companies is voluntary.

Regarding penetration status, the CDP Questionnaires obtained the highest number of respondents: about 7,000 companies in 2018. The GRI Standards had the second-highest number: nearly 4,000 companies voluntarily complied with or referred to the standards when they prepared reporting materials, such as corporate social responsibility (CSR) or sustainability reports. The CDP Questionnaires and the GRI Standards have a long history and have successfully penetrated companies globally.

In contrast, the <IR> Framework is newer (released in 2013), but about 1,700 companies from 72 countries have already conducted integrated reporting. Even newer are the TCFD Recommendations Report (released in 2017) and the SASB Standards (first codified version, 2018) but they have already started influencing corporate disclosure practices.

Regarding the scope of disclosure, the GRI Standards, the <IR> Framework, the International Organization for Standardization (ISO)26000, and the SASB Standards cover environmental, social, and governance (ESG) issues, while the CDP Questionnaires, the Climate Disclosure Standards Board (CDSB) Framework, and the TCFD Recommendations Report focus on climate-related issues and other environmental issues.

The ISO26000 is not a disclosure-focused framework but guidance on social responsibility. Many companies, however, have used ISO26000 for extra-financial disclosure. The CDP Questionnaires takes a different

Table 2.1: Overview of Framework Developers and Standard Setters

	CDP	CDSB	GRI	IIRC	ISO	SASB	TCFD
Headquarters	London	London	Amsterdam	London	Geneva	San Francisco	n/a
Founded	2000	2007	1997	2010	1947	2011	2016
Form of organization	NGO	NGO	NGO	NGO	NGO	NGO	n/a
Name of the framework or standard (latest version)	CDP Questionnaires	CDSB Framework	GRI Standards	International Integrated Reporting Framework	ISO26000	SASB Standards	TCFD Recommendations Report
Scope	Climate, Water, Forests	Environment, Climate	ESG overall	Financial and ESG overall	ESG overall	ESG overall	Climate
Company penetration status globally	7,018 companies reported in 2018	374 companies across 32 countries	3,966 organizations adopt or refer in the reporting year 2017	1,700 organizations in 72 countries	(No data)	314 companies refer in YTD 2019 (31 August 2019)	299 business firm supporters

CDSB = Climate Disclosure Standards Board, GRI = Global Reporting Initiative, IIRC = International Integrated Reporting Council, ISO = International Organization for Standardization, NGO = nongovernment organization, SASB = Sustainability Accounting Standard Board, TCFD = Task Force on Climate-related Financial Disclosures, YTD = year to date.

Notes:

1. TCFD is a less formal entity then others.
2. The figure of TCFD supporters relates only to business firms. Supporters that are categorized as financial, government, professional services, proxy firm, law firm, real estate, and other are not included.

Source: Author, based on the CDP (https://www.cdp.net/en/companies/companies-scores [accessed 20 November 2019]), the CDSB (https://www.cdsb.net/what-we-do/reporting-frameworks [accessed 20 November 2019]), the GRI (https://database.globalreporting.org/ [accessed 20 November 2019]), the IIRC (https://integratedreporting.org/news/richard-howitt-on-what-really-drives-value-pivot-magazine-and-cpa-canada/ [accessed 20 November 2019]), and the TCFD (https://www.fsb-tcfd.org/tcfd-supporters/ [accessed 20 November 2019]) as well as the information provided by the SASB.

approach: it sends questionnaires to companies to obtain extra-financial information on behalf of investors or other companies. But the content of the questionnaires influences what is disclosed publicly. We therefore incorporate the ISO26000 and the CDP Questionnaires in our research scope.

2.2.2 How Are the Framework Developers and Standard Setters Different from Each Other?

Frameworks and standards have different features. This chapter categorizes them by examining (i) the nature of disclosure information and (ii) the differences in standard-setting approaches.

Differences in Disclosure Information

Disclosure information can be divided into that related to (i) the company's financial performance such as operating performance and/or financial conditions, and (ii) the company's environmental and/or societal impacts. While the CDSB Framework, the <IR> Framework, the TCFD Recommendations Report, and the SASB Standards fall under the first group, the ISO26000, the CDP Questionnaires, and the GRI Standards are classified under the second.

Differences in Standard-Setting Approaches

The principle-based and rule-based approaches have advantages and disadvantages. Under the principle-based approach, "norms are formulated as guidelines; the exact implementation is left to the subject of norm" (Burgemeestre, Hulstijn, and Tan, 2009), allowing companies flexible disclosure. Too much flexibility, however, may confuse the implementation of principles and may result in disparity of disclosure levels among companies. Conversely, the rule-based approach "prescribes in detail how to behave" (Burgemeestre, Hulstijn, and Tan, 2009) which makes it easier for companies to understand what to disclose because there is less room to interpret the rules. However, applying strict rules may result in mere formality and undermine substantial disclosure.

The ISO26000, the CDSB Framework, the <IR> Framework, and the TCFD Recommendations Report are all principle-based frameworks that allow more flexibility, i.e., more tailored disclosure reflecting each company's situation. Conversely, the GRI and the SASB Standards are rule-based standards that define a series of concrete disclosure items and indicators. Similarly, the CDP Questionnaires consists of questions that ask for specific matters or indicators.

Table 2.2: Classification of Frameworks and Standards

		Nature of disclosure information	
		Information about environmental and/or societal impact brought by a company	Information related to a company's financial performance
Standard-setting approach	Principle-based	- ISO26000	- CDSB Framework - <IR> Framework - TCFD Recommendations Report
	Rule-based	- CDP Questionnaires - GRI Standards	- SASB Standards

Source: Author.

Table 2.2 summarizes the above analysis. Frameworks and standards are dispersed among four areas, suggesting that they have different characteristics. The ISO26000 and the SASB Standards have unique characteristics, while the CSDB Framework, the <IR> Framework, and the TCFD Recommendations Report, as well as the CDP Questionnaires and the GRI Standards, have similar characteristics.

2.2.3 Differences among Frameworks and Standards

This section focuses on the information users, i.e., investors' demands for extra-financial disclosure.

Recently, an increasing number of investors have been using ESG information to manage ESG investment. The global asset volume of ESG investment has been expanding and reached $30.7 trillion in 2018, accounting for 48.8% of total managed assets in Europe and 25.7% in the United States. However, there is no single approach to using ESG information. Rather, the approach has been diversifying.[1]

In judgmental investment strategies, where ESG information is used mainly for fundamental analysis (Van Duuren, Plantinga, and Scholtens

---

[1]   CFA Institute and the PRI provide case studies about how institutional investors incorporate ESG factors into investment analysis and/or portfolio construction process (see CFA Institute and PRI [2018]).

2016) or, more specifically, valuation of companies (Schramade 2016), the ESG information demanded is likely to be specific to the individual company. For example, the information may be about corporate governance, which suggests the quality of management, as well as information about how companies tackle environmental and social issues and/or deal with the interest groups, which suggests the quality of strategic planning (Van Duuren, Plantinga, and Scholtens 2016). Such information helps financial analysts or investment managers obtain a clearer view of the company's future. Principle-based frameworks, such as the <IR> Framework, which promote disclosure tailored to each company, are more likely than rule-based standards to meet such information demand.

ESG information is used not only for judgmental investment strategies. Recently, ESG indexes have also been gaining popularity, where constituents are selected objectively, usually based on ESG ratings or ESG scores created by ESG rating agencies (e.g., Escrig-Olmedo, Muñoz-Torres, and Fernandez-Izquierdo [2010]). Quantitative investment strategies, including smart beta, are increasingly paying attention to ESG information (e.g., Giese, Ossen, and Bacon [2016]; Grene [2016]; Bender, Sun, and Wang [2017]). ESG information demand for such strategies should be easier to quantify and easier to compare among peer companies. To ensure that it is quantifiable and comparable, ESG information should be disclosed in a standardized way. Therefore, rule-based standards such as the SASB Standards would be especially welcomed in such strategies.

A new form of ESG investment—impact investing—has been rapidly expanding since the second half of the 2000s (e.g., Höchstädter and Scheck [2015], Trelstad [2016], Clarkin and Cangioni [2016]). The Global Impact Investing Network (GIIN, 2019) defines impact investing as "investments made to generate positive, measurable social and environmental impact alongside a financial return." Impact investments' global market size was estimated at $502 billion as of the end of 2018. Based on the GIIN's definition, information about impact may be assumed to be necessary for impact investors' decision making. Of the seven frameworks and standards researched for this chapter, the GRI Standards, which aim for disclosure of economic, environmental, and/or societal impact, are conceptually the most relevant to impact investors' demand for information.

Figure 2.2 shows that ESG investment approaches have diversified and have varied information demand, which is a reason why various frameworks and standards can coexist. Different characteristics of frameworks and standards can be interpreted as strategies to differentiate themselves from others.

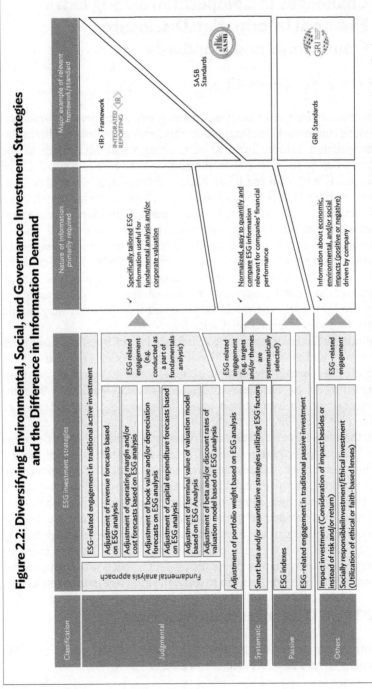

Figure 2.2: Diversifying Environmental, Social, and Governance Investment Strategies and the Difference in Information Demand

Note: The figure indicates only the most basic ESG information for each strategy. Other types of ESG information not mentioned in the figure might also be utilized.

Source: Author, based on CFA Institute and PRI (2018). Reprinted from GPIF (2019a: 14).

2.3 Challenges in Competition among Extra-Financial Information Disclosure Frameworks and Standards

2.3.1 Nature of Competition

Before examining the competition among extra-financial information disclosure frameworks and standards, this section reviews the literature on competition among financial accounting standards. Much of the literature has been issued in response to policy trends toward global convergence with International Financial Reporting Standards (e.g., Dye and Sunder [2001]; Ball [2006]; Watts [2006]; Sunder [2002, 2010, 2011]) and may be informative in examining competition among extra-financial information disclosure frameworks and standards.

One common message of the above literature is that convergence will make disclosure information more comparable but not necessarily more relevant for investors' decision making. Uniformity and quality of standards are not synonymous. Comparability is only one aspect of disclosure information's usefulness for investors. The same may be said of extra-financial information disclosure.

While the convergence of extra-financial information disclosure frameworks and standards could reduce complexity, and thus relieve companies' reporting burden, it should never be pursued without paying attention to the quality of frameworks and standards. Bottom-up convergence via competition among frameworks and standards, i.e., selection by companies through comparison of alternatives, could be better than top-down convergence, where a central authority develops unified frameworks or standards and forces companies to adopt them.

However, unlike financial accounting standards that companies are forced to adopt, extra-financial information disclosure frameworks and standards are adopted completely voluntarily. Companies may adopt more than two frameworks and standards, pick and choose certain elements from them, or not even adopt any of them. Hence, the intensity of competition, i.e., selective pressure, could likely be less than for financial accounting standards. Ensuring a sufficient level of competition intensity could be a prerequisite to fostering effective convergence.

2.3.2 Three Challenges to Be Addressed

To sufficiently raise the intensity of competition, three possible challenges should be addressed (Figure 2.3).

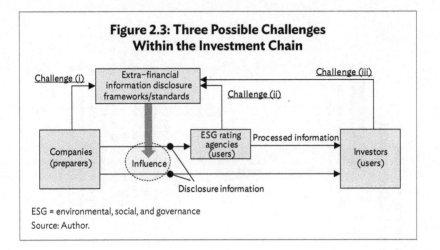

**Figure 2.3: Three Possible Challenges
Within the Investment Chain**

ESG = environmental, social, and governance
Source: Author.

Improve Consistency Among Frameworks and Standards at the Level of Individual Disclosure Items and Indicators

Many disclosure items and indicators in the frameworks and standards, while not identical, have certain common elements. For instance, the GRI Standards and the SASB Standards provide disclosure items and indicators that are (i) mixtures of these standards and are partially matched, (ii) related in a complex manner to three or more disclosure items and/or indicators, and (iii) a subset of others (Figure 2.4).

Such complexity is not surprising since the frameworks and standards have different aims and were developed at different times by different entities in different countries, but it is not easy to clearly identify common elements and differences. This fact could discourage companies from navigating frameworks and standards carefully to choose the best one (or ones) for extra-financial reporting. Comparing and choosing appropriate disclosure item(s) and/or indicator(s) from the universe could be burdensome, and that could decrease the competition intensity among frameworks and standards, i.e., decrease the selective pressure from companies.

To foster healthy competition, reducing complexity among frameworks and standards (i.e., clarifying common elements and differences at the level of individual disclosure items and indicators) could be helpful, and direct communication among framework developers and standard setters such as through the Better Alignment Project initiated by the International Integrated Reporting Council would be necessary.

Figure 2.4: Complexity Between Disclosure Items and Indicators of the Global Reporting Initiative and the Sustainability Accounting Standards Board

Partially matched

SASB Standards: Oil and gas (exploration and production)
Percentage of (i) proved and (ii) probable reserves in the 20 lowest ranked countries in Transparency International's Corruption Perception Index

GRI Disclosure 205-1
The reporting organization shall report the following information:
a. Total number and percentage of operations assessed for risks related to corruption
b. Significant risks related to corruption identified through the risk assessment

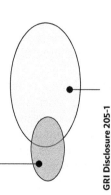

Three or more intricately related

SASB Standards: Hardware
Percentage of tier-1 supplier facilities audited in the RBA Validated Audit Process or equivalent, by (i) all facilities and (ii) high-risk facilities
*The RBA audit covers labor of the suppliers (human rights), health and safety, environmental protection and ethics, etc.

GRI Disclosure 308-2 Negative environmental impacts in the supply chain and actions taken
GRI Disclosure 407-1 Operations and suppliers in which the right to freedom of association and collective bargaining may be at risk
GRI Disclosure 408-1 Operations and suppliers at significant risk for incidents of child labor
GRI Disclosure 409-1 Operations and suppliers at significant risk for incidents of forced or compulsory labor
GRI Disclosure 414-2 Negative social impacts in the supply chain and actions taken
*In the above, specific reporting requirements are omitted.

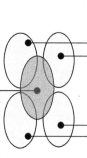

Subset

SASB Standards: Automobiles
Number of vehicles recalled

GRI Disclosure 416-2
Incidents of noncompliance concerning the health and safety impacts of products and services
a. Total number of incidents of noncompliance with regulations and/or voluntary codes concerning the health and safety impacts of products and services within the reporting period [...]
b. If the organization has not identified any noncompliance with regulations and/or voluntary codes, a brief statement of this fact is sufficient.

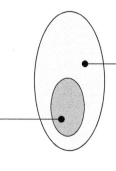

GRI = Global Reporting Initiative, SASB = Sustainability Accounting Standards Board.
Source: Author, based on the GRI Standards and the SASB Standards (Version 2018–10). Reprinted from GPIF (2019a: 25).

More Transparency Between Evaluation Items and Criteria of Environmental, Social, and Governance Rating Agencies and Frameworks and Standards

The second challenge to tackle is the relationship between ESG rating agencies and frameworks and standards.

ESG rating agencies are key users of extra-financial information. They analyze corporate disclosure materials and produce outputs such as ESG analysis reports, ESG scores, and ESG ratings, for their institutional investor clients.

However, details of evaluation items and criteria of ESG rating agencies are generally not publicly disclosed,[2] thus the relationship is less visible between each evaluation item and criterion and each disclosure item and indicator set by frameworks and standards. Such information could be an important indicator for companies to decide which frameworks or standards to adopt. The transparency between ESG rating agencies and frameworks and standards, therefore, could increase selective pressure from companies.

Such transparency could also improve frameworks and standards. To meet the information demands of ESG rating agencies, framework developers and standard setters may modify their disclosure items and/or indicators to align more, and eventually such modifications could also affect selection by companies.

Publicly available sources have little information on communication between ESG rating agencies and framework developers and standard setters.[3] To improve transparency between them, promoting communication is key.

Further Involvement of Asset Owners and Asset Managers in Developing and Improving Frameworks and Standards

Besides ESG rating agencies, institutional investors (asset owners and asset managers) are also key extra-financial information users, and their information demands should be incorporated into frameworks and standards.

---

[2]   Many scholars have pointed out the lack of transparency of the methodologies adopted by ESG rating agencies (Chatterji and Levine, 2006; Escrig-Olmedo, Muñoz-Torres, and Fernandez-Izquierdo, 2010; Scalet and Kelly, 2010; Saadaoui and Soobaroyen, 2018). A questionnaire survey reveals that many sustainability professionals recognize the need for greater transparency of methodologies (Wong, Brackley, and Petroy, 2019).

[3]   This review has found limited information. The SASB's webpage, for example, shows that some research analysts from several ESG rating agencies were involved in setting SASB's standards by participating in industry-by-industry working groups.

Although some institutional investors have become actively involved in framework development and standard-setting processes, more should do so to reflect their information demands.

Institutional investors should more publicly express their preference for frameworks and standards to signal to companies which should be used. The result will be improved selective pressure by companies.

2.4 Concluding Remarks

This study examines the extra-financial information disclosure frameworks and standards from the perspective of competition and finds that the difference in their characteristics can be interpreted as their differentiation strategies to meet their clientele's demands.

Complexity and lack of coordination among frameworks and standards have been intensifying. Consistency must be improved and convergence pushed to relieve companies' burden of reporting and to increase the comparability of disclosure information.

One way to achieve convergence is via competition among extra-financial information disclosure frameworks and standards. Because such competition is different from that among financial accounting standards, however, and competition intensity in extra-financial information disclosure is likely to be lower, we should pay attention to the competitive environment

To ensure sufficient levels of competition, three possible challenges should be tackled: (i) improve consistency among frameworks and standards at the level of individual disclosure items and indicators, (ii) increase transparency between evaluation items and criteria of ESG rating agencies and frameworks and standards, and (iii) further involve asset owners and asset managers in developing standards and improving processes. These propositions are not fully demonstrated here so further analysis and discussion are warranted.

References

Ball, R. 2006. International Financial Reporting Standards (IFRS): Pros and Cons for Investors. *Accounting and Business Research* 36(sup1): 5–27.

Barker, R., and R. G., Eccles. 2018. *Should FASB and IASB Be Responsible for Setting Standards for Nonfinancial Information? Green Paper.* Oxford: University of Oxford. https://www.sbs.ox.ac.uk/sites/ default/files/2018-10/Green%20Paper_0.pdf (accessed 20 November 2019).

Barker, R., and R. G. Eccles. 2019. Charting the Path to Standards for Nonfinancial Information. https://www.sbs.ox.ac.uk/sites/default /files/2019-09/Charting%20the%20Path%20to%20Standards %20for%20Nonfinancial%20Information%20081919.pdf (accessed 20 November 2019).

Bender, J., X. Sun, and T. Wang. 2017. Thematic Indexing, Meet Smart Beta! Merging ESG into Factor Portfolios. *The Journal of Index Investing* 8(3): 89–101.

Bernow, S., J. Godsall, B. Klempner, and C. Merten. 2019. More Than Values: The Value-Based Sustainability Reporting That Investors Want. McKinsey & Company. https://www.mckinsey.com/business -functions/sustainability/our-insights/more-than-values-the-value -based-sustainability-reporting-that-investors-want# (accessed 20 November 2019).

Burgemeestre, B., J. Hulstijn, and Y. H. Tan. 2009. Rule-Based Versus Principle-Based Regulatory Compliance. Paper presented at the 22nd Annual Conference (JURIX 2009), Netherlands, July 2009.

Cambourg, P. 2019. Ensuring the Relevance and Reliability of Non-Financial Corporate Information: Ambition and a Competitive Advantage for a Sustainable Europe. Autorité des Normes Comptables. http://www .anc.gouv.fr/files/live/sites/anc/files/contributed/ANC/4.%20 Qui%20sommes-nous/Communique_de_presse/Report-de -Cambourg_extra-financial-informations_May2019_EN.pdf (accessed 20 November 2019).

CDP. Guidance & Questionnaires. https://www.cdp.net/en/guidance (accessed 20 November 2019).

CDSB. 2018. CDSB Framework: For Reporting Environmental Information, Natural Capital and Associated Business Impacts. https://www.cdsb.net/sites/default/files/cdsb_framework_2.1.pdf (accessed 20 November 2019).

CFA Institute and PRI. 2018. Guidance and Case Studies for ESG integration: Equities and Fixed Incomes. https://www.unpri.org /download?ac=5962 (accessed 20 November 2019).

Chatterji, A., and D. Levine. 2006. Breaking Down the Wall of Codes: Evaluating Non-Financial Performance Measurement. *California Management Review* 48(2): 29–51.

Clarkin, J. E., and C. L. Cangioni. 2016. Impact Investing: A Primer and Review of the Literature. *Entrepreneurship Research Journal* 6(2): 135–173.

Corporate Register Ltd. Tools. http://www.corporateregister.com /livecharts/?chart=1&cou=All&sec=All&sub=All&our=All (accessed 20 November 2019).

Douma, K., and G. Dallas. 2018. Investor Agenda for Corporate ESG Reporting: A Discussion Paper by Global Investor Organisations on Corporate ESG Reporting. PRI and ICGN. https://www.unpri.org /download?ac=6181 (accessed 20 November 2019).

Dye, R. A., and S. Sunder. 2001. Why Not Allow FASB and IASB Standards to Compete in the US? *Accounting Horizons* 15(3): 257–271.

Escrig-Olmedo, E., M. J. Muñoz-Torres, and M. A. Fernandez-Izquierdo. 2010. Socially Responsible Investing: Sustainability Indexes, ESG Rating and Information Provider Agencies. *International Journal of Sustainable Economy*: 2(4): 442–461.

Giese, G., A. Ossen, and S. Bacon. 2016. ESG As a Performance Factor for Smart Beta Indexes. *The Journal of Index Investing* 7(3): 7–20.

Global Impact Investing Network (GIIN). What Is Impact Investing? https://thegiin.org/impact-investing/need-to-know/#what-is -impact-investing (accessed 22 August 2019).

Global Impact Investing Network (GIIN). 2019. Sizing the Impact Investing Market. https://thegiin.org/assets/Sizing%20the%20 Impact%20Investing%20Market_webfile.pdf (accessed 20 November 2019).

Global Reporting Initiative (GRI) Standards. GRI Standards Download Center. https://www.globalreporting.org/standards/gri-standards -download-center/ (accessed 5 June 2019).

GPIF. 2019a. Study of ESG Information Disclosure: Summary. https://www.gpif.go.jp/en/investment/research_2019_EN.pdf (accessed 20 November 2019).

GPIF. 2019b. Study of ESG Information Disclosure. https://www .gpif.go.jp/en/investment/research_2019_full_EN.pdf   (accessed 20 November 2019).

Grene, S. 2016. Quants Are New Ethical Investors. *Financial Times*. 24 January.

Höchstädter, A. K., and B. Scheck. 2015. What's In a Name: An Analysis of Impact Investing Understandings by Academics and Practitioners. *Journal of Business Ethics* 132(2): 449–475.

International Integrated Reporting Council. 2013. International Integrated Reporting Framework. http://integratedreporting.org /wp-content/uploads/2015/03/13-12-08-THE-INTERNATIONAL -IR-FRAMEWORK-2-1.pdf (accessed 20 November 2019).

ISO26000. https://www.iso.org/iso-26000-social-responsibility.html (accessed 20 November 2019).

Jamal, K., M. Maier, and S. Sunder. 2003. Regulations and the Marketplace. *Regulation: The CATO Review of Business and Government* 26(4): 38–41.

Jamal, K., M. Maier, and S. Sunder. 2005. Enforced Standards Versus Evolution by General Acceptance: A Comparative Study of E-Commerce Privacy Disclosure and Practice in the United States and the United Kingdom. *Journal of Accounting Research* 43(1): 73–96.

Jamal, K., and S. Sunder. 2014. Monopoly Versus Competition in Setting Accounting Standards. *Abacus* 50(4): 369–385.

Kolk, A. 2004. A Decade of Sustainability Reporting: Developments and Significance. *International Journal of Environmental and Sustainable Development*: 3(1): 51–64.

KPMG. 2017. The Road Ahead: The KPMG Survey of Corporate Responsibility Reporting 2017.

Sustainability Accounting Standards Board (SASB) Standards (Version 2018-10). https://www.sasb.org/standards-overview/download -current-standards/ (accessed 20 November 2019).

Saadaoui, K., and T. Soobaroyen. 2018. An Analysis of the Methodologies Adopted by CSR Rating Agencies. *Sustainability Accounting, Management and Policy Journal* 9(1): 43–62.

Scalet, S., and T. F. Kelly. 2010. CSR Rating Agencies: What Is Their Global Impact? *Journal of Business Ethics* 94(1): 69–88.

Schramade, W. 2016. Integrating ESG into Valuation Models and Investment Decisions: The Value-Driver Adjustment Approach. *Journal of Sustainable Finance & Investment* 6(2): 95–111.

Sunder, S. 2002. Regulatory Competition Among Accounting Standards Within and Across International Boundaries. *Journal of Accounting and Public Policy* 21(3): 219–234.

Sunder, S. 2010. Adverse Effects of Uniform Written Reporting Standards on Accounting Practice, Education, and Research. *Journal of Accounting and Public Policy* 29(2): 99–114.

Sunder, S. 2011. IFRS Monopoly: The Pied Piper of Financial Reporting. *Accounting and Business Research* 41(3): 291–306.

Task Force on Climate-related Financial Disclosures (TCFD). 2017. Final Report: Recommendations of the Task Force on Climate-Related

Financial Disclosures (June 2017). https://www.fsb-tcfd.org/wp -content/uploads/2017/06/FINAL-2017-TCFD-Report-11052018 .pdf (accessed 20 November 2019).

Trelstad, B. 2016. Impact Investing: A Brief History. *Capitalism & Society* 11(2): Article 4.

Van Duuren, E., A. Plantinga, and B. Scholtens. 2016. ESG Integration and the Investment Management Process: Fundamental Investing Reinvented. *Journal of Business Ethics* 138(3): 525–533.

Watts, R. L. 2006. What Has the Invisible Hand Achieved? *Accounting and Business Research* 36(sup1): 51–61.

Wong, C., A. Brackley, and E. Petroy. 2019. Rate the Raters 2019: Expert Views of ESG Ratings. SustainAbility. https://sustainability.com /wp-content/uploads/2019/02/SA-RateTheRaters-2019-1.pdf (accessed 20 November 2019).

World Economic Forum (WEF). 2019. Seeking Return on ESG: Advancing the Reporting Ecosystem to Unlock Impact for Business and Society. White Paper. http://www3.weforum.org/docs/WEF _ESG_Report_digital_pages.pdf (accessed 20 November 2019).

3

Environmental, Social, and Governance Factors and Their Implications for Equity Investments

Yasuyuki Kato

3.1 Is Environmental, Social, and Governance Evaluation Factored into Corporate Value?

3.1.1 Environmental, Social, and Governance Evaluation and Capital Cost

Is the hypothesis that the higher the environmental, social, and governance (ESG) evaluation, the higher the corporate value correct? The answer is critical. If the hypothesis does not hold, investors seeking returns will not use ESG evaluation in their investment decisions. They will also not seek stocks whose ESG evaluation will increase and companies will have no incentive to improve ESG evaluation if it is unrelated to corporate value. If the hypothesis is correct, investors will be able to obtain excess returns by investing in companies whose ESG evaluation will improve. Or if the ESG evaluation of the company already held increases, excess returns can be obtained. Of course, investors need to be able and make the effort to select companies whose ESG evaluation will increase, or to increase the ESG evaluation of companies held through engagement. Therefore, the hypothesis is extremely important for both investors and companies and must be verified. It is not easy to determine which variables should be factored into corporate value. Even if a variable seems to be working, it may not be factored into corporate value. For example, in recent years, earnings surprise has been declining (that is, the degree of incorporation of profit forecasts into the corporate value decreased) (Gu and Lev, 2017). The most important variable for corporate value is not necessarily certain. The structure of the economy changes over time. It will always need to be verified.

3.1.2 Method of Verification

First, we describe the verification method used in this study. Corporate value can be measured by the market value of shareholder capital. But the level of market value depends on the size of the company. Corporate value changes due to capital increase or decrease. Therefore, a proxy variable of corporate value must be used that can measure the relationship with ESG evaluation regardless of the company size or capital increase or decrease. According to the discounted cash flow (DCF) model, corporate value can be considered the present value of future cash flow (profit):

$$V = \frac{CF_1}{(1+r)} + \frac{CF_2}{(1+r)^2} + \frac{CF_3}{(1+r)^3} + \cdots$$

where V is the corporate value, CF_i (i = 1, ..., N, ...) is the cash flow for each period, and r is the discount rate (capital cost). This equation shows that the corporate value is a function of the capital cost and cash flow growth rate. If the capital cost is higher, the corporate value is lower. Conversely, if the capital cost is lower, the corporate value is higher. In terms of the growth rate, the relationship with the corporate value is reversed. If the growth rate is higher, the corporate value is higher. Conversely, if the growth rate is lower, the corporate value is lower. The cost of capital is risk-free return plus the risk premium and is related to the risk of the company. Improvement of ESG evaluation is generally considered to be useful for reducing corporate risk. Even in the FTSE Russell survey, the biggest item for ESG investment is the reduction of investment risk.

It would be natural, therefore, to think that ESG evaluation affects the cost of capital. We examine the relationship between ESG evaluation and capital cost, where capital cost is used as a proxy variable for corporate value. Cross-sectional regression verifies whether the capital cost of companies with higher ESG evaluation is lower and, conversely, the capital cost of companies with lower ESG evaluation is higher. Indicators such as price earnings ratio and price book value ratio are also candidates as proxy variables for corporate value. These indicators are derived from the DCF model. But here we examine capital cost, which is considered to have a clearer effect for ESG evaluation. Next, the capital cost of each company must be estimated. Under the capital asset pricing model theory, capital cost can be represented by capital asset pricing model beta.

Much research has been done on ESG evaluation and capital cost verification. For example, Ghoul et al. (2011) used the evaluation of ESG ratings to classify companies into two groups according to ESG rating and calculate the average value of the capital cost for each group. The results show that the capital cost of companies with high ESG ratings is significantly lower, while the corporate value of companies with low ESG ratings is higher.

3.1.3 Environmental, Social, and Governance Evaluation

What should we use for ESG evaluation? Financial information, such as sales and profits, is available in corporate disclosure and data are standardized and compared using a unified accounting standard. Financial information can be easily obtained and used for various evaluations. Regarding ESG evaluation, the disclosure of company data is not enough and few disclosure standards are used widely. In the United States (US), ESG information disclosure standards such as those of the Sustainability Accounting Standards Board have been proposed and tend toward unification, but it will take time for them to be standardized. It is not always easy for investors to obtain ESG evaluation information directly from corporate disclosure. This is a major obstacle to ESG investment. We hope that ESG information disclosure by companies will advance and that ESG evaluation information and financial information will be easily available to any investor.

In such an environment, two types of organizations create ESG evaluation information for companies: investment management organizations and ESG rating organizations. ESG evaluations are used by investment managers to select stocks and are generally not disclosed outside the company. What is available to general investors is rating information from ESG rating agencies.

3.1.4 Verification Results in the Japan Market

To determine whether ESG evaluation is incorporated into the corporate value, we use cross-sectional regression between ESG evaluation and beta, which is a proxy of the capital cost. If the coefficient of ESG evaluation is significantly negative, the ESG evaluation can be considered to be factored into the capital cost. Companies with higher ESG evaluation have lower capital cost and higher corporate value and, conversely, companies with lower ESG evaluation have higher capital cost and lower corporate value. In cross-sectional regression, we consider that beta is affected by factors other than ESG evaluation and add three control variables: shareholder equity ratio, total assets, and sales growth rate. With beta as an explanatory variable, cross-sectional regression is performed with four variables: ESG evaluation, shareholder capital ratio, total assets, and sales growth. Then the coefficient of the ESG evaluation variable is verified as significantly negative. Beta is estimated by regressing the weekly return data for the last 2 years against the market return of each market benchmark.

The following analysis uses two pieces of ESG evaluation information. The first is disclosure evaluation published by the Securities Analysts Association of Japan, which is considered a proxy variable for governance evaluation. The second is the ESG ratings published by FTSE Russell, where E, S, and G are used separately for this analysis. The regression analysis is performed simultaneously using the data from 2007 to 2014 as the panel data for the former analysis. The latter is performed separately for 2016, 2017, and 2018 so that the timing differences can be verified. Table 3.1 and Table 3.2 show the results of analysis using the disclosure rating as governance evaluation. This analysis is based on the work of Satoshi Kasai at the Kato Study Group on the Tokyo Stock Exchange (Kasai, 2015).

Table 3.1: Disclosure and Cost of Capital (Japanese companies)

(Regression model)

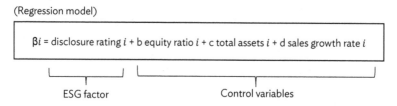

βi = disclosure rating i + b equity ratio i + c total assets i + d sales growth rate i

ESG factor   Control variables

Note: Analysis method
- Data: Overall rating for Excellence in Corporate Disclosure announced by the Securities Analysts Association of Japan
- Period: FY2007–FY2014 (1 July to 30 June the following year)
- Sample size: 1,846 companies. Industries covered: 17, including banking, construction, food, pharmaceuticals, iron and steel, electrical and precision machinery, and start up company stocks, among others
- Evaluation items differed in each industry, and average score and standard deviation were different → Overall evaluation converted into deviation value to perform analysis across fiscal years and industries
- Cost of capital regressed on disclosure evaluation [(1) deviation value of overall evaluation; (2) top 3 dummy variables for each industry] and control variables

ESG = environmental, social and governance, FY = fiscal year.
Source: Kasai (2015).

Table 3.2: Disclosure and Cost of Capital

Explanatory variables (x)	Overall disclosure evaluation			Disclosure top 3 dummy variables		
	Regression coefficient	Significance	t value	Regression coefficient	Significance	t value
Disclosure rating	↓ -0.85	◎	-3.0	↓ -0.52	◎	-2.9
Equity ratio	↓ -2.84	◎	-7.1	↓ -2.87	◎	-7.2
Total assets	↑ 0.58	◎	4.9	0.58	X	4.9
Net sales growth rate	↑ 0.01	○	2.2			
Adjusted R-squared	0.50					
Intercept	12.4	○	2.2			15.0

Cost of capital is lower for companies with higher disclosure ratings

Regression coefficient: ↑ = plus (when variable x increases, cost of equity also increases)
↓ = minus (when variable x increases, cost of equity decreases)
Significance: ◎ = 99% significant, ○ = 95% significant, x = not significant

Source: Kasai (2015).

This rating uses two methods: the disclosure evaluation value (disclosure rating) as the explanatory variable, and the dummy variable that gives 1 to the top-rated companies. As a result of the analysis, the coefficient of the variable for disclosure rating is negative, and the t– value shows a significant result at the 0.5% significance level. Companies with higher disclosure ratings have lower beta and higher corporate value. Next, we use the ESG rating of a rating agency as an ESG evaluation. Table 3.3, Table 3.4, and Table 3.5 show the results of analysis using the ESG rating by FTSE Russell. The results for the Japan market show that the governance (G) rating is significant and seems to be incorporated into the corporate value. However, the environmental (E) and social (S) ratings were far from significantly negative. The Corporate Governance Code introduced by the Japan Financial Services Agency and the Tokyo Stock Exchange in 2015 can explain why the governance factor works. Thanks to the code, companies have made progress in disclosure of corporate governance, and the market started to evaluate corporate governance. Regarding environmental (E) and social (S) factors, corporate disclosure is still not sufficient, so the market is not fully evaluated. In the future, corporate disclosure will progress as ESG investment progresses.

Table 3.3: Environmental, Social, and Governance Ratings and Cost of Capital (Japanese Companies), 2016 (regression coefficient t-value)

t-value	ESG Rating	Equity Ratio	Total Assets	Sales Growth
E	4.286	−5.078	1.496	−0.754
S	3.527	−5.343	1.595	−0.984
G	−1.057	−5.452	1.810	−1.470

Note: Analysis method
- Explained variable: Historical beta (weekly from 9 January 2015 to 30 December 2016)
- Explanatory variable: FTSE ESG ratings (as of 30 December 2016)
- Control variables: Equity ratio, total assets, net sales growth rate (financial results for the fiscal year ended 31 March 2016)
- Sample size: 477 leading Japanese companies

ESG = environmental, social, and governance.
Source: Data from FTSE and FACTSET.

Table 3.4: Environmental, Social, and Governance Ratings and Cost of Capital (Japanese Companies), 2017 (regression coefficient t-value)

t-value	ESG Rating	Equity Ratio	Total Assets	Sales Growth
E	4.280	−6.449	1.299	−2.662
S	3.949	−6.664	1.349	−2.655
G	−2.758	−6.740	1.601	−3.225

Note: Analysis method
- Explained variable: Historical beta (weekly from 25 December 2016 to 22 December 2017)
- Explanatory variable: FTSE ESG ratings (as of 22 December 2017)
- Control variables: Equity ratio, total assets, net sales growth rate (financial results for the fiscal year ended 31 March 2017)
- Sample size: 495 leading Japanese companies

ESG = environmental, social, and governance.
Source: Data from FTSE and FACTSET.

Table 3.5: Environmental, Social, and Governance Ratings and Cost of Capital (Japanese Companies), 2018 (regression coefficient t-value)

t-value	ESG Rating	Equity Ratio	Total Assets	Sales Growth
E	1.235	−2.338	−1.691	1.438
S	1.554	−2.389	−1.700	1.397
G	−1.496	−2.377	−1.533	1.543

Note: Analysis method
- Explained variable: Historical beta (weekly from 23 December 2017 to 30 December 2018)
- Explanatory variable: FTSE ESG ratings (as of 31 December 2018)
- Control variables: Equity ratio, total assets, net sales growth rate (financial results for the fiscal year ended 31 March 2018)
- Sample size: 489 leading Japanese companies

ESG = environmental, social, and governance.
Source: Data from FTSE and FACTSET.

3.1.5 Verification in the United States and the United Kingdom Markets

In the US, ESG investment is progressing rapidly. The United Kingdom (UK) is one of the most advanced ESG markets. We analyze the US and UK markets as we did the Japan market, using the ESG rating data of FTSE Russell. The US results are shown in Table 3.6, Table 3.7, and Table 3.8, and the UK results are shown in Table 3.9, Table 3.10, and Table 3.11. In the US, governance (G) clearly shows significant results, but environment (E) also shows a weak relationship. What about the UK, a country with an advanced ESG market? Surprisingly, no results were significant. How should this be interpreted?

Table 3.6: Environmental, Social, and Governance Ratings and Cost of Capital (US Companies), 2016 (regression coefficient t-value)

t-value	ESG Rating	Equity Ratio	Total Assets	Sales Growth
E	−1.236	0.125	2.780	−0.697
S	0.388	0.226	2.482	−0.533
G	−2.788	−0.203	2.683	−0.496

Note: Analysis method
- Explained variable: Historical beta (weekly from 9 January 2015 to 16 December 2016)
- Explanatory variable: FTSE ESG ratings (as of 30 December 2016)
- Control variables: Equity ratio, total assets, net sales growth rate (financial results for the fiscal year ended 31 March 2016)
- Sample size: 599 leading US companies

ESG = environmental, social, and governance.

Source: Data from FTSE and FACTSET.

Table 3.7: Environmental, Social, and Governance Ratings and Cost of Capital (US Companies), 2017 (regression coefficient t-value)

t-value	ESG Rating	Equity Ratio	Total Assets	Sales Growth
E	−2.001	−0.800	3.317	1.893
S	0.317	−0.719	2.852	1.798
G	−2.470	−1.103	3.036	1.770

Note: Analysis method
- Explained variable: Historical beta (weekly from 25 December 2016 to 22 December 2017)
- Explanatory variable: FTSE ESG ratings (as of 22 December 2017)
- Control variables: Equity ratio, total assets, net sales growth rate (financial results for the fiscal year ended 31 March 2017)
- Sample size: 601 leading US companies

ESG = environmental, social, and governance.

Source: Data from FTSE and FACTSET.

Table 3.8: Environmental, Social, and Governance Ratings and Cost of Capital (US Companies), 2018 (regression coefficient t-value)

t-value	ESG Rating	Equity Ratio	Total Assets	Sales Growth
E	1.349	−0.391	1.453	5.570
S	3.295	−0.325	1.366	5.844
G	−2.320	−0.608	2.103	5.153

Note: Analysis method
- Explained variable: Historical beta (weekly from 22 December 2017 to 30 December 2018)
- Explanatory variable: FTSE ESG ratings (as of 31 December 2018)
- Control variables: Equity ratio, total assets, net sales growth rate (financial results for the fiscal year ended 31 March 2018)
- Sample size: 562 leading US companies

ESG = environmental, social, and governance.
Source: Data from FTSE and FACTSET.

Table 3.9: Environmental, Social, and Governance Ratings and Cost of Capital (UK Companies), 2016 (regression coefficient t-value)

t-value	ESG Rating	Equity Ratio	Total Assets	Sales Growth
E	2.756	−0.869	0.708	−0.148
S	3.274	−1.328	0.975	0.190
G	−0.244	−1.109	1.531	−0.118

Note: Analysis method
- Explained variable: Historical beta (weekly from 26 December 2015 to 18 December 2016)
- Explanatory variable: FTSE ESG ratings (as of 30 December 2016)
- Control variables: Equity ratio, total assets, net sales growth rate (financial results for the fiscal year ended 31 March 2016)
- Sample size: 122 leading UK companies

ESG = environmental, social, and governance.
Source: Data from FTSE and FACTSET.

Table 3.10: Environmental, Social, and Governance Ratings and Cost of Capital (UK Companies), 2017 (regression coefficient t-value)

t-value	ESG Rating	Equity Ratio	Total Assets	Sales Growth
E	2.140	−0.445	1.177	2.992
S	2.516	−0.713	1.516	2.804
G	0.692	−0.760	1.837	2.693

Note: Analysis method
- Explained variable: Historical beta (weekly from 25 December 2016 to 22 December 2017)
- Explanatory variable: FTSE ESG ratings (as of 22 December 2017)
- Control variables: Equity ratio, total assets, net sales growth rate (financial results for the fiscal year ended 31 March 2017)
- Sample size: 122 leading UK companies

ESG = environmental, social, and governance.
Source: Data from FTSE and FACTSET.

**Table 3.11: Environmental, Social, and Governance Ratings and Cost of
Capital (UK Companies), 2018 (regression coefficient t-value)**

t-value	ESG Rating	Equity Ratio	Total Assets	Sales Growth
E	−0.731	−0.406	0.383	1.481
S	0.181	−0.333	0.141	1.835
G	0.294	−0.296	0.159	1.860

Note: Analysis method
- Explained variable: Historical beta (weekly from 23 December 2017 to 30 December 2018)
- Explanatory variable: FTSE ESG ratings (as of 31 December 2018)
- Control variables: Equity ratio, total assets, net sales growth rate (financial results for the fiscal year ended 31 March 2018)
- Sample size: 111 leading UK companies

ESG = environmental, social, and governance.
Source: Data from FTSE and FACTSET.

Figure 3.1 compares average country ESG evaluation scores. As expected, the average ESG rating of the UK, an advanced ESG market, is higher and the standard deviation lower. The analysis conducted this time is a cross-section analysis, which shows whether the difference in

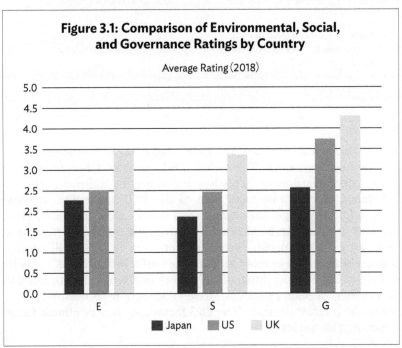

**Figure 3.1: Comparison of Environmental, Social,
and Governance Ratings by Country**

Average Rating (2018)

continued on next page

Figure 3.1 *continued*

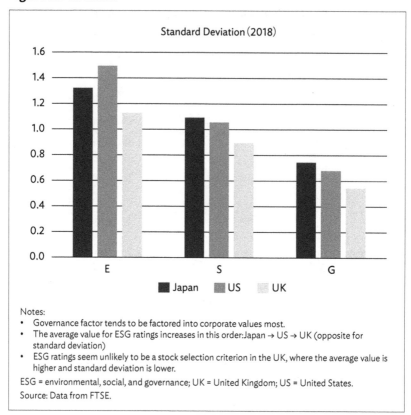

Notes:
- Governance factor tends to be factored into corporate values most.
- The average value for ESG ratings increases in this order:Japan → US → UK (opposite for standard deviation)
- ESG ratings seem unlikely to be a stock selection criterion in the UK, where the average value is higher and standard deviation is lower.

ESG = environmental, social, and governance; UK = United Kingdom; US = United States.
Source: Data from FTSE.

ESG evaluation among companies is related to the difference in capital cost among companies. The overall ESG rating of UK companies is high and standard deviation is low and it may be difficult to see the difference in corporate value due to the ESG evaluation. If some companies have high ESG ratings and others have low ones, cross sections are likely to be affected. However, if ESG ratings have been high in most companies, investors' interests in ESG will decline because differences in cross sections are unlikely to occur. A study by Bebchuk, Cohen, and Wang, (2013) shows that when the attention to corporate governance declines, shareholder proposals decline, that is, investors' interest declines. The ESG factor may be a nonlinear factor depending on the level.

3.1.6 Environmental, Social, and Governance Factors in Asian Markets

Figure 3.2 shows the average and the standard deviation of ESG ratings of the FTSE Russell in the Australian, US, UK, and Asian economies. Table 3.12 shows the results of analyses if ESG ratings are factored into corporate value. All ESG ratings are factored into corporate value in some markets such as India and Hong Kong, China.

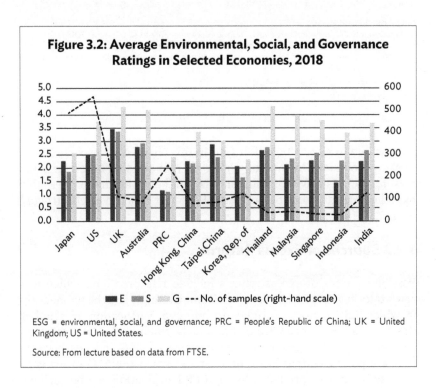

Figure 3.2: Average Environmental, Social, and Governance Ratings in Selected Economies, 2018

ESG = environmental, social, and governance; PRC = People's Republic of China; UK = United Kingdom; US = United States.

Source: From lecture based on data from FTSE.

3.2 Do Environmental, Social, and Governance Factors Generate Excess Returns?

3.2.1 Risk Factors and Excess Returns

The hypothesis is that the ESG factor is a risk factor, that extra returns can be obtained by investing in stocks with higher ESG ratings. Excess

Table 3.12: Are Environmental, Social, and Governance Ratings Factored into Corporate Value? (2018)

t-value	Australia	Hong Kong, China	India	Korea, Rep. of	Singapore	Taipei,China	Thailand
E	−0.062	−1.438	−1.096	1.227	−0.470	0.518	0.823
S	−0.025	−0.080	−2.226	2.329	−0.379	1.663	1.504
G	−0.809	−2.277	−3.545	1.535	−1.469	1.819	1.595
No. of samples	90	80	126	123	32	86	39

Note: Analysis method
• Explained variable: Historical beta (weekly from 23 December 2017 to 30 December 2018)
• Explanatory variable: FTSE ESG ratings (as of 31 December 2018)
• Control variables: Equity ratio, total assets, net sales growth rate (financial results for the fiscal year ended 31 March 2018)

ESG = environmental, social, and governance.

Source: Data from FTSE.

returns due to risk factors discussed in this chapter are excess returns as reward obtained by investing in stocks that are discounted for some reason, such as having additional risk or being an anomaly. If this hypothesis holds, it can be said that ESG smart beta can be constructed using ESG factors.

3.2.2 Sources of Excess Returns

Possible sources of excess returns include risk premium, which is a reward for higher risk taking; a persistent anomaly; and the momentum in which ESG factors continues to improve. Verification of whether this ESG factor is a risk factor are widely conducted. Many research studies have investigated the performance of ESG indexes because they are portfolios that incorporate stocks when the ESG rating goes up. Excess returns produced by high ESG evaluation can be verified. For example, Liao and Campagna (2014) reported that there was no significant difference between the return and volatility of the major US ESG indexes and of market indexes. A portfolio with a higher ESG rating does not lead to excess returns. Nagy, Kassam, and Lee (2015) show that the performance of the Morgan Stanley Capital International (MSCI) portfolio with a tilted higher ESG rating is above the market average. There are various opinions but no consensus about the verification of this excess return. Results may differ depending on conditions such as which evaluation items of which rating agencies are used for ESG evaluation, how a portfolio is created, how a portfolio is rebalanced, and in which period. It is difficult to draw a conclusion. It is natural to think that if a company's ESG rating is higher, the risk of that company is lower. It would be difficult to expect excess return as risk premium with highly rated companies which are considered low-risk. However, there may be momentum such as slow incorporation into corporate value or continued improvement in ESG evaluation. This is the same reason that excess returns are observed in quality factors in developed markets. Higher-quality companies generally have low risk, so risk premium is unlikely, and anomaly and momentum are considered. Momentum has been observed in governance factors in Japan. Given the recent changes in the country's companies, this momentum may continue for some time.

3.2.3 Excess Return Verification

We will verify the performance of the ESG indexes. Those indexes produced by major index providers are portfolios with exposure to ESG factors and have relatively long data. An ESG index is a portfolio that incorporates stocks with higher ESG ratings after their ratings are increased, resulting in a portfolio with higher exposure to ESG factors. By measuring the portfolio's performance, it is possible to evaluate whether ESG factors cause excess returns. Therefore, we evaluate the performance of ESG indexes of MSCI, FTSE Russell, and S&P Dow Jones, which are major index providers, using a test of excess returns against the market index and a risk-adjusted alpha test with the three-factor model.

The ESG indexes analyzed are in three markets: Japan, the US, and the UK. The data period is the FTSE4Good Index October 2001–October 2017 (September 2004–October 2017 for Japan), the MSCI ESG Leader Index October 2007–October 2017, and the Dow Jones Sustainable Index February 2008–October 2017. The market index is TOPIX for Japan, Russell 3000 for the US, and the FTSE UK Index for the UK. Table 3.13 shows a test of excess returns of the market portfolio versus the market portfolio and the excess returns and t-values. This result does not indicate that all ESG indexes in the three markets have significant excess returns. Table 3.14 shows the results of the regression analysis of the ESG index with three factors for each market. The value factor uses the return difference between the MSCI value factor index and the growth factor index, and the size factor uses the return difference between the MSCI large factor index and the small factor index. The results show that alpha (excess return) after three-factor adjustment is not significantly positive. The above two results do not show ESG index excess return. The FTSE has a positive exposure to the value factor in the three markets and is significant for Japan and the UK. MSCI has negative exposure (i.e., growth

Table 3.13: Excess Returns of Environmental, Social, and Governance Indexes

Monthly Excess Return vs. Market	Japan	US	UK	Period (monthly)
FTSE4Good	-0.011	-0.041	-0.012	Oct 2001–Oct 2017
MSCI ESG	-0.016	0.048	-0.307	Oct 2007–Oct 2017
DJ Sustainable	-0.168	0.011	-0.021	Feb 2008–Oct 2017

Notes: ESG Indexes:
• Portfolios that include companies with high ESG ratings
• Whether ESG rating produces excess returns can be verified

ESG = environmental, social, and governance; UK = United Kingdom; US = United States.
Note: Market returns in Japan (TOPIX), the US (Russell3000), and the UK (FTSE-UK).
Source: Data from FTSE, MSCI, and S&P Dow Jones.

Table 3.14: Risk-Adjusted Returns (t-values) of Environmental, Social, and Governance Indexes

| Japan Market | 3 factor model, t-value | | | | |
	Alpha	Market	Value	Size	Period (monthly)
FTSE4Good	-0.185	112.512	4.194	-11.427	Sep 2004–Oct 2017
MSCI ESG Leaders	0.606	106.398	-2.863	-6.992	Oct 2007–Oct 2017
DJ Sustainable	-0.223	29.343	1.062	-5.654	Feb 2008–Oct 2017

| US Market | 3 factor model, t-value | | | | |
	Alpha	Market	Value	Size	Period (monthly)
FTSE4Good	-0.469	64.240	0.901	-6.615	Oct 2001–Oct 2017
MSCI SRI	-0.089	14.992	-0.508	0.672	Oct 2007–Oct 2017
DJ Sustainable	0.322	37.628	1.701	-2.922	Feb 2008–Oct 2017

| UK Market | 3 factor model, t-value | | | | |
	Alpha	Market	Value	Size	Period (monthly)
FTSE4Good	-0.789	137.840	4.441	6.109	Oct 2001–Oct 2017
MSCI ESG Leaders	-1.742	12.486	-0.689	5.020	Oct 2007–Oct 2017
DJ Sustainable	-0.053	63.698	-1.670	-2.750	Feb 2008–Oct 2017

DJ = Dow Jones; ESG = environmental, social, and governance; UK = United Kingdom; US = United States.
Note: Market returns calculated from TOPIX (Japan), Russell3000 (the US), and FTSE-UK (the UK), and value/size factor calculated from MSCI Factor Indices.
Source: From lecture based on data from FTSE, MSCI, and S&P Dow Jones.

exposure). Regarding size factors, all Japan indexes tend to be large but other markets vary. Japan's high-ESG companies tend to be large, possibly because large companies tend to perform ESG disclosure. This difference in factor exposure will result in short-term performance differences.

ESG investment has a short history and is immature, so it is premature to draw conclusions from the verification results in this section. However, if ESG evaluation information is being incorporated into the market (corporate value), excess returns may not be observed in the ESG index. An increase in ESG evaluation leads to a decrease in corporate risk, so expected returns will decrease. It will take more time to reach any conclusion because companies are in the middle of improving disclosure and markets are still insufficiently factored into the market.

3.3 Classification of Environmental, Social, and Governance Investment Methods and Benchmarking

3.3.1 Classification of Environmental, Social, and Governance Investment Methods

Concept of classification. In general, ESG investment selects stocks based on a company's approach to ESG factors. However, this alone may be a shortage of information on ESG investment methods. The classification used by the Global Sustainable Investment Alliance (GSIA), an international organization that promotes ESG investment publishing ESG investment balances, is often cited. However, this classification method does not indicate the source of returns. The current ESG index, however, does not have excess returns. The answer to the question "Can we expect an excess return with ESG investment?" is important. Investors must know what return to earn and how to categorize their investment methods based on the source of return. In this chapter, instead of sticking to the final form of a specific investment method, we focus on the source of return to classify investment methods. By contrasting with the source of return, it becomes easier to understand what the investment method is aimed at. According to the invested amount of assets by the GSIA classification, negative screening is largest globally, and voting rights and engagement are the largest in Japan. This is an interesting difference. ESG investment in Europe originated from negative screening, i.e., the exclusion of immoral companies in asset management by religious institutions. Japanese ESG investment, however, started in the exercise of voting rights focusing on governance. As ESG integration that represents active management ranks second both globally and in Japan, we can see that ESG investment is becoming an important part of the active asset management process. In the following, investment methods are categorized based on the sources of return.

Source of environmental, social, and governance investment return. ESG investment returns can be divided into the following:

(i) If ESG evaluation is factored into corporate value, a higher corporate ESG rating would bring about a higher corporate value.

(ii) If ESG is a risk factor that brings systematic excess returns (risk premium, anomaly, among others), excess returns can be obtained by investing in a portfolio with companies that have a higher ESG rating.

3.3.2 Investment Method when Environmental, Social, and Governance Evaluation Is Factored into Corporate Value

Assuming ESG evaluation is factored into corporate value, if ESG evaluation increases, excess returns can be expected. To obtain these excess returns, future ESG ratings must be forecast and those stocks held in advance. Excess returns would not bring additional risk. Excess returns are alpha. If the ESG rating of most companies in the market improves, the overall market return will improve. "Beta improvement" becomes possible. Here we will consider two categories: alpha seeking by selecting stocks and improvement of beta applied to the entire market.

3.3.3 Alpha Seeking

Alpha is obtained by selecting a stock that brings about returns that exceed the market average without additional risk. Based on the hypothesis that improved ESG evaluation improves corporate value, alpha can be acquired by selecting stocks that are expected to improve ESG evaluation. Alpha is based on the premise that managers have a high ability to select stocks. The alpha methods are divided into three.

Stock Selection by Environmental, Social, and Governance Factors

This is the simplest investment method using ESG evaluation: select and invest in stocks that are expected to improve ESG evaluation. If it improves, then the corporate value will also improve and excess returns can be expected. Since we need to predict it, we are not necessarily taking additional risks. It is excess returns with no additional risk. The ability to forecast ESG evaluation of individual companies is required. This stock selection includes positive screening that selects and incorporates stocks that will improve ESG evaluation and, conversely, negative screening that selects and eliminates stocks that are expected to lower ESG evaluation.

Environmental, Social, and Governance Integration

ESG integration is the incorporation of ESG evaluation into the existing asset management process. Many investors think that ESG evaluation is useful as complementary information for traditional active management methods such as earnings forecasts. The various ways of incorporating ESG evaluation into asset management can be roughly divided into those based on complementary information on earnings forecast (growth forecast) and on complementary information for capital cost estimation.

When calculating the theoretical price of stock, the discounted cash flow (DCF) model is often assumed. The important variables are growth rate and capital cost, which are estimated based on company analysis. ESG information is used as complementary information during the estimation.

The growth rate forecast based on the existing analysis method is revised in such a way that, for example, companies with higher ESG evaluations are revised upward, while those with lower evaluations are revised downward. Capital cost that is the basis for estimating corporate value is corrected with ESG evaluation information. For example, if the ESG evaluation is higher, the capital cost is corrected to be lower and, conversely, if the ESG evaluation is lower, the capital cost is corrected to be higher. An investment judgment is made by comparing the theoretical price predicted by this method with the current market price.

ESG investment may be set as a new fund for asset managers, but in many cases asset owners are required to support ESG for existing funds. In European public fund management, there are cases where ESG compliance is required by law and existing funds are converted to ESG. The existing management method and ESG investment method are merged, resulting in ESG integration.

Active Investment, Including Concentrated Investment and Smart Beta, Plus Environmental, Social, and Governance Engagement

The third alpha method is one that selects stocks based on ESG engagement. Companies select and invest in stocks that are likely to improve ESG evaluation through ESG engagement. The portfolio becomes active in selecting stocks. It is also possible to engage companies with smart beta. In the case of concentrated investment, companies that are likely to have a higher engagement effect are selected. If the target companies are narrowed down, the number of companies will decrease, so it will be possible to maintain strong commitments to each target company and engage effectively. It is possible to select smart beta with a factor that can increase the alpha acquisition effect of engagement. Some of the major factors have positive and negative correlation with ESG factors. For example, value and size (small) factors have a negative correlation with ESG factors, and low volatility and profitability factors are positive. Therefore, many smart beta with value and size factor exposures have low ESG ratings, and there is room to improve ESG ratings through engagement. Many smart betas with low volatility and profitability factor exposure have high ESG ratings, and there is little room to improve them through engagement. If the objective is to make ESG engagement more effective, value or size factor smart beta will be a better choice. If ESG evaluation is improved through engagement, it will lead to higher corporate value and alpha. There is no additional risk in this case.

3.3.4 Beta Improvement

This is particularly important for Japan's stock market, whose performance has been inferior to that of other markets in the past decades. Japan's stock market has been stagnant since the collapse of the bubble at the end of the 1980s. As of the end of 2017, US stock prices (Dow average and S&P 500 index) had reached record highs, while Japan's stock prices (Nikkei average and TOPIX) were about half the record highs just before the bubble burst. (Stock price levels and returns are different.) It is not active management that selects only good stocks that are expected to have higher future returns. Beta improvement is, in a sense, a macro story, so one might wonder whether it is a government economic policy and not an investor story. Abenomics' corporate governance reform is a policy to improve overall corporate governance of Japan's companies and consequently increase their corporate value.[1] We show, however, an investment method aimed at improving beta, not government policy. Two methods are introduced.

---

[1]   Abenomics refers to the economic policies advocated by Prime Minister Shinzō Abe since Japan's December 2012 general election. Abenomics is based on "three arrows" of monetary easing, fiscal stimulus, and structural reforms.

Market Passive Management Plus Environmental, Social, and Governance Engagement

This method adds ESG engagement to general market passive management, which is passive management for an index, including a wide range of stocks such as TOPIX and Russell 3000. ESG engagement is carried out for these passive investment targets. ESG engagement is carried out for stocks held to improve ESG evaluation and to obtain excess returns. Since ESG evaluation is assumed to be factored into corporate value, the higher the ESG evaluation, the higher the corporate value. Only stocks that have undergone ESG engagement will cause excess returns. However, if ESG engagement is carried out for a broad group of stocks that are subject to passive management, the overall market returns will increase and beta will improve. Although this investment method is passive management, it uses an active method called ESG engagement, so it may be called "active passive management."

Environmental, Social, and Governance Index Management

Another method for improving beta is ESG index management. An ESG index is a portfolio consisting of stocks with a higher ESG rating or a portfolio with higher exposure to ESG factors. ESG index management is passive management. Investment is focused on stocks with higher ESG ratings. Why does this lead to improved beta? Three conditions must be present:

(i)   Institutional investors must have a significant impact on the market and they must use ESG index management.
(ii) The stocks included in the ESG index and the criteria for inclusion must be made public.
(iii) Most companies must have strong incentives to join the ESG index.

When an influential institutional investor uses the ESG index, stable investment in the companies in the index can be expected. It is an honor for a company to be included in the index, and being included in the index can improve corporate image. If the criteria for inclusion in the ESG index are clearly stated, companies can work to meet them. If many companies have an incentive to improve their ESG evaluation and do so, their ESG evaluation will increase as will their corporate value. As a result, the return of the entire market can be expected to increase. Such an index is not common as a benchmark index in traditional investment theory. Incentives for companies are not assumed in traditional investment theory. Therefore, the index is known as an "incentive index." The JPX-Nikkei 400 index, which focuses on returns on equity, would be considered an incentive index, one of the purposes of which is to give companies incentives to increase returns on equity.

Research to support the concept of the incentive index has been conducted in relation to the FTSE4Good Index, for example (Mackenzie, Rees, and Rodionova, 2013), and the JPX-Nikkei 400 (Chattopadhyay, Shaffer, and Wang, 2017). Both studies verify the incentives. The second study's title contains the word "shame," which is the key to the investment method: it is a "shame" for a company not to be included in the index or to be excluded from it. Using shame is suitable for Japan's companies. In her famous book *The Chrysanthemum and the Sword*, Benedict (1946) said Japan had a shame culture. It is characterized by an emphasis on the inner feelings of other people and one's own "face."

Issues in Beta Improvement

Two issues in beta improvement are:
  (i) Who pays the cost of improving beta?
  (ii) How do we know when beta has been improved?

Let us consider each.

Who pays for the cost of improving beta? Who will implement this investment method? Given a choice, investors would rather not pay. Passive management plus ESG engagement have more costs than passive management alone. Passive management, however, delivers the same performance. Who bears this additional cost? What about passive management of the ESG index? The purpose of this investment method is to give a wide range of companies incentives to improve ESG. The ESG index usage cost is expected to be higher than for a general market index. Investors who have an incentive to adopt this investment method even if it is costly are those who need to manage huge assets over a long period. They generally have a large amount of passive investment in the market index and limited options for active management and need to keep investing in the entire market for a long time. Such investors benefit greatly from increased market returns over the long term. Principles for Responsible Investment, an organization that promotes ESG investment internationally, calls such investors "universal owners," who are expected to play a central role in ESG investment (PRI 2011). An example of a universal owner is a pension fund with large assets. The cost of improving beta can be thought of as the cost for universal owners to participate in the market.

How do we know when beta has been improved? Investment performance is usually measured by comparing it with the market index, but there is no point in comparing the market index when evaluating market return itself. We should measure not investment performance but the degree of improvement of a company's ESG evaluation. It is necessary, however, to show that it is ultimately reflected in investment performance. In the long run, the absolute performance of the stock market should be compared with that of overseas markets. A factor model could be built that incorporates ESG factors and evaluates global market returns cross-sectionally.

3.4 Conclusion

As modern capitalism reaches its limit, ESG investment is expanding to make capital markets more sustainable. ESG evaluation is reflected in corporate value with a focus on governance factors, but the higher the companies' ESG evaluation, the lower the potential impact on corporate value cross-sectionally.

ESG investment management methods can be classified as follows:
  (i)   active management aiming for excess returns,
  (ii) beta improvement aiming for improving market returns, and
  (iii) sustainable investment aiming for social returns.
  (iv) As ESG investment progresses, assessing social returns becomes more important and is based on the Sustainable Development Goals.

References

Bebchuk, L. A., A. Cohen, and C. C. Y. Wang. 2013. Learning and the Disappearing Association Between Governance and Returns. *Journal of Financial Economics* 108(2): 323–348.

Benedict, R. 1946. *The Chrysanthemum and the Sword*. Boston, MA: Houghton Mifflin.

Chattopadhyay, A., M. D. Shaffer, and C. C. Y. Wang. 2017. Governance Through Shame and Aspiration: Index Creation and Corporate Behavior in Japan. Harvard University Working Paper, 18–01. Cambridge, MA: Harvard University.

Ghoul, S., O. Guedhami, C. C. Y. Kwok, and D. Mishra. 2011. Does Corporate Social Responsibility Affect the Cost of Capital? *Journal of Banking and Finance* 35(9): 2388–2406.

Gu, F., and B. Lev. 2017. Time to Change Your Investment Model. *Financial Analysts Journal* 73(4): 23–33.

Laio, L., and J. Campagna. 2014. Socially Responsible Investing: Delivering Competitive Performance. New York, US: TIAA–CRIEF.

Mackenzie, C., W. Rees, and T. Rodionova. 2013. Do Responsible Investment Indices Improve Corporate Social Responsibility? FTSE4Good's Impact on Environmental Management. *Corporate Governance: An International Review* 21(5): 495– 512.

Nagy, Z., A. Kassam, and L-E. Lee. 2015. Can ESG Add Alpha? An Analysis of ESG Tilt and Momentum Strategies. *Journal of Investing* 25(2): 113–124.

Principles for Responsible Investment (PRI). 2011. *Universal Ownership: Why Environmental Externalities Matter to Institutional Investors*. London: PRI.

Kasai, S. 2015. The Impact of Disclosure on the Cost of Equity, Japan Exchange Group, Inc. Internal study group materials.

4

How Will Environmental, Social, and Governance Factors Affect the Sovereign Borrowing Cost?

Naoko Nemoto and Lian Liu

4.1 Introduction

The sovereign borrowing cost is crucial as it affects the soundness of fiscal policy and debt sustainability of a country. The theoretical literature (Longstaff et al., 2011; Hilscher and Nosbusch, 2010; Crifo, Diaye, and Oueghlissi, 2017; Jeanneret, 2018; Margaretic and Pouget, 2018) attributes sovereign borrowing costs to three factors: (i) financial performance measured by public debt and other fundamental indicators; (ii) investors' sentiments and risk aversion trends; and (iii) nonfinancial factors, including political stability and policy effectiveness.

Recently, an increasing number of investors have incorporated nonfinancial factors measured by environmental, social, and governance (ESG) issues into their investment decision making (World Bank, 2018). This trend started in equity investment and gradually expanded into the fixed-income area. Investors' motivation is of three kinds:

(i) Many investors believe ESG performance has a material effect on investment risks and returns (Crifo, Diaye, and Oueghlissi, 2017). A country with better access and management of its natural resources, human resources, and financial resources is able to implement economic policies to generate more revenue, which could, in turn, affect the country's ability to repay the sovereign debt (Margaretic and Pouget, 2018). Poor governance is associated with inefficient use of fiscal revenue rather than use of funds to repay debt.

(ii) Some investors seek to attain certain nonfinancial objectives through ethical, political, and societal values without hampering financial objectives.

(iii) Certain investors are willing to sacrifice some or all financial returns to achieve social or environmental benefits (Kitzmueller and Shinmshack, 2012; Crifo, Diaye, and Oueghlissi, 2017)

This chapter intends to empirically gauge the effect of sovereign ESG performance on government borrowing costs based on panel regression models with a data set of 85 countries during 2008–2016. As a proxy of borrowing costs, we use the spreads on sovereign credit default swap (CDS) .

Prevailing ESG investment and more accessible ESG data have led to an increasing amount of research on ESG performance and financial indicators. However, most of the research focuses on equities[1] and few focus on nonequity assets (Friede et al., 2015).

Empirical studies focusing on sovereign bonds and ESG factors are limited. More than 60% of fixed-income research shows that high ESG performance is linked with lower borrowing costs, while the rest indicate neutral or opposite results (Friede et al., 2015).

The chapter will shed light on sovereign borrowing costs in emerging markets, particularly in Asia. In Asia, average credit ratings have been improving but are still lower than those in Europe and the United States (US), indicating higher default probability. It is critical for the government to ensure stable borrowing costs while dependence on foreign capital market is increasing. ESG issues are particularly acute for emerging countries. Based on the research by Morgan Stanley Capital International (MSCI) and Beyond Ratings, which are external providers of ESG scores, the average ESG performance of Asian countries trails that of Organisation for Economic Co-operation and Development (OECD) countries. Asia and the Pacific economies are home to about 40% of the world's extremely poor. Of the 10 countries most exposed to climate change, environmental stress, and natural disaster risk, 7 are in Asia (ADB, 2017).

Our research shows good ESG performance as associated with lower sovereign CDS spreads, a result that is useful for policy makers interested in the determinants of the sovereign borrowing costs.

The literature focuses on specific aspects of qualitative factors such as government corruption, while Crifo, Diaye, and Oueghlissi (2017) and Margaretic and Pouget (2018) examined the effects of comprehensive

---

[1]   Ng and Rezaee (2015) investigated the correlation between corporate ESG performance and cost of equity capital and detected a significantly negative link between them. Atan et al. (2018) found a significantly positive relationship between a firm's ESG rating and its weighted average cost of capital.

ESG factors on sovereign bond spreads. Our chapter aims to contribute to the literature from three perspectives. First, we examine the possible effect of ESG performance on sovereign borrowing costs in different regions and disentangle Asia and the Pacific from other developed countries. Most researches focus on OECD or European countries. Second, our research explores not only the link between overall ESG performance and sovereign borrowing cost but also accounts for the role of each ESG dimension separately. Third, given varied ESG criteria and methodologies worldwide, this chapter tests the results using ESG scores of two major providers.

Section 4.2 describes recent developments in ESG investment. Section 4.3 reviews the literature. Section 4.4 explains the data and methodology. Section 4.5 presents empirical results and the robustness check. The final section concludes with policy implications.

4.2 Recent Developments in Environmental, Social, and Governance Investment

ESG investment is increasing in the global market, accelerated by United Nations initiatives such as the Principles for Responsible Investment (PRI) [2] and the Sustainable Development Goals (SDGs).[3] A key feature of the SDGs is that they position private companies as the main players in solving social and environmental problems. While the SDGs guide governments and private corporations, the PRI targets investors. Companies that achieve the SDGs are always highly evaluated for ESG investment because they are managed in an ESG-friendly way. Guided by the PRI, more investment will be directed to these ESG-friendly companies (Figure 4.1). The PRI and the SDGs introduce incentives to incorporate ESG factors into the investment chain, starting with investors and ending with investee companies. ESG investment, the SDGs, and the PRI are designed to work together for sustainable development.

Key issues for consideration typically include the following:
  (i) E: climate change, carbon emissions, pollution, resource efficiency, biodiversity;

---

[2]   The PRI were launched in 2006 to encourage investors to incorporate ESG issues into investment practice through six principles. The PRI are voluntary, sponsored by investors, and developed by an international group of institutional investors.

[3]   The SDGs were adopted by all 193 member countries of the UN in 2015 as part of its 2030 Agenda for Sustainable Development. The SDGs encompass a broad range of social and economic topics of great importance for developing a sustainable society.

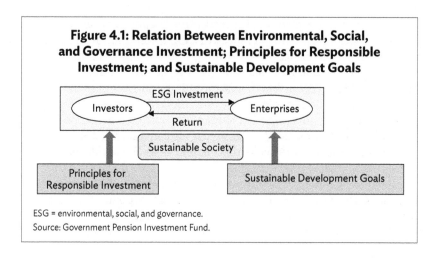

Figure 4.1: Relation Between Environmental, Social, and Governance Investment; Principles for Responsible Investment; and Sustainable Development Goals

ESG = environmental, social, and governance.
Source: Government Pension Investment Fund.

(ii) S: human rights, labor standards, health and safety, diversity policies, community relations, development of human capital; and

(iii) G: corporate governance, corruption, rule of law, institutional strength, transparency.

ESG investing has been widely adopted by institutional investors such as pensions, mutual funds, and endowments and become one of the most important strategies of responsible investment. ESG investment has continuously expanded and reached $30.68 trillion in the five major markets in 2018, increasing from $18.23 trillion in 2014 (Table 4.1). The largest contributors to ESG investment are Europe ($18.23 trillion) and the US ($12.00 trillion).

In Asia and the Pacific, Australia, New Zealand, and Japan are the largest players in the ESG investment market. Japan witnessed the strongest growth of ESG investment, from $7 billion in 2014 to $2,180 billion 2018, making the country the world's third-largest center for ESG investment. Following Japan, Australia and New Zealand witnessed the second-largest growth of 395.95% from 2014 to 2018, holding $734 billion ESG assets. Australia and New Zealand have the largest ratio of ESG investment assets to total managed assets, where 63% of total managed assets are invested through ESG strategies.

ESG investment in the rest of Asia and the Pacific is still in the early stage of development. Malaysia is most active, where $15.63 billion of assets were managed using the ESG strategy in 2016, followed by Hong Kong, China ($13.55 billion) and the Republic of Korea ($7.29 billion). The People's Republic of China saw the largest increase in ESG

Table 4.1: Environmental, Social, and Governance Investment Assets by Region, 2014–2018 ($ billion)

Region	2014	2016	2018	Growth per Period 2014–2018	Growth per Period 2016–2018
Europe	10,775	12,040	14,075	30.63%	16.90%
United States	6,572	8,723	11,995	82.52%	37.51%
Japan	7	474	2,180	31,042.86%	359.92%
Canada	729	1,086	1,699	133.06%	56.45%
Australia and New Zealand	148	516	734	395.95%	42.25%
Asia excluding Japan	45	52	–	–	–
Total	18,276	22,891	30,683	–	–

Note: This research employs the sustainable investment data from the Global Sustainable Investment Alliance (GSIA) as a proxy measure of environmental, social, and governance (ESG) investment, as sustainable investment, defined in GSIA (2018), is "an investment approach that consider ESG factors in portfolio selection and management."
Source: Global Sustainable Investment Alliance (2016, 2018).

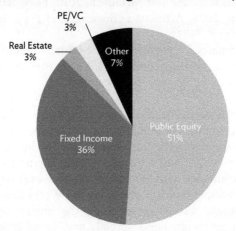

Figure 4.2: Global Environmental, Social, and Governance Investing Asset Allocation, 2018

PE/VC 3%
Real Estate 3%
Other 7%
Public Equity 51%
Fixed Income 36%

PE = private equity, VC = venture capital.
Notes: 1. This figure shows the asset allocation in Europe, the United States, Japan, and Canada.
2. "Other" includes hedge funds, cash and/or deposits, commodities, infrastructure, and not otherwise specified.
Source: Global Sustainable Investment Alliance (2018).

investment, with 105% growth from 2014 to 2016. Given the People's Republic of China's growing interest in green finance, it is expected to further advance into ESG investment.

ESG investment started among equity investors and recently expanded to bond markets. More investors incorporate ESG-related issues into fixed-income investment. As a result, the portion of fixed income to total ESG-related assets increased from 40% to 64% in Canada and Europe during 2014–2016, with 64% of assets invested in bonds in 2016, increasing from 40% in 2014 (see Global Sustainable Investment Alliance [2016]). The Russell Investments survey shows that 92% of Europe-based fixed-income managers have an ESG-related investment policy but only 58% of US-based managers do. As of 2018, fixed income comprised 36% of global ESG investing.

4.3 Literature Review

Despite the quantity of research, the debate on the determinants of sovereign borrowing costs is far from settled (Crifo et al., 2017). The factors affecting costs can be classified into three groups:

  (i)   country-specific macroeconomic factors such as inflation rate, gross domestic product (GDP) growth, foreign reserves, current account balance;
  (ii) global factors such as global risk aversion, international interest rates, among others (Uribe and Yue, 2010; Longstaff et al., 2011; Hilscher and Nosbusch, 2010; Baek, Bandopadhyaya, and Du, 2005; Aizenman, Jinjarak, and Park, 2016; Kennedy and Palerm, 2014);
  (iii) extra-financial performance, which could potentially determine sovereign credit risk and, in turn, the cost of capital as well.

The studies choose a specific aspect of extra-financial performance such as corruption control or human resource development and examine their impact on the sovereign borrowing cost. For instance, Ciocchini, Durbin, and Ng, (2003) and Connolly (2007) focused on corruption and found that countries with better corruption scores pay a lower risk premium when issuing bonds. Relying on the World Bank Governance Indicators, Jeanneret (2018) investigated the impact of government effectiveness on sovereign bond spreads and found that government effectiveness has a significant economic impact on sovereign credit risk. Bundala (2013) concluded that countries with a better equality-adjusted human development index and lower unemployment rate were associated with lower default risk and thus had lower borrowing costs.

The studies on ESG performance and sovereign borrowing costs focus on nonfinancial factors, although most of the studies use specific factors rather than holistic indicators such as ESG scores. As integration of ESG factors into fixed-income investment is new, research on it is not abundant. Only a few studies investigate how a broad measure of ESG factors could affect the sovereign borrowing cost. Crifo, Diaye, and Oueghlissi (2017) used the Vigeo ESG index to estimate the effect of a country's ESG ratings on sovereign borrowing cost. They collect data for 23 OECD countries from 2007 to 2012. Their results reveal that better sovereign ESG ratings can reduce the sovereign borrowing cost, but the effect is three times weaker than that of financial rating, measured by Standard and Poor's (S&P) sovereign ratings. Capelle-Blancard et al. (2016) also researched OECD countries and found a strong link between ESG performance and sovereign bond spread, especially for long-term bonds. Better ESG performance is associated with lower bond yield. Margaretic and Pouget (2018) examined how ESG factors affect sovereign bond spreads and demonstrate that good social and governance performance is associated with lower cost of debt among emerging countries.

Based on the previous studies, we expand the coverage to emerging countries such as those in Asia and incorporated recent data about when ESG investment gained momentum. We investigate the impact of each ESG component over different regions. The results are tested by using ESG scores of two major providers. We verified the link between ESG performance and sovereign CDS spread as a proxy of sovereign borrowing costs.

4.4 Data and Methodology

4.4.1 Data

Dependent Variable: Sovereign Borrowing Cost

The data in this analysis span 2008–2018 on a yearly basis. The sovereign CDS spread is used as a proxy measure of sovereign borrowing cost, which functions as an insurance contract for the buyer against the sovereign default on its debt. One of the important advantages to using sovereign CDS data, instead of the sovereign bond yield, is that the sovereign CDS may give more accurate estimates of credit spreads and returns, since the CDS market is typically more liquid than the underlying sovereign bond market. Besides, Chan-Lau (2003) has also demonstrated the link between the CDS spread and sovereign default probability.

Main Independent Variable: Government Environmental, Social, and Governance Score

Due to MSCI's broad coverage, wide usage, and transparent criteria, we employ ESG scores calculated by MSCI, a world-leading index company. As part of the robustness check, we also employ the sustainability profile provided by Beyond Ratings, a specialist sustainability research firm that is now integration into FTSE Russell, part of the London Stock Exchange Group.

MSCI ESG government ratings. MSCI and Sustainalytics are market leaders (World Bank, 2018) in fixed income and investors regard their assessment as benchmarks[4] (METI, 2019). MSCI government ESG ratings reflect one country's exposure to ESG risks, as well as the country's performance and capacity to manage them. The risk exposure and management scores are computed based on the country's performance with respect to 27 subfactors with 99 data points (Table A4.2).

Finally, the overall ESG score is calculated based on the following formula:

$$\frac{\text{Government}}{\text{ESG Score}} = \min \left\{ \begin{array}{c} (Risk\ Management + 1) \\ Average\ (10 - Risk\ Exposure\ Score, Risk\ Management\ Score) \end{array} \right\} \quad (1)$$

Government ESG scores range from 0 to 10, with a higher score indicating stronger ESG performance. This formula assumes that a country with poor risk management cannot utilize its resources effectively even though the resources are abundant.

MSCI does not disclose the aggregate score of each component. To examine the different impacts from each ESG dimension, we replace the overall ESG score in formula (1) with E (environmental quality index), S (social quality index), and G (governance quality index) to construct the performance score for each dimension.

Beyond Ratings ESG scores. Beyond Ratings ESG scores have been calculated quarterly using a systematic, quantitative approach based on 40 indicators from the end of 1999. To calculate an aggregate ESG score, individual ESG scores are weighted 30:30:40. The weights for each indicator (Table A4.1, Appendix) are estimated using an econometric modeling technique called partial least squares, with a score for variable

---

[4]   According to Russell Investments (2017), 52 of the respondent fixed-income managers utilize third-party vendors exclusively to obtain ESG scores, 35 utilize external vendors with in-house ESG analysis, and 15 use only internal analysis.

importance in projection added on. The methodology assesses ESG risks, taking into account qualitative factors as well as a country's state of development. The sovereign ESG scores of Beyond Ratings range from 0 to 100, with higher scores representing better ESG performance.

The informational content of MSCI and Beyond Ratings ESG scores is qualified and transparent. However, the scores' scope and criteria are not identical. We derived the Pearson correlation coefficients of these two scores. The correlation coefficient of aggregate ESG score is very high at 0.90.[5] However, the correlation of environment is low at 0.63 and that of social and governance scores 0.89 and 0.83. The difference in scores means that their methodology and criteria are varied. For instance, the MSCI environment score puts weight on risk management, including energy productivity and energy consumption efficiency. Beyond Ratings scores, however, incorporate qualitative assessment as well as the stage of development besides quantitative factors. The MSCI score is calculated based on fixed weight while Beyond Ratings uses econometric modeling. Although ESG information on government is becoming available from UN bodies, the World Bank, and other multinational organizations, ESG factors, particularly environmental factors, are often difficult to grasp and compare.

Control Variables

To control for each country's economic characteristics, based on previous researches (Aizenman et al., 2016; IMF, 2013) this analysis includes seven country-specific macroeconomic factors and one global factor as control variables: GDP growth, foreign reserves, government debt, inflation rate, current account balance, Chicago Board Options Exchange (CBOE) volatility, and quantitative easing (QE) policy.

Following the literature (Beirne and Fratzscher, 2013; Remolona et al., 2008), we control for the CBOE volatility index (VIX) as a key driver of change in the sovereign borrowing cost. Calculated by the CBOE by taking the weighted average of the implied volatility of a subset of S&P 500 Index options, VIX is widely used as the proxy measure of global investor sentiment. A higher reading of the VIX suggests greater market anxiety, which raises the sovereign borrowing cost.

As important indicators of a country's economic health, the current account balance, foreign reserves, and the inflation rate are used as control variables. A current account surplus signals that a country's net foreign assets are increasing and a deficit that they are shrinking.

---

5   For the correlation matrix of MSCI and Beyond Ratings ESG scores, see Table A4.3, Appendix.

Table 4.2: Mean Distribution of All Variables

	Asia and the Pacific				OECD countries				All Countries			
	Mean	Std. Dev.	Min	Max	Mean	Std. Dev.	Min	Max	Mean	Std. Dev.	Min	Max
CDS	153	237	16	1,997	93	107	10	890	191	571	10	11,311
ESG	5.1	1.8	1.2	8.2	6.5	1.4	2.9	9.1	5.6	1.7	1.2	9.1
E	4.4	1.4	2.6	7.6	5.2	1.2	2.6	7.7	5.1	1.3	2.6	7.7
S	6.3	1.9	2.1	8.6	7.6	0.9	4.7	9.2	6.7	1.5	1.8	9.2
G	6.2	1.6	2.8	8.8	7.2	1.4	3.0	9.7	6.4	1.7	2.1	9.7
BESG	58.5	17.3	26.8	82.8	74.8	8.8	44.5	87.4	65.5	15.5	26.5	87.4
BE	52.1	8.2	39.8	69.6	61.9	6.5	41.7	75.2	58.7	7.8	39.8	75.2
BS	56.5	17.8	26.5	79.4	70.5	10.8	40.0	87.1	63.2	15.1	24.8	87.1
BG	64.4	28.8	15.3	99.3	87.2	13.2	35.3	99.7	72.2	25.6	13.2	99.7
VIX	19.7	6.8	11.1	32.7	19.3	6.6	11.1	32.7	19.1	6.5	11.1	32.7
Cab	2.8	6.5	-9.2	23.4	0.9	5.1	-24.6	15.8	0.5	6.3	-26	23.4
Inf	3.3	4.0	-6.0	20.7	1.8	2.1	-5.2	11.9	2.9	3.9	-6.0	38.9
Debt	56.5	47.8	13.3	223.2	65.7	37.9	4.9	223.2	61.6	38.9	4.9	223.2
Res	7.5	4.9	1.2	25.7	3.5	3.6	0.0	18.4	5.0	4.6	0.0	25.7
Growth	4.1	2.9	-5.4	15.2	1.8	2.9	-8.3	25.6	2.4	3.2	-9.8	25.6
QE	0.0	0.2	0.0	1.0	0.3	0.4	0.0	1.0	0.2	0.4	0.0	1.0

BE = Beyond Ratings environmental index, BESG = Beyond Ratings ESG composite index, BG = Beyond Ratings governance quality index, BS = Beyond Ratings social quality index, Cab = current account balance as a percentage of GDP, Debt = government debt as a percentage of GDP, E = MSCI environmental index, ESG = MSCI ESG composite index, G =MSCI governance quality index, Growth = GDP growth rate, Inf = inflation rate, QE = adoption of quantitative easing policy, Res = foreign reserve as a percentage of imports, S = MSCI social quality index, VIX = CBOE volatility, CDS = sovereign CDS spread.

Sources: Sovereign CDS spread data extracted from Bloomberg; data on government debt extracted from S&P database; data on current account balance, inflation rate, foreign reserves, and GDP growth extracted from World Bank database.

Similarly, foreign reserves are key to a country's defense against external shocks. A higher inflation rate is usually associated with economic instability and thus reduces the creditworthiness of a country. Therefore, an improved current account balance, foreign reserves and inflation rate should increase a country's credibility and is expected to reduce the sovereign borrowing cost.

The government debt-to-GDP ratio measures the financial leverage of a country. A low government debt ratio indicates that the country can produce and sell goods and services sufficient to pay back its debt. A higher level of government debt ratio is expected to raise the country's default risk and, consequently, the sovereign borrowing cost.

Due to the economic slowdown after the 2008 global financial crisis, a number of developed economies adopted quantitative easing (QE) to help unlock liquidity directly into the economy through large-scale asset purchases in capital markets such as the US, Japan, and several European countries. Theoretically, increasing demand for government bonds may raise bond prices and, in turn, reduce bond yields, which has been proved by the empirical analysis of Krishnamurthy and Vissing-Jorgensen (2011). As a result, the QE policy is included as the control variable and assumed to decrease the sovereign borrowing cost.

Table 4.2 displays the mean distribution of all the variables. The average ESG score is 5.1 for Asia and the Pacific, 6.5 for OECD countries. All the economies perform better in a social matrix. On average, OECD countries have the lowest credit default swap (CDS) spreads and better ESG ratings. Asia and the Pacific economies have the largest foreign reserves and highest economic growth. Based on a Pearson correlation matrix of the independent variables (Table A4.4, Appendix), control variables and ESG scores do not exhibit high correlations. Thus, we assume our estimates will not suffer from multi-collinearity.

4.4.2 Methodology

Using the data sets explained in Section 4.1, we developed the following panel data regression model to estimate the sovereign CDS spreads. Because the data is available, we include 85 countries in our research. They are grouped into 16 economies in Asia and the Pacific and 35 OECD countries.[6] Based on the researches of the International Monetary Fund (IMF, 2013), Hilscher and Nosbusch (2010), and Aizenman, Jinjarak, and Park (2016), seven variables are chosen as control variables in the baseline estimation, which include GDP growth, foreign reserves, government debt, inflation rate, current account balance, CBOE volatility, and QE policy. The general model is given by the following equation:

$$CDS_{it} = \alpha_0 + \alpha_1 ESG_{it} + \alpha_2 Cab_{it} + \alpha_3 Inf_{it} + \alpha_4 Debt_{it} \qquad (2)$$
$$+ \alpha_5 Res + \alpha_6 Growth_{it} + \alpha_7 QE_{it} + \gamma_t + \mu_{it}$$

Where, i denotes the economies and t the time indexes. γ_t represents the unobserved time specific effect. μ_{it} represents the random error term. CDS_{it} denotes sovereign CDS spreads. ESG_{it} denotes ESG scores. E_{it} denotes environmental quality scores. S_{it} denotes social quality scores. G_{it} stands for governance quality scores. VIX_{it} stands for CBOE

---

[6]   The region classification is sourced from the World Bank (See Table A4.5, Appendix)..

volatility. Cab_{it} stands for current account balance as a percentage of GDP. Inf_{it} stands for inflation rate. $Debt_{it}$ stands for government debt as a percentage of GDP. Res_{it} stands for foreign reserve as a percentage of imports. $Growth_{it}$ stands for GDP growth rate. QE_{it} stands for the adoption of QE policy.

4.5 Empirical Results

4.5.1. Results

In order to choose an appropriate estimation model for the panel data, the Hausman test is performed to check whether a fixed effects model or random effects model is preferable for the panel data estimation. The result shows that the random effects model is more suitable for the estimation. The results are reported in Table A4.6 and Table A4.7 (Appendix). All the specifications control for global risk aversion, the country-specific macroeconomic factors and the time effect.

The following are evaluations that can be inferred from the results of the verification:

- The overall ESG rating of MSCI has significantly negative signs, which suggests that higher ESG performance is associated with lower sovereign CDS spreads. This result confirms the researches of Capelle-Blancard et al. (2016) and Reznick et al. (2019). As a robustness check, we also tested estimation using Beyond Ratings ESG scores, which does not alter the previous result. ESG performance seems to have a more significant impact than macroeconomic indicators such as current account balance and public debt.
- Most of the control variables show the expected signs, suggesting the validity of the model. In Asia and the Pacific, public debt to GDP, inflation rate, and foreign reserves have significant impact, while public debt to GDP, foreign reserves, GDP growth and quantitative policy are significant for OECD countries.
- To assess the effect of each ESG component, we replace the overall ESG index with E (environmental quality index), S (social quality index), and G (governance quality index). In the global context, governance performance has a significantly negative correlation with sovereign borrowing cost. This result is unchanged based on Beyond Ratings ESG scores. However, we detected a significant positive relationship between environmental performance and sovereign CDS spreads when applying MSCI ESG scores.

- We applied the model to subregions. Although the aggregate ESG score is significantly negative for both Asia and the OECD, the coefficient significance of each component is different depending on the region. In Asia and the Pacific, the estimation using MSCI ESG scores shows that social factors have a significant negative effect on sovereign borrowing cost, probably because human capital, education, and knowledge capital are critical to future growth. These social factors are extremely important for Asia and the Pacific, which still have a large number of emerging economies with less developed social infrastructure. In Asia and the Pacific, the environmental score shows negative signs but is not significant, which might mean that social factors have a more imminent impact on sovereign default risk while environmental factors such as climate change risk will emerge in the long term.[7] The estimation using Beyond Ratings ESG scores shows that environmental and governance factors have a significantly negative effect on sovereign borrowing costs in Asia and the Pacific. But the social factors have a significantly positive impact. The different result is probably attributable to different scopes and criteria of ESG evaluation, which could be expressed more clearly in each component score.[8]
- Among OECD countries, governance performance of MSCI is found to be negatively correlated with sovereign borrowing cost, while the impact of social indicator is not significant. This is in line with research by Capelle-Blancard et al. (2016). The results are unchanged based on Beyond Ratings ESG scores. Various studies on European sovereign borrowing cost pointed out the governance side of country ESG performance such as corruption, and political stability had larger effects on the sovereign borrowing cost (Bernoth and Erdogan, 2012; Arghyrou and Kontonikas, 2012). However, there is a significant positive relationship between environmental performance and sovereign CDS spreads when regressing on MSCI ESG scores.

---

[7] Different ESG factors will present greater risks over different time periods. In the longer term, ESG trends such as demographic changes and climate change are likely to have a significant impact on borrowing costs, but to what extent is uncertain. Analysts tend to give social factors greater weight than environmental factors because of links between political stability, governance, and a country's ability to raise taxes or implement reforms (World Bank, 2018).

[8] The MSCI governance score has incorporated a few numerical financial indicators such as current account surplus, which might account for the difference in results.

4.6 Conclusion

This chapter studies the link between ESG performance of a country and its CDS spreads. We focus on emerging countries, particularly in Asia, as they are more vulnerable to unstable borrowing costs and ESG risk.

The analysis shows a significantly negative relationship between overall sovereign ESG performance and sovereign CDS spreads. Given varied ESG criteria, we verified the results using ESG scores of two leading companies—MSCI and Beyond Ratings.

We applied the model to subregions and confirmed that the aggregate ESG scores are significantly negative across regions. However, the coefficient significance of each component shows different results depending on the region. In Asia and the Pacific, social factors have a significant negative effect on sovereign borrowing cost, while in OECD countries, governance is significant. The environmental score shows negative but not significant signs in Asia and the Pacific. The impact of each component is not constant between vendors in Asia.

The policy implications are that the government should be aware that ESG factors have gained more importance for investment decisions and that improved ESG performance could stabilize borrowing costs. In Asia and the Pacific, it is particularly crucial to improve social factors such as human rights, education, gender equality, and infrastructure.

Investors perceive social factors as closely linked with political stability, social cohesiveness, and a country's ability to pay debt. These social factors are generally enhanced by a country's wealth and development. Considering the potential tradeoff between some environmental and social factors, policy makers need to have an optimal balance of economic development and environment protection or energy consumption.

Future research could investigate how different ESG criteria and methodologies are incorporated into investors' behavior and debt pricing. It is worthwhile to estimate the model over a longer time and explore if each ESG component would affect borrowing costs in different time frames.

References

Aizenman, J., Y., Jinjarak, and D. Park. 2016. Fundamentals and Sovereign Risk of Emerging Markets. *Pacific Economic Review* 21(2): 151–177.

Arghyrou, M. G., and A. Kontonikas. 2012. The EMU Sovereign-Debt Crisis: Fundamentals, Expectations and Contagion. *Journal of International Financial Markets* 22(4): 658–677.

Asian Development Bank (ADB). 2017. *ADB Annual Report.* Manila: ADB. https://www.adb.org/documents/adb-annual-report-2017 (accessed 5 August 2019).

Atan, R., M. Alam., J. Said., and M. Zamri. 2018. The Impacts of Environmental, Social, and Governance Factors on Firm Performance: Panel Study of Malaysian Companies. *Management of Environmental Quality: An International Journal* 29 (2): 182–194.

Baek, I.-M., A. Bandopadhyaya, and C. Du. 2005. Determinants of Market-Assessed Sovereign Risk: Economic Fundamentals or Market Risk Appetite? *Journal of International Money and Finance* 24(4): 533–548.

Beirne, J., and M. Fratzscher. 2013. The Pricing of Sovereign Risk and Contagion During the European Sovereign Debt Crisis. *Journal of International Money and Finance* 34 (2013): 60–82.

Bernoth, K., and B. Erdogan. 2012. Sovereign Bond Yield Spreads: A Time-Varying Coefficient Approach. Journal of International Money and Finance, 31(3): 639–656.

Beyond Ratings. 2019. *Sovereign Rating Methodology.* Paris: Beyond Ratings. https://beyond-ratings.com/www-site/uploads/2019/03 /sovereign-rating-methodology.pdf (accessed 18 August 2019).

Bundala N. N. 2003. Do Economic Growth, Human Development and Political Stability Favour Sovereign Creditworthiness of a Country? A Cross Country Survey on Developed and Developing Countries. *International Journal of Advances in Management and Economics* 1(1): 32–46.

Capelle-Blancard, G., P. Crifo, M. Diaye, R. Oueghlissi, and B. Scholtens. 2016. Environmental, Social and Governance (ESG) Performance and Sovereign Bond Spreads: An Empirical Analysis of OECD Countries. EconomiX Working Papers. 2017-7. Nanterre, France: Paris Nanterre University. https://papers.ssrn.com/sol3/papers. cfm?abstract_id=2874262 (accessed 16 July 2019).

Chan-Lau, J. 2003. Anticipating Credit Events Using Credit Default Swaps, with an Application to Sovereign Debt Crises. IMF Working Papers 03/106. International Monetary Fund.

Ciocchini, F., E. Durbin, and D.T.C. Ng. 2003. Does Corruption Increase Emerging Market Bond Spreads? *Journal of Economics and Business* 55(5): 503–528.

Connolly, M., 2007. Measuring the Effect of Corruption on Sovereign Bond Ratings. *Journal of Economic Policy Reform* 10(4): 309–323.

Crifo, P., M.A. Diaye, and R. Oueghlissi. 2017. The Effect of Countries' ESG Ratings on Their Sovereign Borrowing Costs. *The Quarterly Review of Economics and Finance* 66(2017): 13–20.

Friede, G., T. Busch, and A. Bassen. 2015. ESG and Financial Performance: Aggregated Evidence from More Than 2000 Empirical Studies. Journal of Sustainable Finance & Investment, 5(4): 210–233. Global Sustainable Investment Alliance (GSIA). 2016. *Global Sustainable Investment Review.* GSIA. http://www.gsi-alliance.org/wp-content/uploads/2017/03/GSIR_Review2016.F.pdf (accessed 16 July 2019).

Global Sustainable Investment Alliance (GSIA). 2018. *Global Sustainable Investment Review.* GSIA. http://www.gsi-alliance.org/wp-content/uploads/2019/03/GSIR_Review2018.3.28.pdf (accessed 16 July 2019).

Government Pension Investment Fund. https://www.gpif.go.jp/investment/esg/#a (accessed 17 July 2019).

Hilscher, J., and Y. Nosbusch. 2010. Determinants of Sovereign Risk: Macroeconomic Fundamentals and the Pricing of Sovereign Debt. *Review of Finance* 14(2): 235–262.

Inderst, G., and F. Stewart. 2018. Incorporating Environmental, Social and Governance Factors into Fixed Income Investment. World Bank.

International Monetary Fund (IMF). 2013. A New Look at the Role of Sovereign Credit Default Swaps. In *Global Financial Stability Report: Old Risks, New Challenges. Global Financial Stability Report.* Washington, DC: IMF.

Jeanneret, A. 2018. Sovereign Credit Spreads Under Good/Bad Government. *Journal of Banking and Finance* 98(2018): 230–246.

Kennedy, M., and A. Palerm. 2014. Emerging Market Bond Spreads: The Role of Global and Domestic Factors from 2002 to 2011. *Journal of International Money and Finance* 43(C): 70–87.

Kitzmueller, M., and J. Shimshack. 2012. Economic Perspectives on Corporate Social Responsibility. *Journal of Economic Literature* 50(1): 51–84.

Krishnamurthy, A., and A. Vissing-Jorgensen. 2011. The Effects of Quantitative Easing On Interest Rates: Channels and Implications for Policy. NBER Working Paper No. 17555. Cambridge, MA: National Bureau of Economic Research. https://www.nber.org/papers/w17555 (accessed 6 August 2019).

Longstaff, F. A., J. Pan, L. H. Pedersen, and K. J. Singleton. 2011. How Sovereign Is Sovereign Credit Risk? *American Economic Journal: Macroeconomics* 3(2): 75–103.

Margaretic, P. and S. Pouget. 2018. Sovereign Bond Spreads and Extra-Financial Performance: An Empirical Analysis of Emerging Markets. *International Review of Economics & Finance*, 58(C): 340–355.

Morgan Stanley Capital International (MSCI). 2019. MSCI ESG Government Ratings Methodology. https://www.msci.com/documents/10199/123a2b2b-1395-4aa2-a121-ea14de6d708a (accessed 6 August 2019).

Ng, A. C., and Z. Rezaee. 2015. Business Sustainability Performance and Cost of Equity Capital. *Journal of Corporate Finance* 34(2015): 128–149.

Reznick, M., M. Viehs, N. Chockalingam, T. Panesar, G. A. Lizarazu, and J. Moussavi. 2019. *Pricing ESG Risk in Sovereign Credit*. Hermes Investment Management. https://www.hermes-investment.com/wp-content/uploads/2019/07/bd03720-credit-research-paper-pricing-esg-in-sovereign-credit-q3-2019.pdf (accessed 19 November 2019).

Russell Investments. 2017. *Fixed Income ESG Survey Results*. London: Russel Investments. https://russellinvestments.com/-/media/files/us/insights/institutions/fixed-income/fixed-income-esg-survey-results.pdf (accessed 19 November 2019).

Uribe, M., and V.Z. Yue. 2010. Country Spreads and Emerging Countries: Who Drives Whom? *Journal of International Economics* 69(1): 6–36.

Appendix

Table A4.1: Beyond Rating's Environmental, Social, and Governance Government Rating Framework

Pillar	Weight (%)		Theme
Environmental Performance	30%	Energy	Energy Policy
			Fossil Fuel Risks
			Energy Independency
		Climate	Physical Risks
			Transition Risks
		Resources	Natural Resources
			Air and Water
Social Performance	30%	Human Capital	
		Health	
		Societal	
		Inequality	
		Employment	
Governance	40%	Control of Corruption	
		Government Effectiveness	
		Rule of Law	
		Regulatory Quality	
		Voice and Accountability	
		Political Stability and Absence of Violence	

Source: Beyond Ratings (2019).

Table A4.2: Morgan Stanley Capital International's Environmental, Social, and Governance Government Rating Framework

Pillar	Risk Factor	Weight (%)	Risk Exposure	Weight (%)	Risk Management	Weight (%)
Environmental Risk	Natural resource risk	18%	Energy security risk	6%	Energy resource management	6%
			Productive land and mineral resources	6%	Resource conservation	6%
			Water resources	6%	Water resource management	6%
	Environmental externalities and vulnerability risk	7%	Vulnerability to environmental events	3%	Environmental performance	3%
			Environmental externalities	4%	Management of environmental externalities	4%
Social Risk	Human capital risk	15%	Basic human capital	5%	Basic needs	5%
			Higher education and technology readiness	6%	Human capital infrastructure	3%
					Human capital performance	3%
			Knowledge capital	4%	Knowledge capital management	4%
	Economic environment risk	10%	Economic environment	10%	Wellness	10%
Governance Risk	Financial governance risk	20%	Financial capital and trade vulnerability	20%	Financial management	20%
	Political governance risk	30%	Institution	10%	Stability and peace	10%
			Judicial and penal system	10%	Corruption control	10%
			Governance effectiveness	10%	Political rights and civil liberties	10%

MSCI = Morgan Stanley Capital International.
Source: MSCI (2019).

Table A4.3: Pearson Correlation Matrix of Environmental, Social, and Governance Scores

		1	2	3	4	5	6	7	8
1	ESG	1.00							
2	E	0.46	1.00						
3	S	0.87	0.20	1.00					
4	G	0.95	0.24	0.81	1.00				
5	BESG	0.90	0.27	0.94	0.84	1.00			
6	BE	0.64	0.63	0.56	0.48	0.66	1.00		
7	BS	0.80	0.19	0.89	0.74	0.88	0.58	1.00	
8	BG	0.86	0.19	0.89	0.83	0.97	0.51	0.78	1.00

BE = Beyond Ratings environmental index, BESG = Beyond Ratings ESG composite index, BG = Beyond Ratings governance quality index, BS = Beyond Ratings social quality index, E = MSCI environmental index, ESG = MSCI ESG composite index, G = MSCI governance quality index, S = MSCI social quality index.

Source: Authors, based on Stata.

Table A4.4: Pearson Correlation Matrix

		1	2	3	4	5	6	7	8	9	10	11	12	13	14	15
1	ESG	1.00														
2	E	0.46	1.00													
3	S	0.87	0.20	1.00												
4	G	0.95	0.24	0.81	1.00											
5	BESG	0.90	0.27	0.94	0.84	1.00										
6	BE	0.64	0.63	0.56	0.48	0.66	1.00									
7	BS	0.80	0.19	0.89	0.74	0.88	0.58	1.00								
8	BG	0.86	0.19	0.89	0.83	0.97	0.51	0.78	1.00							
9	VIX	0.09	0.08	0.13	0.14	0.07	0.02	0.01	0.08	1.00						
10	Cab	0.40	-0.07	0.34	0.48	0.31	0.09	0.32	0.31	-0.07	1.00					
11	Inf	-0.38	0.03	-0.50	-0.36	-0.48	-0.19	-0.38	-0.52	0.15	-0.17	1.00				
12	Debt	-0.10	-0.27	0.14	-0.10	0.16	-0.10	0.12	0.22	-0.10	-0.10	-0.33	1.00			
13	Res	-0.29	-0.14	-0.28	-0.27	-0.41	-0.28	-0.16	-0.48	-0.09	0.01	0.18	-0.07	1.00		
14	Growth	-0.25	-0.13	-0.36	-0.19	-0.33	-0.25	-0.30	-0.31	-0.23	0.09	0.27	-0.29	0.25	1.00	
15	QE	0.12	-0.18	0.20	0.13	0.27	0.18	0.22	0.27	-0.28	0.17	-0.20	0.40	-0.17	-0.09	1.00

BE = Beyond Ratings environmental index, BG = Beyond Ratings governance quality index, BS = Beyond Ratings social quality index, Cab = current account balance as a percentage of GDP, Debt = government debt as a percentage of GDP, E = MSCI environmental index, ESG = MSCI ESG composite index, ESG = Beyond Ratings, G = MSCI governance quality index, Growth = GDP growth rate, Inf = inflation rate, QE = adoption of quantitative easing policy, Res = foreign reserve as a percentage of import, S = MSCI social quality index, VIX = Chicago Board Options Exchange volatility index.

Source: Authors, based on Stata.

Table A4.5: Economies Included in the Analysis

Asia and the Pacific	Australia; China, People's Republic of; Hong Kong, China; India; Indonesia; Japan; Republic of Korea; Malaysia; Mongolia; New Zealand; Pakistan; Philippines; Sri Lanka; Thailand; Viet Nam
Organisation for Economic Co-operation and Development	Australia; Austria; Belgium; Canada; Chile; Czech Republic; Denmark; Estonia; Finland; France; Germany; Hungary; Iceland; Ireland; Israel; Italy; Japan; Korea, Republic of; Latvia; Lithuania; Mexico; Netherlands; New Zealand; Norway; Poland; Portugal; Slovak Republic; Slovenia; Spain; Sweden; Switzerland; Turkey; United Kingdom; United States
Europe and Central Asia	Austria, Belgium, Czech Republic, Denmark, Estonia, Finland, France, Germany, Hungary, Iceland, Ireland, Italy, Latvia, Lithuania, Netherlands, Norway, Poland, Portugal, Slovak Republic, Slovenia, Spain, Sweden, Switzerland, Turkey, United Kingdom
Latin America, Caribbean and North America	Canada, Chile, Mexico, United States
Middle East	Israel

Source: World Bank (2018).

Table A4.6: Regressions of Sovereign CDS Spread (with Morgan Stanley Capital International environmental, social, and governance data)

	All samples		Asia and the Pacific		OECD	
	(1)	(2)	(3)	(4)	(5)	(6)
ESG	−89.80**		−53.57***		−93.65***	
	(39.97)		(14.20)		(32.73)	
E		86.89*		27.15		59.46*
		(46.53)		(22.77)		(35.16)
S		−58.45		−53.22**		40.13
		(51.36)		(23.44)		(66.68)
G		−81.81*		−22.69		−155.8***
		(47.61)		(23.10)		(45.24)
VIX	−4.708	−3.280	1.582	2.254	−7.234	−4.026
	(5.116)	(5.156)	(2.374)	(2.365)	(7.170)	(7.264)
Cab	1.023	3.875	−2.790	−1.868	8.914	16.68*
	(5.902)	(6.002)	(3.319)	(3.269)	(8.714)	(8.890)
Inf	27.28***	25.73***	20.13***	18.82***	12.17	10.72
	(6.279)	(6.312)	(3.759)	(3.625)	(16.40)	(16.42)
Debt	1.022	1.260	1.158*	1.426*	3.372***	3.287***
	(1.796)	(1.793)	(0.693)	(0.805)	(1.170)	(1.151)
Res	−23.07**	−22.81**	−11.94**	−10.83*	−20.15*	−17.59
	(11.49)	(11.40)	(5.283)	(6.230)	(11.49)	(11.25)
Growth	−50.52***	−48.82***	−5.907	−4.549	−60.88***	−56.74***
	(9.365)	(9.565)	(7.214)	(6.965)	(13.01)	(12.92)
QE	−123.3	−108.0	−81.33	−68.01	−277.3***	−257.3***
	(112.4)	(112.5)	(88.52)	(83.77)	(100.1)	(99.66)
Constant	832.2***	724.6*	334.3***	365.0**	848.9***	650.8
	(305.9)	(405.4)	(115.6)	(164.7)	(306.6)	(416.5)
Time effect	Yes	Yes	Yes	Yes	Yes	Yes
Obs	702	702	133	133	341	341

Cab = current account balance as a percentage of GDP, CDS = credit default swap, Debt = government debt as a percentage of GDP, E = MSCI environmental index, ESG = MSCI ESG composite index, G =MSCI governance quality index, Growth = GDP growth rate, Inf = inflation rate, QE = adoption of quantitative easing policy, Res = foreign reserve as a percentage of import, S = MSCI social quality index.

Notes: 1. Standard errors in parentheses.
2. *, **, and *** mean significance at 10%, 5%, and 1% levels, respectively, and standard errors.

Source: Authors, based on Stata.

Table A4.7: Regressions of Sovereign CDS Spread
(with Beyond Ratings environmental, social, and governance data)

	All sample countries		Asia and the Pacific		OECD	
	(1)	(2)	(3)	(4)	(5)	(6)
BESG	−16.32***		−6.463***		−15.55***	
	(4.660)		(1.613)		(4.633)	
BE		13.61		−5.186*		8.357
		(9.919)		(3.116)		(6.932)
BS		6.876		4.079**		−7.241
		(5.520)		(2.039)		(5.229)
BG		−18.15***		−5.927***		−7.780*
		(4.076)		(1.511)		(4.249)
VIX	−3.454	−2.943	1.037	1.657	−5.244	−7.685
	(5.181)	(5.516)	(2.373)	(2.335)	(7.200)	(7.556)
Cab	2.704	2.686	−2.388	−6.495*	8.411	8.805
	(5.996)	(6.298)	(3.303)	(3.596)	(8.435)	(8.971)
Inf	25.74***	22.80***	20.94***	25.86***	7.969	7.107
	(6.509)	(7.302)	(3.694)	(4.188)	(16.43)	(17.05)
Debt	2.017	2.901	1.454**	1.709**	3.932***	4.333***
	(1.783)	(1.879)	(0.674)	(0.668)	(1.101)	(1.139)
Res	−27.97**	−37.50***	−12.82**	−18.56***	−20.76*	−17.33
	(11.60)	(12.40)	(5.184)	(5.753)	(11.33)	(11.91)
Growth	−52.08***	−52.10***	−8.426	−5.477	−58.11***	−57.78***
	(9.379)	(10.03)	(7.332)	(7.359)	(12.86)	(13.13)
QE	−91.30	−114.9	−82.14	−100.4	−243.5**	−281.4**
	(113.6)	(124.9)	(88.69)	(85.04)	(100.0)	(111.2)
Constant	1,304***	323.9	441.2***	485.4***	1,322***	847.2*
	(348.1)	(541.0)	(131.8)	(183.7)	(392.6)	(480.3)
Time effect	Yes	Yes	Yes	Yes	Yes	Yes
Obs	692	692	133	133	341	331

BE = Beyond Ratings environmental index, BESG = Beyond Ratings ESG composite index, BG = Beyond Ratings governance quality index, Cab = current account balance as a percentage of GDP, CDS = credit default swap, Debt = government debt as a percentage of GDP, Growth = GDP growth rate, Inf = inflation rate, QE = adoption of quantitative easing policy, Res = foreign reserve as a percentage of imports.

Note: 1. Standard errors in parentheses

2. *, **, and *** mean significance at 10%, 5%, and 1% levels, respectively, and standard error

Source: Authors, based on Stata.

5

Optimal Portfolio Selection for Environmental, Social, and Governance Investment

Naoyuki Yoshino, Farhad Taghizadeh-Hesary, and Miyu Otsuka

5.1 Introduction

5.1.1 Overview of Sustainable Development Goals

The Sustainable Development Goals (SDGs), targeted for 2030, are interconnected and aim to "leave no one behind." They provide a blueprint for peace and prosperity and envision (i) no poverty, (ii) zero hunger, (iii) good health, (iv) quality education, (v) gender equality, (vi) clean water and sanitation, (vii) clean energy, (viii) decent work and economic growth, (ix) industry and infrastructure, (x) reduced inequality, (xi) sustainable cities, (xii) responsible consumption and production, (xiii) climate action, (xiv) sustainable marine environment, (xv) sustainable land ecosystems, (xvi) peace and justice, and (xvii) partnerships (United Nations, 2019).

To build a sustainable global economy, companies' business operations must pay attention not only to economic aspects but also ecological and social criteria. Environmental, social, and governance (ESG) criteria enable investors to determine if a company contributes to creating a sustainable economy.

Environmental factors include level of energy use, share of renewable energy sources, and climate change strategies. Carbon dioxide (CO_2) or nitrogen oxide (NOx) emission targets are set by each company, however, and investors have difficulty comparing enterprises' targets. Although many companies, countries, and regions are demonstrating their skill, commitment, and ingenuity in achieving their targets, they must use science-based data to clarify how much and how quickly they need to reduce their greenhouse gas (GHG) emissions (UN Global Compact, 2019). SDG 7 aims to ensure access to affordable, reliable, sustainable, and modern energy for all, and to increase the share of renewable energy in the global energy mix by 2030. Global emissions of CO_2 have increased by almost 50% since 1990 and they grew more quickly in 2000–2010 than in each of the previous 3 decades. Climate change, including global warming, is a serious issue and SDG 13 stresses taking urgent action to tackle it.

There are several examples of commitment to ESG around the world. The city of Berlin, for example, aimed to meet CO_2 and NOx emission targets by establishing a low-emissions zone (The Partnerships for SDGs, 2019) of 88 square kilometers, divided into four, and home to one third of Berlin's inhabitants. Monetary and traffic registry penalties are enforced if vehicles do not meet the emission standards of each zone. Berlin targets NOx emissions from motor traffic 14% lower than those in 2010, 70% fewer high-polluting private cars, and 50% fewer old commercial carriers by 2020.

Enel, a huge Italian electricity company established in 1962, has committed to achieving certain targets by 2020 to reduce atmospheric emissions such as sulfur dioxide and NOx by 30% and dust by 70% compared with 2010 levels. Possible strategies are the installation or improvement of pollutant abatement systems and progressive decommissioning of inefficient plants.

The examples of Berlin and Enel show that environmental target setting depends on an entity's size, business strategy, and social responsibilities.

5.1.2 Environmental, Social, and Governance Criteria

Investors use ESG criteria for indicator-based measurements of a company's sustainability, focusing on environmental and social measures as well as corporate governance. Common environmental criteria include level of energy use, share of renewable energy sources, climate change strategy, and emissions. Social aspects focus on human rights, forced labor, labor environment diversity, workplace design, among others. The governance criterion is based on the extent to which sustainability is structurally implemented in a company.

Investors pay more attention to the sustainability of companies, improving the risk assessment of their investment and possibly increasing the performance of the investment pool. Considering ecological and social aspects does not mean a reduced rate of return, as enterprise values have been changing in the global economy. As companies improve their potential, especially in sustainability, the trend of including ESG criteria in investment decisions will continue to intensify.

5.1.3 Consulting Firms' Environmental, Social, and Governance and Sustainable Development Goal Criteria

Different consulting companies have different criteria for assessing ESG and SDG investment, which means that institutional investors have different portfolio allocations. We examine the criteria that three major consulting companies use to assess ESG and SDG investment.

KPMG is a multinational professional service (financial audit, tax, and advisory) network, and one of the Big Four accounting organizations. KPMG uses the SDG Industry Matrix to encourage the private sector to help achieve the SDGs. The SDG Industry Matrix is jointly managed by the United Nations Global Compact and KPMG. The SDGs give companies an opportunity to create values for their own business and for society by investing in ethical, resource-efficient, and resilient businesses such as renewable energy and other low-carbon infrastructure projects. To determine whether the businesses are consistent with the SDGs, four points are considered: *demographics* (population prediction in a country or region); *income growth*; *technology* (including renewable energy sources, knowledge-sharing cultures); and *collaboration* (among, for example, governments, companies, international organizations, academia). The higher the four indicators' levels are, the more active SDG investment can be (United Nations Global Compact and KPMG, 2016).

Nomura Research Institute (NRI), the largest Japanese management consulting and economic research firm, states that consistency and level of contribution to the SDGs should be quantitatively defined. The NRI uses four key performance indicators in investigating business activities: *innovation, business opportunity, impact,* and *cost*. For example, technological growth through innovation is essential to create the hydrogen energy market. When a company succeeds activating a hydrogen energy business, opportunities can be broadly expanded. The social impact of hydrogen energy is huge and can help achieve the SDGs. Risk factors, however, should be taken into account, such as the rise of energy prices or high product costs (NRI, 2019).

PricewaterhouseCoopers International Limited (PwC) is the world's second largest professional service (financial audit, tax, and advisory) firm and a Big Four accounting company. PwC has developed indicators that consider business level to achieve global goals, including the SDGs.

Deciding on the right company to meet the SDG strategy is crucial in the global market. The indicators include *leadership* (business and financial strategies); *employee engagement* (awareness and bottom-up initiatives); *reporting* (risk assessment and management); and *collaboration* (among suppliers, consumers, government, nongovernment organizations) (PwC 2016).

5.2 Theoretical Model of Environmental, Social, and Governance Needs and Portfolio Selection

5.2.1 A Model Incorporating Environmental, Social, and Governance Indicators in Investors' Utility Function

We modify the conventional portfolio utility function by incorporating ESG indicators. First, the traditional portfolio utility function can be written as equation (1), which includes the risk and rate of return:

$$U(R_t, \sigma_t^2) = R_t - \beta \sigma_t^2 \tag{1}$$

Second, we can think of the new portfolio utility function considering ESG investment as the following:

Rate of return:

$$R_t = \alpha_t R_t^A + (1 - \alpha_t) R_t^B \text{ where A = Company A, B=Company B} \tag{2}$$

Risk:

$$\sigma_t^2 = \alpha_t^2 (\sigma_t^A)^2 + (1 - \alpha_t)^2 (\sigma_t^B)^2 + 2\alpha_t (1 - \alpha_t) \sigma_t^{AB} \tag{3}$$

ESG:

$$ESG_t^A = a_t^1 (CO_{2\,t}^A) + a_t^2 (NO_{X\,t}^A) \tag{4}$$

$$ESG_t^B = b_t^1 (CO_{2\,t}^B) + b_t^2 (NO_{X\,t}^B) \tag{5}$$

where 1 = CO_2 emitted by company A and company B, 2 = NO_X emitted by company A and company B. In equations (4) and (5), the coefficient of (a_t^1, a_t^2) and (b_t^1, b_t^2) are different from one consulting company to another.

The level of total ESG can be described as follows:

$$ESG_t = \alpha_t(ESG_t^A) + (1 - \alpha_t)(ESG_t^B) \tag{6}$$

Here, we set the utility function as in equation (7), which includes all three elements above: rate of return, risk, and ESG variable subject to the constraints as in equation (8):

$$U(R_t, \sigma_t^2, ESG_t) = R_t - \beta\sigma_t^2 + \gamma(ESG_t) \tag{7}$$

$$\text{s.t. } R_t = \alpha_t R_t^A + (1 - \alpha_t)R_t^B \tag{8}$$

$$\sigma_t^2 = \alpha_t^2(\sigma_t^A)^2 + (1 - \alpha_t)^2(\sigma_t^B)^2 + 2\alpha_t(1 - \alpha_t)\sigma_t^{AB} \tag{9}$$

Substituting equations (6), (8), and (9) into equation (7), we have the optimal level of portfolio function as expressed in equation (10).

$$U = \alpha_t R_t^A + (1 - \alpha_t)R_t^B - \beta\{\alpha_t^2(\sigma_t^A)^2 + (1 - \alpha_t)^2$$
$$(\sigma_t^B)^2 + 2\alpha_t(1 - \alpha_t)\sigma_t^{AB}\} + \gamma\{\alpha_t(ESG_t^A) + (1 - \alpha_t)(ESG_t^B)\} \tag{10}$$

Obtaining the first-order conditions with respect to the ratio between asset A and asset B (α_t), equation (11) can be shown as follows:

$$\frac{\partial U}{\partial \alpha_t} = (R_t^A - R_t^B) - \beta\{2\alpha_t(\sigma_t^A)^2 + 2(1 - \alpha_t)(\sigma_t^B)^2\}$$
$$+ (2 - 4\alpha_t)\sigma_t^{AB} + \gamma(ESG_t^A - ESG_t^B) = 0 \tag{11}$$

Writing equation (11) for results in equation (12):

$$\alpha_t = \frac{\frac{1}{2\beta}(R_t^A - R_t^B) - (\sigma_t^B)^2 - \sigma_t^{AB} + \frac{\gamma}{2\beta}(ESG_t^A - ESG_t^B)}{(\sigma_t^A)^2 - (\sigma_t^B)^2 - 2\sigma_t^{AB}} \tag{12}$$

Equation (12) indicates the share of allocation into asset A. The last term in the numerator is an additional component, which affects allocation between asset A and asset B. If ESG_t^A is larger than ESG_t^B, portfolio allocation to asset A will be larger (Figure 5.2). Figure 5.1 shows traditional portfolio investment, which is determined by rate of return and risk; point "e" is the optimal portfolio allocation. In Figure 5.2, SDGs are included in the utility function, where point "f" will become the optimal portfolio allocation since asset A has a higher ESG score than asset B.

However, the ESG measure is different from one consulting company to another. Investors select a consulting company to allocate their portfolio based on the company's ESG definition. Each investor's asset allocation results in distorted portfolio allocation based on different weight of (a_t^1, a_t^2) and (b_t^1, b_t^2) as in equations (4) and (5). Each investor will choose different portfolio (f) based on which consulting company it chooses.

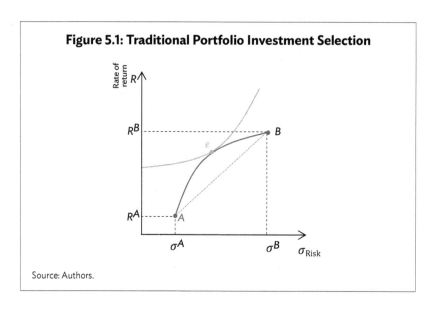

Figure 5.1: Traditional Portfolio Investment Selection

Source: Authors.

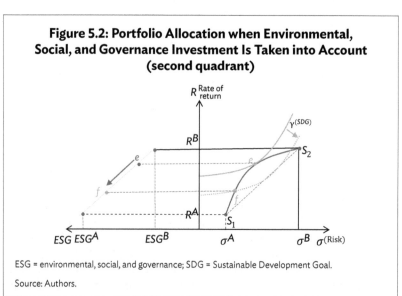

Figure 5.2: Portfolio Allocation when Environmental, Social, and Governance Investment Is Taken into Account (second quadrant)

ESG = environmental, social, and governance; SDG = Sustainable Development Goal.

Source: Authors.

5.2.2 Greenhouse Gas Taxation and Optimal Portfolio Allocation for Environmental, Social, and Governance Investment

Greenhouse gas (GHG) (CO_2 and NO_x) taxation is a suitable tool for preventing fossil fuel projects' growth and for financing green energy projects (Taghizadeh-Hesary and Yoshino, 2019, 2020). Global GHG taxation based on the same tax rate will give us a new rate of return on asset A and asset B. Tax rates can be adjusted based on the progress of pollution reduction. If it is slower than the target, the tax rate can be adjusted globally by the same rate.

$$U\left(\tilde{R}_t, \tilde{\sigma}_t^2\right) = \tilde{R}_t - \beta \tilde{\sigma}_t^2 \tag{13}$$

$$T_A = t_1\left(CO_{2\,t}^A\right) + t_2\left(NO_{X\,t}^A\right) \tag{14}$$

$$T_B = t_1\left(CO_{2\,t}^B\right) + t_2\left(NO_{X\,t}^B\right) \tag{15}$$

Equation (13) shows the new utility function of investors, which is based on "after-tax rate of return" and "after-tax risk." Equations (14) and (15) show the tax rates on CO_2 and NO_x, which are the same globally. The tax rate on CO_2 is the same for company A and company B and the tax rate of NO_x is same for company A and company B. These rates need to be same globally to avoid distortion of investments from one country to another.

$$\tilde{R}_t^A = R_t^A - T_A \tag{16}$$

$$\tilde{R}_t^B = R_t^B - T_B \tag{17}$$

Equations (16) and (17) show the after-tax rate of return of company A and company B. We can compute the optimal allocation of assets between company A and company B as in equations (18) and (19), which show the optimal rate of return and risk, respectively:

$$\tilde{R}_t = \tilde{\alpha}_t \tilde{R}_t^A + (1 - \tilde{\alpha}_t)\tilde{R}_t^B \tag{18}$$

$$\tilde{\sigma}_t^2 = \tilde{\alpha}_t^2(\tilde{\sigma}_t^A)^2 + (1 - \tilde{\alpha}_t)^2(\tilde{\sigma}_t^B)^2 + 2\tilde{\alpha}_t(1 - \tilde{\alpha}_t)\tilde{\sigma}_t^{AB} \tag{19}$$

To find the optimal portfolio allocation ratio between asset A and asset B, we get the first-order condition of the utility function with respect to $\tilde{\alpha}$:

$$\frac{\partial U}{\partial \tilde{\alpha}_t} = (\tilde{R}_t^A - \tilde{R}_t^B) - \beta\{2\tilde{\alpha}_t(\tilde{\sigma}_t^A)^2$$
$$+ 2(1 - \tilde{\alpha}_t)(\tilde{\sigma}_t^B)^2\} + (2 - 4\tilde{\alpha}_t)\tilde{\sigma}_t^{AB} = 0 \qquad (20)$$

Finally, we get the optimal level of portfolio allocation as in equation (21):

$$\tilde{\alpha}_t = \frac{\frac{1}{2\beta}(\tilde{R}_t^A - \tilde{R}_t^B) - (\tilde{\sigma}_t^B)^2 - \tilde{\sigma}_t^{AB}}{(\tilde{\sigma}_t^A)^2 - (\tilde{\sigma}_t^B)^2 - 2\tilde{\sigma}_t^{AB}} \qquad (21)$$

As is clear in equation (21), investors need not take into account ESG investment as an additional item shown in equation (12). Instead, investors maximize their utility based only on the rate of return and the risk after the GHG tax. The optimal portfolio allocation is as in equation (21). The $\tilde{\alpha}_t$ will give us the optimal portfolio, which is shown in Figure 5.3 by point f, the optimal point after adoption of the international GHG taxation scheme.

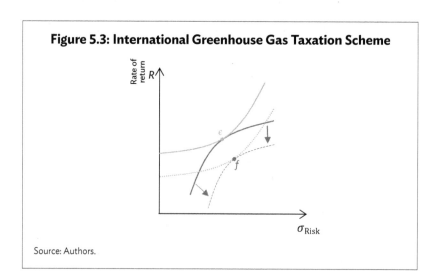

Figure 5.3: International Greenhouse Gas Taxation Scheme

Source: Authors.

5.3 Empirical Analysis

The empirical section assesses investors' pro-environment preferences. Green bonds are suitable for funding ESGs. To provide policy implications, we examine the possible association between (i) ESG indicators as a proxy for investors' pro-environment preferences, and (ii) the rate of return of green bonds and issuers' stock market performance.

5.3.1 Empirical Model

We consider the state of ESG investment in Japan. In ESG fields of interest, GHGs and climate change are brought up in the environmental aspect (E), effective use of human resources in social issues (S), and corporate board structure in governance (G) (Soga, 2016). According to the Japan Sustainable Investment Forum, the third sustainable investment survey, conducted in 2017, found that sustainable investment in Japan had increased to ¥136.6 trillion, or 2.4 times the amount from the previous survey (2016). The percentage of total sustainable assets held by institutional investors grew from 16.8% in 2016 to 35% in 2017.

The empirical model of this study is shown as equation (22):

$$(SPG)_{it} = \alpha_{it} + \beta_1(ROR_{it}) + \beta_2(BIA_{it})$$

$$+ \beta_3 (ESG_{it}) + \beta_4(RSK_{it}) + \varepsilon_{it} \tag{22}$$

Where SPG denotes growth rate of stock prices of companies that issued green bonds, ROR denotes rate of return of green bonds, BIA stands for volume of green bond issuance (2016–2018), and ESG denotes ESG indicator expressed as CO_2 emissions by the companies that issued green bonds. RSK is risk expressed as credit rating of the green bonds, ranging from AA to BBB (based on the evaluation of Rating and Investment Information, Inc).

5.3.2 Empirical Results and Discussion

In running the empirical analysis, we used 24 Japanese institutions that issued green bonds in 2016–2018. Table 5.1 shows the descriptive analysis. The panel ordinary least square (OLS) results of three regressions based on different risk levels are in Table 5.2.

The empirical results in Table 5.2 show that the rate of return of green bonds is positively correlated with stock price growth of the companies issuing green bonds. The larger the rate of return, the

Table 5.1: Descriptive Statistics of Variables

Variable	Unit	Mean	Std. Dev.	Min	Max
SPG	Growth rate of stock prices (%)	4.82	30.63	−33.84	102.74
ROR	Rate of return (%)	0.47	0.49	0	2.53
BIA	Green bond issuance amount (¥)	1.55e+10	1.54e+10	4.00e+09	5.45e+10
ESG	ESG indicator (CO_2 emissions reduction rate, %)	−3.75	18.92	−73.28	28.87
RSK	Credit rating of the green bonds (AA, A, and BBB)	–	–	–	–

BIA = bond issuance amount; ESG = environmental, social, and governance; ROR = rate of return; RSK = risk; SPG = stock price growth.
Source: Authors.

Table 5.2: Panel Ordinary Least Square Regression Results

	SPG	SPG	SPG
Explanatory Variable			
ROR	43.08**	44.81**	45.40**
	(3.17)	(3.06)	(3.15)
BIA	−1.3e−09**	−1.3e−09*	−1.33e−09**
	(−2.99)	(−2.63)	(−2.91)
ESG	0.04**	0.04*	0.04*
	(2.83)	(2.70)	(2.78)
RSK (AA)		−2.30	
		(−0.18)	
RSK (BBB)			2.84
			(0.18)
Constant	−0.67	−0.84	−2.63
	(−0.09)	(−0.08)	(−0.31)
R-squared	0.47	0.49	0.49

BIA = bond issuance amount; ESG = environmental, social, and governance; ROR = rate of return; RSK = risk; SPG = stock price growth.
Notes: The numbers in parentheses are t-values. ** Indicates statistically significant result in 1%.
* Indicates statistically significant result in 5%.
Source: Authors.

greater investors' demand, which will elevate the stock price index. A negative correlation was shown between green bond issuance amount and stock price growth. A possible interpretation is that the stock price of green bond issuance companies tends to decline just 1 year after the bond issuance because of the risk and uncertainty surrounding the completion of green projects or because of the temporary current account deficit. As for the ESG indicator expressed as CO_2 emissions by the companies that issued green bonds, the reduction rate of CO_2 emissions is positively associated with companies' stock price growth. More environmentally-friendly companies that satisfy investors' pro-environment preferences would see stock prices increase. Finally, risk expressed as credit rating of green bonds does not have a statistically significant correlation with stock price growth. A major reason behind this insignificant association is that high risk projects and those projects that get a low credit rating, do not get eligibility by the capital market authorities to issue bonds publicly.

5.4 Conclusion and Policy Implications

To build a sustainable global economy, companies' business operations must pay attention to not only economic aspects but also ecological and social criteria. ESG criteria enable investors to determine if a company contributes to creating a sustainable economy. By adopting ESG goals, institutional investors consider three factors: rate of return, risk, and ESG goals for investment allocations. The term ESG is not clearly defined among investors, but investment decision making was traditionally based only on rate of return and risk.

We argue that each consulting company has its own criteria for ESG investment. Institutional investors include ESG aspects in their investment portfolios based on the criteria of the consulting firm they receive services from, which will distort portfolio allocation as there is no global standardized criteria for ESG measurement.

Our main policy recommendation is to adopt a global GHG taxation scheme. Based on the theoretical models provided here, we investigated the portfolio investment scheme, taking into consideration ESG goals. The best policy to achieve clean energy and pro-environment ESG goals is taxing GHGs (CO_2 and NOx, globally) and plastics. This will make investors focus on the rate of return and risk (after tax) only. This international taxation system will ultimately lead to optimal asset allocation and achieve sustainable growth. Our empirical analysis shows that the rate of return of green bonds as well as CO_2 emissions reduction rate are positively associated with stock price growth of companies issuing green bonds. This means that pro-environment preferences are becoming important among investors, whose demand for environmentally-friendly companies is increasing. Improving firms' environmental performance could lead to rising stock prices. Finally, although imposing an emission tax will reduce the rate of return, private investors will become more willing to invest in environmentally-friendly companies, which will partly or wholly offset losses caused by carbon taxation.

References

Nomura Research Institute (NRI). 2019. How to Quantify the Contribution Level to SDGs by Organization Units (in Japanese).

PricewaterhouseCoopers (PwC). 2016. *Navigating the SDGs: A Business Guide to Engaging with the UN Global Goals.* https://www.pwc.com /gx/en/sustainability/publications/PwC-sdg-guide.pdf   (accessed 19 March 2020).

Soga, K. 2016. *Scale of ESG investment in Japan.* Nikko Research Review, Research Report February 2016. Tokyo: Nikko Research Center Inc. Taghizadeh-Hesary F., and N. Yoshino. 2019. The Way to Induce Private Participation in Green Finance and Investment. *Finance Research Letters* 31: 98–103.

Taghizadeh-Hesary, F., and N. Yoshino, 2020. Sustainable Solutions for Green Financing and Investment in Renewable Energy Projects. *Energies* 13: 788.

United Nations. 2019. About the Sustainable Development Goals. https://www.un.org/sustainabledevelopment/sustainable -development-goals/ (accessed 10 December 2019).

United Nations Global Compact and KPMG. 2016. *SDG Industry Matrix—Energy, Natural Resources and Chemicals.* https://assets .kpmg/content/dam/kpmg/xx/pdf/2017/01/SDG-industry-matrix .pdf (accessed 19 March 2020).

6

Measuring the Effect of Environmental, Social, and Governance Investment on Banking in Indonesia and How Fiscal Policies Contribute

Abdul Aziz

6.1 Introduction

Environmental, social, and governance (ESG)-based investment has grown rapidly all over the world. Many countries have applied ESG factors to every investment. In Indonesia, ESG investment in banks started in 2009 although not all banks today engage in it. Triyono (2018) explains: "ESG investment is a set of operational standards that refers to three main criteria in measuring the sustainability and impact of an investment in a company, namely, environmental, social, and governance criteria."

Several authors have related ESG investment company finance, assets, and financial health. Novethic (2013) surveyed more than 100 asset owners in Europe every year since 2008, asking how they integrate ESG criteria into asset management. The study concluded that asset owners increasingly consider the urgency of integrating ESG criteria into their investments. Bernardi and Stark (2015: 7) said that "our results also provide support for the idea that specific aspects of ESG performance are more important than others for some sets of firms in understanding future performance."

Thomson Reuters/Refinitiv (2019) introduced a method of calculating ESG scores separating the factors (E, S, and G) and aggregating them (ESG), essentially measures the level of reporting of a company's ESG information. Environmental data are used to develop water, energy, waste, emissions, and operational policies. Social data are used to build social relationships, especially with the work force, humanity, and the community. Governance data are related to the structure and functions of company boards, executive compensation, and corporate political involvement.

6.2 Problems and Objectives

This chapter considers ESG investment as the main independent variable in the regression equation, with several other independent variables as control variables (such as total income and total assets). Stock prices and deposits are dependent variables because they are easily influenced by other variables, including ESG investment.

An estimation equation about the influence of ESG investment in banks should be studied and evaluated urgently. If they show the influence of ESG investment on important factors in banks, the estimation results can be applied to other types of companies to encourage them to consider ESG factors in their investment activities.

However, an estimation of the influence of ESG investment on stock prices and deposits has never been applied to banks in Indonesia, even though they are highly important in the economy.

The government has not encouraged ESG investment in banks or other companies. Therefore, the purposes of this study are the following:

(i) Measure the effect of ESG investment and other control variables on deposits and share prices in banks in Indonesia.

(ii) Describe the form of fiscal incentives that the government should use to support ESG investment in banks and other companies.

6.3 Research Methodology

6.3.1 Analysis Method

This study uses quantitative analysis methods to explain the relationship between independent variables and dependent variables using panel data estimation models. The research uses a descriptive analysis to explain Indonesia's fiscal policy and how it can be used to promote ESG investment.

The initial panel data estimation model follows:

$$Y_{it} = \alpha_i + \beta_1 X_{1it} + \beta_2 X_{2it} + \beta_3 X_{3it} + \beta_4 X_{4it} + \beta_5 X_{5it} + \beta_6 X_{6it} + \varepsilon_{it}$$

Y1 = STC = Stock Prices (share prices) in the sample banking companies
Y2 = DEP = Total Deposits in the sample banking companies
α = Constant
β = Coefficient regression
X_1 = ENV = Environmental Performance with a score from 0 to 100
X_2 = SOC = Social Performance with a score from 0 to 100
X_3 = GOV = Governance Performance with a score from 0 to 100
X_4 = ESG = ESG Performance with a score from 0 to 100
X_5 = INC = Total Income in the sample banking companies
X_6 = ASSET = Total Asset in the sample banking companies
ε = Error term

6.3.2 Data Collection Method

The study used secondary data from banks listed on the Indonesian Stock Exchange and can be accessed in Eikon, which belongs to Thomson Reuters/Refinitiv, including ESG factor data that have been formulated with scores and grades.

The purposive sampling method was used, taking samples of four banks with the largest assets (Table 6.1) and which had completed ESG score data from 2009 to 2017: Bank Rakyat Indonesia (BRI), Mandiri, Bank Central Asia (BCA), and Bank Nasional Indonesia (BNI). In total, there were 36 observational data for the four biggest banks.

Table 6.1: Banks with the Largest Assets, Indonesia

Rank	Bank	Assets (Rp million)
1	Bank Rakyat Indonesia	1,064,730,000
2	Mandiri	645,620,000
3	Bank Central Asia	754,040,000
4	Bank Nasional Indonesia	648,570,000

Source: Centerklik (https://www.centerklik.com/10-daftar-bank-terbesar-di-indonesia-dan-asetnya/amp/).

6.3.3 Operationalization of the Panel Data Analysis Model

Besides the panel data regression model, this chapter presents several test and assessment models (see Appendix 1 for details):

(i)   hypothesis test of each independent variable,
(ii) estimation model selection method,
(iii) statistical testing criteria (diagnostic test), and
(iv) econometric testing criteria.

6.4 Literature Review

6.4.1 Definition of, Opportunities in, and Challenges of Environmental, Social, and Governance Investment in Banks

Yusoff, Hazwani, and Ghani (2018) focus on environmental accountability. The demand for environmental performance data is increasing from stakeholder groups, indicating that more disclosure is needed. The introduction of mandatory requirements by the government for environmental reporting has increased environmental reporting by companies.

Many countries, including Indonesia, have investments that consider nonfinancial factors such as ESG issues, which allow for better conditions and more transparency.

Lundstrom and Svensson (2014) say, "The condition of financial markets around the world in recent times has shown that investors have begun to focus on non-financial factors in their portfolio selection process including the ESG factor." This factor is considered reasonable if included in the mathematical calculation framework to optimize a company's portfolio because: (i) investors pay serious attention to the ESG factor, and (ii) companies that consider ESG issues perform better than those that do not.

Tarmuji, Maelah, and Tarmuji (2016) argue that responsible ESG management builds company integrity and stakeholder trust. Companies in Malaysia and Singapore that disclose their ESG practices in the media have a reputation for being profitable and competitive.

Thomson Reuters/Refinitiv (2019) recognizes "the increasingly critical importance of transparent, accurate and comparable Environmental, Social and Governance (ESG) data for the financial industry." The ESG scores formulated by Thomson Reuters/Refinitiv are designed to transparently and objectively measure ESG performance, commitment, and effectiveness in a company by using 10 indicators: resource use, emissions, innovation, workforce, human rights, community, product responsibility, management, shareholders, and corporate social responsibility (CSR) strategy.

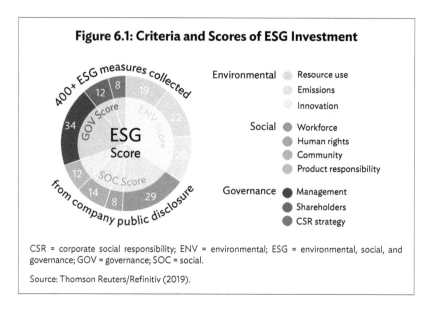

Figure 6.1: Criteria and Scores of ESG Investment

CSR = corporate social responsibility; ENV = environmental; ESG = environmental, social, and governance; GOV = governance; SOC = social.

Source: Thomson Reuters/Refinitiv (2019).

6.4.2 ESG Investment Grades and Scores

Based on company data, Thomson Reuters/Refinitiv (2019) captures and calculates ESG indicators in more than 400 companies, where it has carefully selected 178 of the most comparable and relevant fields to strengthen companies' overall assessment and scoring process. The ESG combined score provides a comprehensive assessment of companies' ESG performance based on information from global media sources (Figure 6.1).

Table 6.2: Environmental, Social, and Governance Grades and Scores (D– to A+; 1–100)

Grade	Score	Grade	Score
A+	$91.67 < \text{score} \leq 100.00$	C+	$41.67 < \text{score} \leq 50.00$
A	$83.33 < \text{score} \leq 91.67$	C	$33.33 < \text{score} \leq 41.67$
A–	$75.00 < \text{score} \leq 83.33$	C–	$25.00 < \text{score} \leq 33.33$
B+	$66.67 < \text{score} \leq 75.00$	D+	$16.67 < \text{score} \leq 25.00$
B	$58.33 < \text{score} \leq 66.67$	D	$8.33 < \text{score} \leq 16.67$
B–	$50.00 < \text{score} \leq 58.33$	D–	$0.00 < \text{score} \leq 8.33$

Source: Thomson Reuters/Refinitiv (2019).

The grades and scores formulated by Thomson Reuters/Refinitiv
(2019) are shown in Table 6.2.

The author recorded scores from Eikon and ESG combined scores
for the four commercial banks sampled (Table 6.3 and Table 6.4).

Table 6.3: Environmental, Social, and Governance Grades and Scores (2009–2017) in Bank Rakyat Indonesia and Mandiri (D– to A+; 1–100)

Year	Bank Rakyat Indonesia				Mandiri			
	ENV	SOC	GOV	ESG	ENV	SOC	GOV	ESG
2009	23	42	28	31	16	57	85	52
2010	24	47	56	42	17	60	84	53
2011	24	46	54	41	26	60	80	55
2012	21	67	59	49	39	58	75	57
2013	23	61	56	46	39	61	74	58
2014	53	75	71	66	44	63	75	60
2015	69	72	61	68	52	75	71	66
2016	80	76	80	79	58	72	70	66
2017	86	79	89	84	56	80	45	61
Average	44,78	62,78	61,56	56,22	38,56	65,11	73,22	58,67
Grade	C+	B	B	B–	C	B	B+	B

ENV = environmental; ESG = environmental, social, and governance; GOV = governance; SOC = social.
Source: Thomson Reuters/Refinitiv (2019).

Table 6.4: ESG Score and Grade (2009 – 2017) in Bank Central Asia and Bank Nasional Indonesia (D– to A+; 1–100)

Year	Bank Central Asia				Bank Nasional Indonesia			
	ENV	SOC	GOV	ESG	ENV	SOC	GOV	ESG
2009	41	24	43	41	52	43	44	46
2010	31	47	61	46	67	51	57	58
2011	31	51	38	40	72	73	42	63
2012	29	65	75	56	70	69	49	63
2013	47	67	78	63	69	74	57	67

continued on next page

Table 6.4 *continued*

	Bank Central Asia				Bank Nasional Indonesia			
Year	ENV	SOC	GOV	ESG	ENV	SOC	GOV	ESG
2014	84	86	69	80	73	79	60	71
2015	61	77	51	64	78	86	68	78
2016	83	81	51	81	83	86	57	76
2017	83	81	75	80	85	83	41	71
Average	54,44	64,33	60,11	61,22	72,11	71,56	52,78	65,89
Grade	B–	B	B	B	B+	B+	B–	B

ENV = environmental; ESG = environmental, social, and governance; GOV = governance; SOC = social.
Source: Thomson Reuters/Refinitiv (2019).

6.4.3 Deposits in Banks

Deposits have a strategic role in channeling loans to customers. Many variables make the amount of deposits in a bank increase or decrease, depending on financial factors (such as interest rates) and nonfinancial factors (such as public confidence in the condition of banking liquidity). ESG factors can influence the ups and downs of the deposits rate.

Fitri (2016) writes that the factors that influence the development of deposit funds from a macro perspective include the level of community income, and from a micro perspective profit sharing in a sharia-based banking system among others (including, I might add, interest in a conventional banking system).

If ESG investment is carried out properly by banks and if the public benefits directly and indirectly, banks will have a positive public image and the public will save their funds in them. This chapter, therefore, analyzes bank deposits, and how they relate to ESG investments, as a dependent variable.

6.4.4 Stock and Share Prices

Many factors affect the ups and downs of stock prices and whether a stock needs to be bought back (stock return). Triyono (2018) tests whether stock returns are affected by ESG scores as measured by the disclosure of CSR information and the application of good corporate governance, and if stock returns are controlled by financial parameters such as leverage, growth, and profitability. Triyono's study uses data from companies listed on the Indonesia Stock Exchange that reveal ESG performance in 2010–2016. The study's results indicate that environmental performance has no significant effect but is positively correlated with stock returns. Social performance also has no significant effect but has a negative correlation with stock returns. Corporate governance significantly and negatively affects stock returns.

Whittaker, Spinoso, and Lee (2018) say that an ESG rating for a company shows the extent of the company's positive momentum in managing ESG investment risks and opportunities. Such companies are not yet "leaders" but their performance on various ESG criteria shows signs that one day they will be. The momentum is an investment strategy of buying shares that have an upward price trend, and selling shares that have had a bad return in recent months, based on the tendency of prices to move in a trend direction.

Based on the studies cited, this chapter uses the stock price, and how it relates to ESG investment, as a dependent variable.

6.4.5 Total Assets and Total Income

Bennani et al. (2018) say that in fact, ESG factors affect investment in two different ways. First, ESG can be seen as a model. In this case, investors manage portfolio risks differently from traditional risk factor models, because the criteria are not the same (extra-financial versus financial risk), and different time horizons (long term versus medium term). If we assume that the ESG investment model does its job well it will produce a better managed portfolio, then this implies that ESG screening has a positive impact on portfolio payments and subsequently on asset timing. Second, ESG is an investment style, not just a risk model. This implies that ESG produces investments that can increase asset prices, and subsequently increase portfolios. In general, positive investment flows result in price increases, while negative investments result in price decreases, due to the law of supply and demand.

Aziz (2006) explained that one indicator to measure the health of a company (in this case, banking) is to look at the condition of the total assets and total income because these two indicators are tools to show the relative net profit (after tax) of total assets. In another definition is an indicator that shows the ability of banks to obtain a return on a number of banks assets. The formula used to measure this is return on assets (ROA) (Aziz 2006). ROA is net income divided by total assets or equal to net income (after tax) divided by total assets:

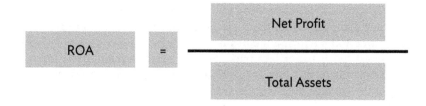

Aziz (2006) explains that although the formula for calculating ROA is simple, the figures it produces give a picture of the ability to manage a bank. Thus, ROA is good enough to assess a bank's performance and prospects.

6.4.6 Concept and Implementation of Fiscal Policy

Indonesia's Ministry of Finance (2019) states: "Fiscal policy is a policy taken by the Government to influence the economy and realize public welfare through revenue (state revenue) and expenditure (state expenditure), and financing (state financing)."

Fiscal policy has three main functions:

(i)   Encourage budget allocation to help realize economic efficiency and provision of public goods.

(ii) Redistribute income to realize economic justice, reduce inequality, and provide social protection for the whole community.

(iii) Maintain macroeconomic balance to maintain economic stability and encourage sustainable economic growth.

Aziz (2018) states that there are three types or sources of fiscal incentives to individuals, businesses, state-owned enterprises (SOEs), among others:

(i)   state revenue such deductible tax, tax holiday incentives;

(ii) state expenditure such as the Smart Indonesia Program, interest subsidies for microcredit programs, construction of school buildings; and

(iii) state financing such as state capital participation (SCP) in international institutions, state companies, business entities, among others.

SCP is central government participation in establishing, developing, and improving the performance of state- and local-owned enterprises or other legal entities (Ministry of Finance of Indonesia, 2019).

6.5 Discussion and Results

The panel data estimation models are the pooled least square (PLS), fixed effect method (FEM), and random effect method (REM).

Various authors, including Wooldridge (2002), argue, "In the traditional approach to panel data models, Ci is called a random effect when it is treated as a random variable and a fixed effect when it is treated as a parameter to be estimated for each cross section observation i." If the parameters to be estimated are all population data, then the FEM is chosen to see the effect of each individual (bank) on the dependent variables. The FEM can be compared with two models to find out if they are better. PLS need not be compared with REM.

After testing and selecting the model (Appendix 2), this study chose the panel data regression equation with the FEM as the best estimation model. The stock/share price regression equation (STC) and the total deposits regression equation (DEP) were simulated several times. After conducting various panel data regression tests required as explained in Appendix 2, including Tables A6.2.1, A6.2.2, A6.2.3, and A6.2.4 two panel data outputs were chosen.

6.5.1 Output of the Stock/Share Price Regression Equation

The output of the first panel data regression equation is the equation that finds out what the influence of ESG variables is, individually and in combination, and what the other control variables are for stock prices in sample banks (Table 6.5).

From the simulation output of STC, the following can be concluded:
  (i) Influence on the constant value (C) of Rp17,207.80 is significant, which means the stock/share price will remain high even though no variables influence it. The stock price of each company (individual effect), however, will be different regardless of time changes:
      (a) BRI's stock price = Rp17,207.80 – Rp2,316.84 = Rp14,890.95
      (b) Mandiri's stock price = Rp17,207.80 + Rp4,151.79 = Rp21,359.59
      (c) BCA's stock price = Rp17,207.80 + Rp3,442.89 = Rp13,764.91
      (d) BNI's stock price = Rp17,207.80 – Rp5,277.84 = Rp11,929.96

If the period (annual) and individual (company) securities are calculated, the annual share price (2009–2017) will be obtained for the four banks (Table 6.6).

Table 6.5: Final Results of Fixed Effect Method Estimates: Effects of Independent Variables Against Dependent Variables in Stock/Share Price Regression
(coefficient = Rp)

Variable	Coefficient	Std. Error	t-Statistic	Prob.
C	17,207.80	4,646.149	3.703670	0.0016
ENV?	178.2522	83.11821	2.144563	0.0459
SOC?	111.2705	77.82587	1.429737	0.1699
GOV?	78.57190	61.21591	1.283521	0.2156
INC?	0.000301	0.000163	1.853254	0.0803
ASSET?	-2.83E-05	5.53E-06	-5.117320	0.0001
ESG?	-345.4457	208.0208	-1.660631	0.1141
Fixed Effects (Cross)				
_BRI--C	-2,316.842			
_MNDR--C	4,151.796			
_BCA--C	3,442.892			
_BNI--C	-5,277.847			
Fixed Effects (Period)				
2009--C	-7,657.942			
2010--C	-5,773.190			
2011—C	-4,584.037			
2012—C	-2,682.799			
2013—C	-1,603.183			
2014—C	1,472.126			
2015—C	2,745.693			
2016—C	6,856.129			
2017—C	1,1227.20			
Effects Specification				
Cross-section fixed (dummy variables)				
Period fixed (dummy variables)				
R-squared	0.955825 Prob(F-statistic)			0.000000
Adjusted R-squared	0.914103			

ASSET = total assets; ENV = environmental performance; ESG = environmental, social, and governance; ESG = ESG performance; GOV = governance performance; INC = total income; SOC = social performance.
Source: Author.

Table 6.6: Annual Stock Prices in Four Sample Banks, Indonesia (from the constant value [C]) (Rp)

Annual Stock Price (Fixed Effects [Period]) Increase/ Decrease		Stock Prices = C + Fixed Effects (Cross)			
		BRI STC = 14,890.95	Mandiri STC = 21,359.59	BCA STC = 13,764.91	BNI STC = 11,929.96
(1)	(2)	(3) = BRI STC + (1)	(4) = Mandiri STC + (1)	(5) = BCA STC + (1)	(6) = BNI STC + (1)
−7,657.94	2009	7,233.01	13,701.65	6,106.97	4,272.02
−5,773.19	2010	9,117.76	15,586.40	7,991.72	6,156.77
−4,584.03	2011	10,306.92	16,775.56	9,180.88	7,345.93
−2,682.79	2012	12,208.16	18,676.80	11,082.12	9,247.17
−1,603.18	2013	13,287.77	19,756.41	12,161.73	10,326.78
1,472.12	2014	16,363.07	22,831.71	15,237.03	13,402.08
2,745.69	2015	17,636.64	24,105.28	16,510.60	14,675.65
6,856.12	2016	21,747.07	28,215.71	20,621.03	18,786.08
11,227.20	2017	26,118.15	32,586.79	24,992.11	23,157.16

BCA = Bank Central Asia, BNI = Bank Nasional Indonesia, BRI = Bank Rakyat Indonesia, STC = stock/share price regression equation.
Source: Author.

The stock price trends of the four banks on an annual basis (2009–2017) are as shown in Figure 6.2: an exact upward trend even with a different nominal amount. The stability and health of the banks are possibly good so they are not much affected by external conditions and factors.

(ii) Each increase in investment of one unit score from environmental performance will cause the stock prices of the banks to increase by Rp178.25.

(iii) Investments made by according to social and governance performance do not affect the increase or reduction of the share prices, nor does the aggregate ESG score.

(iv) A Rp1 million increase in bank assets, however, will reduce the banks' share price by Rp2.83.

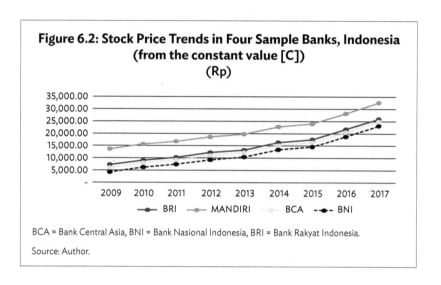

Figure 6.2: Stock Price Trends in Four Sample Banks, Indonesia (from the constant value [C]) (Rp)

BCA = Bank Central Asia, BNI = Bank Nasional Indonesia, BRI = Bank Rakyat Indonesia.

Source: Author.

When banks increase their assets, they do not want to sell their stock or buyers do not need stock from banks whose assets values are always increasing. Environmental performance has a significant effect and is positively correlated with the stock price. Social performance has no significant effect but has a positive correlation with the stock price. Corporate governance has no significant effect but has a positive correlation with the stock price, and combined ESG factors have no significant effect and are negatively correlated with the stock price. This output has similarities with the regression output produced by Triyono (2018) on social performance, i.e., that both independent variables have no effect on the dependent variable in the form of stock returns.

Those who want to buy shares (stock) usually have a high level of education, extensive knowledge, and can think critically. They are mainly concerned with environmental variables, such as whether or not the bank has innovative programs and activities and considers the health of the environment. Only environmental variables, therefore, significantly influence the stock price in each bank sample.

6.5.2 Output of the Total Deposit Regression Equation

The second panel data regression output determined the effect of ESG variables individually and in combination and of other control variables on deposits (Table 6.7).

Table 6.7: Final Results of Fixed Effect Method
Model Estimates: Effects of Independent Variables
Against the Dependent Variable Total Deposits
(coefficient = Rp '000,000)

Variable	Coefficient	Std. Error	t-Statistic	Prob.
C	−79,416,211	36,481,422	−2.176895	0.0430
ENV?	−248,683.4	204,005.7	−1.219002	0.2386
SOC?	757,914.9	281,869.1	2.688890	0.0150
GOV?	265,684.0	143,460.4	1.851967	0.0805
STC?	2,749.863	1,415.505	1.942672	0.0679
INC?	2.905593	0.979026	2.967841	0.0082
ASSET?	0.704349	0.047448	14.84471	0.0000
Fixed Effects (Cross)				
_BRI—C	9,806,781.			
_MNDR—C	−31,805,413			
_BCA—C	14,779,896			
_BNI—C	7,218,737.			
Fixed Effects (Period)				
2009—C	61,334,641			
2010—C	36,432,143			
2011—C	23,892,099			
2012—C	10,104,044			
2013—C	−749,095.6			
2014—C	−19,357,748			
2015—C	−24,366,871			
2016—C	−32,134,277			
2017—C	−55,154,934			
Effects Specification				
Cross-section fixed (dummy variables)				
Period fixed (dummy variables)				
R-squared	0.998665 Prob(F-statistic)			0.000000
Adjusted R-squared	0.997405			

ASSET = total assets, ENV = environmental performance, GOV = governance performance, INC = total income, SOC = social performance, STC = stock price performance.

Source: Author.

From the simulation output of the total deposit panel data regression equation (DEP), the following can be concluded:

(i) It has a significant influence on the constant value (C) but a negative correlation with deposits, which decrease by Rp79,416,211 million. Under normal conditions, total deposits will always decrease in general by that amount, but judging from the total deposits of each company, the total deposits will differ regardless of time changes:

   (a) BRI deposits = Rp79,416,211 million + Rp9.806,781 million = Rp69,609,430 million
   (b) Mandiri deposits = Rp79,416,211 million + Rp31,805,413 million = Rp111,221,624 million
   (c) BCA deposits = Rp79,416,211 million + Rp14,779,896 million = Rp64,636,315 million
   (d) BNI deposits = Rp79,416,211 million + Rp7,218,737 million = Rp72,197,474 million

This means that the banks must carry out strategic policies and programs so that their total deposits are not drastically reduced. This condition is further aggravated by the possibility that deposits may continue to decrease in the last 5 years as indicated by the constant value (C) in each period (annual).

(ii) Each increase in investment of one unit of social performance score will cause total deposits to increase by Rp757.914,90million.

(iii) Each increase in investment of one unit of corporate governance performance score will cause total deposits to increase by Rp265,684 million.

(iv) However, investments carried out with regard to environmental performance and combined ESG performance did not significantly affect deposits.

(v) Each increase in stock price of Rp1 million will affect total deposits by Rp2,749.86 million at each bank.

(vi) Each increase in net income of Rp1 million will affect total deposits by Rp2.90 million at each bank.

(vii) Each increase of Rp1 million in assets will affect total deposits by Rp0.70 million at each bank.

This means that the increase in net income and assets has only a small impact on the amount of deposits at each bank.

Environmental performance , therefore, has no significant effect and is negatively correlated with deposits. Social performance has a significant effect and a positive correlation with deposits. Corporate governance has a significant effect and a positive correlation with deposits. Aggregate ESG factors in the model's output is not an explanatory variable in the regression equation for deposits.

In general, Indonesians (even though many live in rural areas and have a low level of formal education) will decide to keep saving in a bank that has programs and activities that they can easily understand such as job creation, recognition of human rights, good management, a corporate social responsibility program, among others. The performance of social and governance variables is easily appraised, which is probably why they have a significant and positive effect on variable deposits. Environmental and combined ESG variables, however, are difficult to understand and therefore do not influence people's desire to save money in a bank.

6.5.3 Fiscal Incentives for Environmental, Social, and Governance Investment

The form of fiscal incentives for ESG investment in state companies such as banks may vary:

(i) Tax payment relief for companies committed to ESG investment. Such relief is often provided by the government (tax allowance, tax holiday, among others) in certain industrial sectors (especially in investment activities) so that entrepreneurs can be motivated to invest in Indonesia. Of course, the proposal to grant tax incentives must be thought through to be proportionate to the fields that will get this incentive and so as not to burden state finances.

(ii) Financial assistance to build facilities and infrastructure for companies committed to ESG investment.

(iii) SCP, especially in SOEs, both banking and nonbanking.

Fiscal incentives, particularly for SOEs (such as Mandiri, BRI, and BNI), are best provided through SCP.

SCP is given to state enterprises whose government ownership is equal to or more than 51% (SOEs). If government ownership is less than 51%, the companies are called non-SOEs. SCP can be in the form of shares (stock), except for BCA because it is a private company, or without government shares or stock.

The sample banks, except BCA, should have the opportunity to receive capital assistance from the government if they meet the requirements set by the government and the House of Representatives: (i) prioritize capital participation to encourage development of infrastructure; (ii) support energy and food sovereignty; and (iii) support the sustainability of business credit programs and micro, small, and medium-sized enterprises (Indonesian Supreme Audit Board, 2019). The financial condition of state companies that will receive SCP needs to be considered to develop their business and to support development activities. If the state company's financial condition is considered to be healthy and the state company can carry out development programs mandated by the government, the state company cannot receive SCP.

Granting fiscal incentives (SCP, tax allowances, among others) depends on (i) the financial condition of the parties to be given the incentives, (ii) the types of programs and activities implemented support development programs, and (iii) the fiscal incentives will not burden the state.

6.7 Conclusion

Investment programs that consider ESG factors both individually and in aggregate have developed well but still need support, especially from the government. ESG investment can create better and more transparent conditions and can optimize investment. ESG investment can increase company integrity and the trust of stakeholders.

This research used score data on each ESG criterion individually and in aggregate. The ESG score data and other control variables were used to estimate the effect of ESG investments on the stock or share price and deposits in the four sample banks.

The results of this study indicate that environmental performance has a significant effect on stock prices and a positive relationship with stock prices. Social and governance performance has a significant effect and a positive correlation with deposits.

Fiscal policy can be one way out for the development of ESG investment through the provision of fiscal incentives in the field of state revenue or state expenditure or state financing or a combination of the three. The point is that the granting of fiscal incentives (like SCP, tax allowances, etc.) depends on: (i) the financial condition of the parties to be given the incentives (in this case banking), (ii) the types of programs/activities which implemented support Indonesia's development programs, and (iii) the granting of fiscal incentives will not burden the state's financial condition.

6.8 Policy Recommendation

Under certain conditions, ESG investment can have a significant impact on financial variables so that banks in particular and companies in general should start considering ESG-based investments.

The government can support ESG investment by providing appropriate and proportional fiscal incentives so that it can develop better through state revenue or state expenditure or state financing incentives or a combination of all three.

References

Agus, W. 2005. *Econometrics Theories and Applications for Economics and Business.* Yogyakarta, Indonesia: Faculty of Business and Economics, Universitas Islam Indonesia.

Aziz, A. 2006. Role, Performance, and Financial Problem Solving of "Bank Tabungan Negara (BTN)". *Jurnal Keuangan dan Moneter* 9(1).

Aziz, A. 2010. Effect of Government Programs in Education on *"APK WAJAR"*: 2006–2008. *Journal of Financial Economics Studies* 14(1/2010).

Aziz, A. 2018. Vocational Education in Indonesia: Its Problems and Incentives Needed. In *Urbanization, Human Capital & Regional Development: The Indonesian Experience.* Jakarta: Gramedia Pustaka Utama.

Bennani, L., T. L. Guenedal, F. Lepetit, V. Laily, Mortier, T. Roncalli, and T. Sekine. 2018. How ESG Investing Has Impacted the Asset Pricing in the Equity Market. Discussion Paper. http://dx.doi.org/10.2139/ssrn.3316862 (accessed 29 August 2019).

Bernardi, C., and A. W. Stark. 2015. Environmental, Social, and Governance Disclosure, Integrated Reporting, and the Accuracy of Analyst Forecast. Working Paper. Roma Tre University and Manchester Business School, University of Manchester. https://www.iseg.ulisboa.pt/aquila/getFile.do?method=getFile&fileId=671379 (accessed 28 August 2019).

Centerklik. The Ten Largest Banks in Indonesia and Their Assets. https://www.centerklik.com/10-daftar-bank-terbesar-di-indonesia-dan-asetnya/amp/

Fitri, M. 2016. The Role of Third Party Funds in the Performance of Sharia Financing Institutions and the Factors Affecting It. *Journal of Economica* VII(1).

Gujarati, D. 2004. *Basic Econometrics.* 4th edition. New York. The McGraw-Hill Companies.

Hidayat, A. 2014. Explanation of Panel Data Regression Analysis Method. https://www.statisticsian.com/2014/11/regresi-data-panel.html (accessed 1 November 2019).

Indonesian Supreme Audit Board. 2019. The Ministry of Finance of The Republic of Indonesia (MoF Indonesia). *Central Government Financial Report 2018.* https://www.kemenkeu.go.id/media/12590/lkpp-2018.pdf (accessed 1 November 2019).

Lundstrom, E., and C. Svensson. 2014. Including ESG Concerns in the Portfolio Selection Process. Working Paper. Stockholm: KTH Royal Institute of Technology. https://pdfs.semanticscholar.

org/5666/0111dba181b5d3282f7f3 63acd08e5ea0828.pdf (accessed 26 August 2019).

Ministry of Finance. 2019. *The Concept of Fiscal Policy and Budget State. Fiscal Policy and Budget State Drafting Training.* Jakarta: Ministry of Finance.

Nachrowi, D., and U. Hardius. 2006. *Econometrics: Popular and Practical Approaches to Economic and Financial Analysis.* Jakarta: Universitas Indonesia.

Novethic. 2013. ESG Strategies of European Asset Owners: From Theory to Practice. Novethic Group. Working Paper. http://www .responsiblehousing.eu/en/upload/ Generalon_CSR / 2013% 20 -% 20Novethic% 20-% 20ESG% 20strategies% 20 Europe% 204.pdf (accessed 26 August 2019).

Supriyadi, A. Y. 2007. Econometric Eviews Tutorial. Jakarta. University of Indonesia.

Tarmuji, I., R. Maelah, and N. H. Tarmuji. 2016. The Impact of Environmental, Social, and Governance Practices (ESG) on Economic Performance: Evidence from ESG Score. *International Journal of Trade, Economics and Finance* 7(3): 67–74.

Thomson Reuters/Refinitiv. 2019. Environmental, Social, and Governance (ESG) Scores. https://www.refinitiv.com/content /dam/marketing/en_us/documents/methodology/esg-scores -methodology.pdf (accessed 28 August 2019).

Triyono, B. 2018. Analysis of the Impacts of Environmental, Social, and Government Scores on Stock Returns, Study of Companies Listed on the Indonesia Stock Exchange 2010-2016. Gajah Mada University. Undergraduate thesis.

Whittaker, R., M. Spinoso, and A. Lee. 2018. Sustainable Investing, Primary Education: ESG improves Equities. UBS Financial Services Inc. Report Paper. https://www.ubs.com>esg-improves-equities (accessed 28 August 2019).

Wooldridge, J. M. 2002. *Econometric Analysis of Cross Section and Panel Data.* Cambridge, MA: The MIT Press Cambridge.

Yusoff, H., K. S. Hazwani, and E. K. Ghani. 2018. Environmental Reporting Practices of Top Public Listed Companies: Analyzing the Pre-Post CSR Framework. *Indonesian Journal of Sustainability Accounting and Management* 2(1): 50–64.

Appendix 1: Research Methodology

Operations of Panel Data Analysis Model

Aziz (2010) discussed the panel data analysis model, drawing on the work of Gujarati (2004), Wooldridge (2002), Nachrowi and Hardius (2006), Agus (2005), and online articles such as Hidayat (2014). It is hoped that readers will understand that the panel data equation output in the article is the best regression output and has passed the test and model selection required for panel data operations. The following is a brief explanation from Aziz (2010) about the steps in operating the panel data.

Hypothesis Test of Each Independent Variable

To further clarify the direction of this research, it is necessary to test the hypothesis on the dependent variable and the independent variables. In this model, it is expected that the total deposits (DEP) variable and the stock price (STC) variable have a positive and significant relationship with six or seven other independent variables.

The research hypothesis of this model is if

Ho: $\beta = 0$, it means that the independent variable has no influence on the dependent variable STC and/or DEP and if Ha: $\beta \neq 0$, it means that the independent variable has an influence on the dependent variable STC and/or DEP.

Estimation Model Selection Method

There are three model parameter estimation techniques using panel data: pooled least square (PLS or ordinary least square), fixed effect model (FEM), and random effect model (REM).

Pooled least square. The simplest way to process panel data is to use the least square method to make estimates with time series data and cross sections. If we combine the data, we cannot see differences between individuals and between times, which is not the purpose of using panel data. Besides the assumptions above, the intercept (α) and slope (β) in the panel data equation are unchanged or constant between individuals and between time. The PLS model is considered less realistic for estimating panel data.

Fixed effect model. The assumptions of modeling that produce the value of intercept (α) and slope (β) constant are less realistic. Using the FEM, it is possible to change α in each i and t (Nachrowi and Hardius, 2006).

Random effect model. In the FEM, differences in individual characteristics and time are accommodated in the intercept so that the intercept changes between individuals and time. In the REM, however, characteristics and time differences are accommodated in the error of the model. The error of the model is broken down into errors for individual components, time errors, and combined errors.

To choose the most appropriate panel data estimation model, the following test steps should be taken (Hidayat, 2014):

(i) **Conduct a Chow test** to determine whether the PLS or FEM is the most appropriate for estimating panel data. If the result is H0, select PLS, and if Ha, select FEM.

(ii) **Conduct a Hausman test** to choose whether FEM or REM is the most appropriate. If the result is H0, select REM, and if Ha, select FEM.

(iii) **Perform the Lagrange multiplier test** to find out whether the REM is better than the PLS. If the result is H0, select PLS, and if Ha, select REM.

The use of the three tests is illustrated in Figure A6.1:

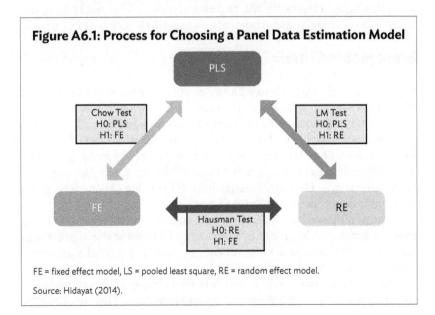

Figure A6.1: Process for Choosing a Panel Data Estimation Model

PLS

Chow Test
H0: PLS
H1: FE

LM Test
H0: PLS
H1: RE

FE

RE

Hausman Test
H0: RE
H1: FE

FE = fixed effect model, LS = pooled least square, RE = random effect model.

Source: Hidayat (2014).

Statistical Testing Criteria (Diagnostic Test)

Test the significance of individual parameters (statistical test t). This test shows the extent of the influence of one independent variable in explaining the dependent variable. The hypothesis is the independent variable, to be tested with the following:

H0: $\beta n = 0$: An independent variable is not a significant explanation of the dependent variable.

Ha: $\beta n \neq 0$: An independent variable is a significant explanation of the dependent variable.

Simultaneous significance test (statistical test F). This test shows whether all independent variables included in the model have an influence together on the dependent variable. The hypothesis to be tested is all parameters contained in the model, to be tested with the following:

H0: $\beta 1 = \beta 2 = \beta 3 = ... = \beta n = 0$: All independent variables are not a significant explanation of the dependent variable.

Ha: $\beta 1 \neq \beta 2 \neq \beta 3 \neq ... \neq \beta n \neq 0$: All independent variables simultaneously constitute a significant explanation of the dependent variable.

Test R^2 (coefficient of determination) and adjusted R^2 (for models that have more than one independent variable). This test is used to find out how much the dependent variable can be explained by all the independent variables included in the model. The R^2 / Adjusted R^2 value has an interval of 0 to 1 ($0 \leq R^2 \leq 1$). The greater the interval (closer to 1), the better results for the regression model. The closer to 0, the independent variables as a whole cannot explain the dependent variable.

Econometric Criteria

Econometric criteria analyze whether or not a model contains violations of regression assumptions and, if it does, it is subjected to econometric testing. The three violations of assumptions are as follows:

Heteroscedasticity. Forecast error variation is not the same for all observations [E $(u2i) = \sigma^2 i$]. Errors can be detected in various ways, including using the statistical test White heteroscedasticity: H0: homoscedasticity; Ha: heteroscedasticity. If the value of obs * R2 $\leq \chi^2$ the decision is to accept Ho (and vice versa).

Multicollinearity. There is a strong correlation between independent variables. It can be detected by (i) looking at a high enough R2 (overall test results are significant but partial test results are not), and (ii) using a correlation matrix.

Autocorrelation. There is a correlation between observational data, the emergence of data influenced by previous data. The consequence of autocorrelation is that although the estimation results are unbiased, the standard error of the regression coefficient is so low that partial test results tend to be significant.

Detecting the autocorrelation can be done using Durbin-Watson statistics. Violations of the autocorrelation assumption generally occur in time-series data but not in cross-section data, so estimates using panel data are not expected to occur because they combine time-series data into their cross-sectional data format.

Even panel data with FEM estimation does not require the assumption that the model is free from serial correlation, so the test of autocorrelation can be ignored (Gujarati, 2003; Nachrowi and Hardius, 2006).

Appendix 2: Discussion and Results

1. Hypothesis Testing of Each Independent Variable

The two panel data equation outputs show that the stock price variable (stock/share price regression equation [STC]) and the total deposits variable (deposit regression equation [DEP]) have a positive and significant relationship with seven or eight independent variables. This is because the value of all parameters is not the same as "0," so it has fulfilled alternative research hypotheses from these two models: Ha: $\beta \neq 0$ means that the independent variables have an influence on the dependent variable STC and/or DEP.

2. Estimation Model Selection Method

The selection of the best estimation method by comparing the fixed effect method (FEM) with pooled least square (PLS) and random effect method (REM) is to confirm the findings and statements of the authors in the methodology section: "In the traditional approach to the panel data models, Ci is called a 'random effect' when it is treated as a random variable and a 'fixed effect' when it is treated as a parameter to be estimated for each cross section observation i" (Wooldridge 2002). If the parameters to be estimated are all individual data (population data) then the chosen model is the FEM and there is no need to test PLS versus REM.

2.1. Pooled Least Square Versus Fixed Effect Model

The Chow test determines whether the PLS or the FEM is most appropriate for estimating panel data. If the result is H0, select PLS, and if Ha, select the FEM, which means that if the chi-square probability value <0.05 then select the FEM, and so on. Both the STC and DEP should, therefore, use the FEM analysis (Table A6.2.1):

Table A6.2.1: Selection of Fixed Effect Method Models Versus Pooled Least Square

Y = Deposits (DEP)				Y = Stock Price			
Redundant fixed effects tests				Redundant fixed effects tests			
Pool: Untitled				Pool: STC			
Test cross-section fixed effects				Test cross-section fixed effects			
Effects Test	**Statistic**	**df.**	**Prob.**	**Effects Test**	**Statistic**	**d.f.**	**Prob.**
Cross-section F	12.690009	(3,26)	0.0000	Cross-section F	28.092235	(3,26)	0.0000
Cross-section chi-square	32.467684	3	**0.0000**	Cross-section chi-square	52.016262	3	**0.0000**
Cross-section fixed effects test equation:				Cross-section fixed effects test equation:			
Dependent variable: DEP?				Dependent variable: STC?			
Method: Panel least squares				Method: Panel least squares			
Date: 10/30/19 Time: 10:38				Date: 10/30/19 Time: 14:07			
Sample: 2009 2017				Sample: 2009 2017			
Included observations: 9				Included observations: 9			
Cross-sections included: 4				Cross-sections included: 4			
Total pool (balanced) observations: 36				Total pool (balanced) observations: 36			

If the value of Prob. cross-section chi-square <0.05 then we will choose the fixed effect method

If the value of Prob. cross-section chi-square <0.05 then we will choose the fixed effect method

d.f. = degree of freedom, DEP = deposit regression equation, prob. = probability, STC = stock/share price regression equation.
Source: Author.

2.2. Random Effect Model Versus Fixed Effect Model

The Hausman test chooses whether the FEM or the REM should be used. If the result is H0, select the REM and if Ha, select the FEM, which means if probability value <0.05, then select the FEM, and so on. The result is that both the STC and DEP should be used in the FEM analysis (Table A6.2.2).

Table A6.2.2: Selection of Fixed Effect Method Versus Random Effect Method

Y = Deposits (DEP)	Y = Stock Price
Correlated random effects—Hausman test	Correlated random effects—Hausman test
Pool: Untitled	Pool: STC
Test cross-section random effects	Test cross-section random effects

Test summary	Chi-Sq. Statistic	Chi-Sq. d.f.	Prob.	Test summary	Chi-Sq. Statistic	Chi-Sq. d.f.	Prob.
Cross-section random	12.690009	3	0.0000	Cross-section random	106.915921	3	0.0000

Cross-section random effects test equation: ⬆	Cross-section random effects test equation: ⬆
Dependent variable: DEP?	Dependent variable: STC?
Method: Panel least squares	Method: Panel least squares
Date: 10/30/19 Time: 12:51	Date: 10/30/19 Time: 14:09
Sample: 2009 2017	Sample: 2009 2017
Included observations: 9	Included observations: 9
Cross-sections included: 4	Cross-sections included: 4
Total pool (balanced) observations: 36	Total pool (balanced) observations: 36

If the Hausman test accepts H1 or p value <0.05, then choose the fixed effect method.	If the Hausman test accepts H1 or p value <0.05, then choose the fixed effect method.

d.f. = degree of freedom, DEP = deposit regression equation, prob. = probability, STC = stock/share price regression equation.
Source: Author.

3. Statistical Testing Criteria (Diagnostic Test)

The two outputs above show that, based on the t statistical test and the F statistical test, the diagnostic test accepts an alternative hypothesis (Ha: $\beta n \neq 0$). The output means that an independent variables individually and together explain the dependent variables. If the R^2 test (coefficient of determination) or adjusted R^2 (for models that have more than one independent variable) shows an interval approaching "1," we can conclude that the overall independent variable can explain the dependent variable.

Table A6.2.3: Statistical Test Criteria (Diagnostic Test)

Test	Y = Stock Price	Y = Deposits (DEP)
"t" statistic	The value of constants (C) and independent variables such as environmental performance (ENV), total income (INC), and total assets (ASSET) are significantly related to the dependent variable stock price (STC).	The value of constants (C) and independent variables such as social performance (SOC), governance performance (GOV), stock price (STC), total income (INC), and total assets (ASSET) are significantly related to the dependent variable: total deposits (DEF).
"F" statistic	Significant	Significant
R^2	0.99	0.95
Adjusted R^2	0.99	0.91

DEP = deposit regression equation.
Source: Author.

4. Econometric Criteria

Violating assumptions in the econometric model will produce values that do not reflect the pure influence of the independent variable on the dependent variable (Aziz 2010). Testing the econometric criteria (violation of classical assumptions) on the characteristics of panel data and, in particular, the FEM estimation method chosen here has proven to be free from all violations of assumptions (in the form of heteroscedasticity, multicollinearity, and autocorrelation) and each independent variable still has a pure influence on the dependent variable.

The econometric criteria can be explained as follows:

(i)   The problem of violating the assumption of heteroscedasticity has been resolved automatically with the assumption that, if in a regression model there is a heteroscedasticity problem while the results of partial tests (t-test) and overall test (F-test) show significant effects, then the problem does not need to be overcome (Supriyadi 2007).

(ii) The problem of violating the assumption of multicollinearity has automatically been resolved because, based on the results of the correlation matrix test above, there are no symptoms of multicollinearity in the model because all the correlation values of each independent variable are below 80%, with only a few in the range of 85%.

Table A6.2.4: Variable Tables Free of Multicollinearity

	ASSET	ENV	ESG	GOV	INC	SOC	STC
ASSET	1.00	0.33	0.54	0.40	0.85	0.55	0.14
ENV	0.33	1.00	0.86	-0.03	0.25	0.71	0.45
ESG	0.54	0.86	1.00	0.40	0.47	0.88	0.48
GOV	0.40	-0.03	0.40	1.00	0.39	0.26	0.02
INC	0.85	0.25	0.47	0.39	1.00	0.48	0.21
SOC	0.55	0.71	0.88	0.26	0.48	1.00	0.44
STC	0.14	0.45	0.48	0.02	0.21	0.44	1.00

ASSET = total assets in the sample banking companies; ENV = environmental performance with a score from 0 to 100; ESG = environmental, social, and governance performance with a score from 0 to 100; GOV = governance performance with a score from 0 to 100; INC = total Income in the sample banking companies; SOC = social performance with a score from 0 to 100; STC = stock prices (share prices) in the sample banking companies.

Source: Author.

(iii) The problem of violating the autocorrelation assumption can be automatically overcome by choosing the FEM, because it does not require the assumption of a model free from serial correlation so that tests on autocorrelation can be ignored (Nachrowi and Hardius, 2006; Gujarati, 2004).

7

The Ineffectiveness of Environmental, Social, and Governance Policies and Incentives: The Impact of the Generalised Scheme of Preferences Plus on Central Asian and South Asian Countries

Muhammad Ayub Mehar

7.1 Objectives and Scope of the Study

Prudent and responsible decision-making by investors for global sustainable development has become an important area of financial economics, and it is recognized in the economics literature that traditional measures (return on investment, internal rate of return, net present value, profitability index, among others) are not sufficient to test the sustainability of projects in long-term business ventures (United Nations Environment Program, 2018; UNCTAD, 2014; UNCTAD, 2015; Yoshino, Helble, and Abidhajaev, 2014; Mehar, 2010). Several issues related to the environment, climate change, women's empowerment, rights of minorities and indigenous peoples, transparency, human rights, drugs trafficking, good governance, and individual liberty have become important in economic cooperation and cross-border investment. Resolving environmental, social and governance (ESG) issues according to global standards ensures sustainable competitiveness and efficiency in the use of economic resources. Compliance with globally accepted ESG standards ensures the sustainability of long-term returns on investment. Global investors, therefore, have to consider ESG-related conventions in preparing their feasibility studies for investment in developing countries.

Several international conventions and policies provide incentives to developing countries to adopt and ratify global conventions that emphasize responsible investment decisions in ESG-related projects. Regulatory and administrative measures have been introduced by some countries to limit environmentally hazardous projects. To measure ESG-related negative externalities and restrict such projects through administrative and regulatory measures, however, is complicated and difficult, particularly in underdeveloped and developing countries. The attractive profits from environmentally hazardous projects induce investors to form political pressure groups and use corrupt practices and bribery. Having too many administrative and regulatory measures is not the way to reach the desired goals. Sustainable development may be achieved by economic policies that link individual benefits with national and global ones.

Several studies link ESG standards with profit motives, but these studies were conducted in developed industrialized countries, where consideration of ESG standards has become common practice in investment decision-making. Investment decisions in developing countries still consider return on investment in purely monetary terms (Duffy and Eberts, 1991; Hideo et al., 2019). This study tests the impacts of ESG compliance on foreign investment and international trade in South Asia and Central Asia. The next section shows that granting Generalised Scheme of Preferences Plus (GSP+) status to a developing country by the European Union (EU) is an indicator of the recipient country's compliance with United Nations' conventions on ESG investment. Section 7.3 covers the research methodology to measure the impacts of ESG compliance on foreign investment and exports. The methodology to estimate the impact of environmental conditions on health expenditures is discussed in section 7.4. Section 7.5 describes the results and conclusions.

7.2 Granting GSP+ Status as an Indicator of Environmental, Social and Governance Compliance

ESG factors are three areas used to measure sustainability and ethical impacts of a business investment. Standards for these areas are used by socially conscious investors to select potential investments. These criteria determine the financial performance of the companies. Individual investors, however, do not consider ESG standards.

In developing and least developed countries, ESG criteria are considered a government responsibility: government should create an administrative and regulatory environment for ESG implementation. Growth of gross domestic product (GDP) or corporate profit is thought to cause income to trickle down: the profit motive, therefore, automatically creates an environment where ESG standards will ultimately be achieved. This way of thinking does not provide incentives or disincentives to foreign investors to engage in ESG investment.

Several international organizations and countries have introduced regulations to implement and monitor ESG standards and provide incentives to countries and companies that adopt them (European Commission, 2012, 2017). The following are included in ESG-related conventions of the World Trade Organization and United Nations Organization: (i) establishment or maintenance of an independent competition authority, (ii) no discriminatory attitudes in production and marketing, (iii) provision of information, (iv) assessment of anticompetitive behavior, (v) progressive liberalization, (vi) no discrimination in public procurement, (vii) liberalization of trade in services, (viii) harmonization of standards, (ix) regulations on criminal offenses in international trade and investment, (x) measures to proscribe anticompetitive business conduct, (xi) development of environmental standards, (xii) enforcement of national environmental laws, (xiii) development of legal frameworks for investment, (xiv) harmonization and simplification of procedures, (xv) establishment of mechanisms to settle disputes, (xvi) regulation of the national labor market, (xvii) affirmation of International Labour Organization commitments, (xviii) liberalization of capital movement, (xix) prohibition of new restrictions, (xx) harmonization of consumer protection laws, (xxi) implementation of civil protection, (xxii) promotion of joint initiatives for cultural promotion, (xxiii) measures to improve the general level of education, (xxiv) rules guiding the granting and administration of financial assistance, (xxv) monitoring of diseases and development of health information systems, (xxvi) respect for human rights, (xxvii) treatment and rehabilitation of drug addicts, (xxviii) technical and administrative assistance in restricting money laundering, (xxix) technical assistance and facilitation in the access to finance to small and medium-sized enterprises, (xxx) coordination of social security systems, (xxxi) no discrimination regarding working conditions, (xxxii) joint research and exchange of information about terrorism, and (xxxiii) drafting of legislation and exchange of information about visas and asylum.

Individuals and internationally established institutional investors (such as the International Finance Corporation) do not finance projects that do not meet ESG criteria. Production or trade in any product or activity deemed illegal under host-country laws or regulations or international conventions and agreements, or subject to international bans, such as pharmaceuticals, pesticides and herbicides, ozone-depleting substances, wildlife or products regulated under the Convention on International Trade in Endangered Species of Wild Fauna and Flora, and production or trade in weapons and ammunitions are among ESG-contradictory investments. Production or trade in alcoholic beverages (excluding beer and wine), tobacco and radioactive materials (excluding those for medical and testing labs), and unbounded asbestos fibers also fall under ESG-contradictory investment. Gambling, casinos, and marine drift-net fishing using nets in excess of 2.5 kilometers are considered ESG-contradictory investment. Investment in companies that practice forced labor or harmful child labor and engage in environmentally hazardous activities are not permitted under ESG criteria. The production or activities that impinge on lands owned or claimed under adjudication by indigenous peoples are not permitted without their fully documented consent.

This study cannot identify all ESG aspects and criteria. Measuring the implementation of ESG criteria in different countries is complex and complicated. Identifying individuals or institutional investors that strictly follow ESG criteria is difficult. For this purpose, we used the EU criterion for granting GSP+ status to countries that follow ESG standards. For international trade purposes, the EU grants the following to underdeveloped and developing countries:

(i)   Standard GSP for low- and lower-middle–income countries (based on per capita income). This means partial or full removal of customs duties on two-thirds of tariff lines.

(ii) GSP+ as a special incentive for countries that promote sustainable development and good governance. GSP+ slashes the same tariffs to 0% for vulnerable low- and lower-middle–income countries that implement 27 international conventions on human rights, labor rights, protection of the environment, and good governance.

(iii) Everything but Arms is a special arrangement for least developed countries, providing them with duty-free, quota-free access for all products except arms and ammunition.

We used item (ii) to categorize Central Asian and South Asian countries and tested the award's impact on the inflow of foreign investment and exports. If a country attracts more foreign investment after achieving GSP+ status, it means that foreign investors consider ESG criteria. The list of GSP+ conventions is in Table 7.1, and the list of countries awarded GSP+ status, by year, is in Table 7.2.

Table 7.1: GSP+ Conventions

A. Core Human and Labor Rights International Labour Organization Conventions
1.   Convention on the Prevention and Punishment of the Crime of Genocide (1948)
2.   International Convention on the Elimination of All Forms of Racial Discrimination (1965)
3.   International Covenant on Civil and Political Rights (1966)
4.   International Covenant on Economic Social and Cultural Rights (1966)
5.   Convention on the Elimination of All Forms of Discrimination Against Women (1979)
6.   Convention Against Torture and Other Cruel, Inhuman regarding Treatment or Punishment (1984)
7.   Convention on the Rights of the Child (1989)
8.   Convention concerning Forced or Compulsory Labor, No 29 (1930)
9.   Convention concerning Freedom of Association and Protection of the Right to Organize, No 87 (1948)
10.   Convention concerning the Application of the Principles of the Right to Organize and to Bargain Collectively, No. 98 (1949)
11.   Convention concerning Equal Remuneration of Men and Women Workers for Work of Equal Value, No. 100 (1951)
12.   Convention concerning the Abolition of Forced Labor, No. 105 (1957)
13.   Convention concerning Discrimination in Respect of Employment and Occupation, No. 111 (1958)
14.   Convention concerning Minimum Age for Admission to Employment, No. 138 (1973)
15.   Convention concerning the Prohibition and Immediate Action for the Elimination of the Worst Forms of Child Labor, No. 182 (1999)

B. Conventions Related to the Environment and to Governance Principles
16.   Convention on International Trade in Endangered Species of Wild Fauna and Flora (1973)
17.   Montreal Protocol on Substances that Deplete the Ozone Layer (1987)
18.   Basel Convention on the Control of Trans boundary Movements of Hazardous Wastes and Their Disposal (1989)
19.   Convention on Biological Diversity (1992)
20.   United Nations Framework Convention on Climate Change (1992)
21.   Cartagena Protocol on Biosafety (2000)
22.   Stockholm Convention on Persistent Organic Pollutants (2001)
23.   Kyoto Protocol to the United Nations Framework Convention on Climate Change (1998)
24.   United Nations Single Convention on Narcotic Drugs (1961)
25.   United Nations Convention on Psychotropic Substances (1971)
26.   United Nations Convention against Illicit Traffic in Narcotic Drugs and Psychotropic Substances (1988)
27.   United Nations Convention Against Corruption (2004)

GSP+ = Generalised System of Preferences Plus.
Source: Annex VIII of Regulation (European Union) No. 978/2012 of 31 October 2012.

Table 7.2: Countries with GSP+ Status

Country	Year					
	2011	2012	2013	2014	2015	2016
Afghanistan	EBA	EBA	EBA	EBA	EBA	EBA
Azerbaijan	GSP+	GSP+	GSP+	0	0	0
Bangladesh	EBA	EBA	EBA	EBA	EBA	EBA
Bhutan	EBA	EBA	EBA	EBA	EBA	EBA
China, People's Rep. of	GSP	GSP	GSP	GSP	0	0
Georgia	GSP+	GSP+	GSP+	GSP+	GSP+	GSP+
India	GSP	GSP	GSP	GSP	GSP	GSP
Iran	GSP	GSP	GSP	GSP	0	0
Kazakhstan	GSP	GSP	GSP	0	0	0
Kyrgyz Republic	GSP	GSP	GSP	GSP	GSP	GSP+
Sri Lanka	GSP	GSP	GSP	GSP	GSP	GSP
Maldives	EBA	EBA	EBA	GSP	0	0
Mongolia	GSP+	GSP+	GSP+	GSP+	GSP+	GSP+
Nepal	EBA	EBA	EBA	EBA	EBA	EBA
Pakistan	GSP	GSP	GSP	GSP+	GSP+	GSP+
Tajikistan	GSP	GSP	GSP	GSP	GSP	GSP
Turkmenistan	GSP	GSP	GSP	GSP	GSP	GSP
Turkey	S Agreement	S Agreement	S Agreement	S Agreement	S Agreement	S Agreement
Uzbekistan	GSP	GSP	GSP	GSP	GSP	GSP

EBA = Everything but Arms; ESG = environmental, social, and governance; GSP = Generalised System of Preferences; GSP+ = Generalised System of Preferences plus some special incentive for countries that promote sustainable development and good governance, S Agreement = special trade agreement between Turkey and the European Union.
Source: European Commission (2012, 2019).

7.3 Impact of Environmental, Social, and Governance Compliance on Foreign Investment and Exports: Methodology

This study covers two dimensions of the impacts of ESG-related conditions. Its first concern is to test the impacts of compliance with

ESG-related international conventions on investment and exports. GSP+ status is used as an indicator of compliance with ESG-related conventions. The second dimension covers the impacts of improvement in environment-related factors on health expenditures. These two aspects establish the study's scope. The dimensions' diverse scopes require different sets of data and methodologies. Therefore, we divided the research methodology into two parts. In the first part, we tested the impacts of ESG-related international conventions on investment and exports of GSP+ countries, and used GSP+ status as an indicator of compliance with ESG conventions.

We studied 16 countries in South Asia and Central Asia for 6 years (2011–2016), for a total of 96 observations. The countries are members of at least one of the following organizations: Central Asia Regional Economic Cooperation, Economic Cooperation Organization, and/or South Asian Association for Regional Cooperation.

The sample provided balanced panel data, so we applied panel least square techniques (fixed effect model) to estimate the effects of explanatory variables.

GSP+ status is assumed to mean that the country has implemented or actively progressed on 27 ESG-related UN conventions. The EU has a special agreement with Turkey, which is different from GSP+ status, but is based on ESG-related conditions. We considered the special agreement as similar to GSP+. To measure the impact of GSP+ status or special agreement, we created a dummy variable (PLUSAG), which is equal to 1 for the years when a country had GSP+ status or a special agreement, and zero otherwise. We tested the impact of GSP+ and special agreement (PLUSAG) on foreign direct investment (FDI$), net inflow of FDI$ (FDIINF$), inflow of portfolio investment (PTFEQ$), and exports (EXPR$).

To measure the impact of ESG compliance on foreign investment, three components of foreign investment were defined as explained variables: total FDI$, net inflow of FDI$ (FIIINF$), and foreign portfolio investment in equities (PRFEQ), gross domestic product (GDP$), exports (EXPR$), total external debt (EBTTOT$), and domestic credit to the private sector as a percentage of GDP (DCPS_GD) were included as control variables. The robustness of estimated parameters was checked using alternative models, where falsification tests were conducted. The results of these models are in Table 7.3 to Table 7.6.

We hypothesized that ESG compliance, GDP, exports, external outstanding debt, and DCPS_GD are the determinants of foreign direct investment, net inflow of FDI$, and foreign portfolio investment in equities. The data for these variables were extracted from the World Development Indicators (World Bank, 2019).

FDI$ refers to direct investment equity flows in the reporting economy and is the sum of equity capital, reinvestment of earnings, and other capital. Direct investment is a category of cross-border investment associated with a resident in one economy having control or a significant degree of influence on the management of an enterprise that is a resident in another economy (World Bank, 2019). Ownership of 10% or more of the ordinary shares of voting stock is the criterion for determining the existence of a direct investment relationship. Data are in current US dollars.

The net inflows of FDI$ are the inflows of investment to acquire a lasting management interest (10% or more of voting stock) in an enterprise operating in an economy other than that of the investor. It is the sum of equity capital, reinvestment of earnings, other long-term capital, and short-term capital as shown in the balance of payments. This series shows total net FDI$. Data are in current US dollars.

Domestic credit to the private sector refers to financial resources provided to the private sector by financial corporations, such as through loans, purchases of nonequity securities, and trade credits and other accounts receivable, which establish a claim for repayment. The financial corporations include monetary authorities and banks, as well as other financial corporations, including leasing companies, moneylenders, insurance corporations, pension funds, and foreign exchange companies. The data on domestic credit provided to the private sector are from the World Development Indicators (World Bank, 2019), which is based on the financial corporation survey of the International Monetary Fund.

The impact of economic strength on foreign investment was measured through GDP in billion US dollars (GDP$). Everything but Arms and GSP status are granted by the EU on the basis of the country's per capita income, which cannot, therefore, be used as an explanatory variable.

Table 7.3: Dependent Variable Foreign Direct Investment (US$ billion), Panel Least Squares (Fixed Effect Model)

Explanatory Variable	Model: I		Model: II		Model: III		Model: IV	
	β	T	β	T	β	T	β	T
Constant	−13.600	−1.348	−19.700	−1.904*	−10.200	−1.734*	−10.100	−1.673*
GDP$	0.085	18.383***	0.087	18.707***	0.090	21.681***	0.090	21.542***
PLUSAG	0.733	0.142	0.586	0.116			−0.542	−0.109

continued on next page

Table 7.3 *continued*

Explanatory Variable	Model: I β	Model: I T	Model: II β	Model: II T	Model: III β	Model: III T	Model: IV β	Model: IV T
EXPR$	-0.406	-11.268***	-0.341	-7.054***	-0.350	-7.376***	-0.350	-7.321***
DCPS_GD	0.206	1.002	0.231	1.144				
DBTTOT$			-0.059	-1.968*	-0.057	-1.905*	-0.057	-1.895*
R2	0.9391		0.9413		0.9418		0.9411	
F-statistic	78.0665		77.1585		86.4220		80.8234	
AIC	49.0509		49.0214		48.9971		49.0178	
D-W Statistic	1.7004		2.0705		2.01373		2.0151	

β = coefficient, AIC = Akaike information criterion, D-W = Durbin Watson, DBTTOT$ = total outstanding debt in billion US dollars, DCPS_GD = domestic credit to private sector as a percentage of GDP, EXPR$ = exports in billion US dollars, GDP$ = gross domestic product in billion US dollars, PLUSAG = dummy variable equal to 1 if country has been granted GSP+ status or special agreement by European Union, T = T-statistics.

*p < 0.1; **p < 0.05; ***p < 0.01.

Note: Periods: 6; cross-sections: 16; total observations: 96. Sample: 2011–2016.

Source: Author.

Table 7.4: Dependent Variable: Net Inflow of Foreign Direct Investment (US$ billion), Panel Least Squares (Fixed Effect Model)

Explanatory Variable	Model: I β	Model: I T	Model: II β	Model: II T	Model: III β	Model: III T	Model: IV β	Model: IV T
Constant	13.200	1.902*	10.200	1.524	7.550	1.871*	7.600	1.928*
GDP$	-0.031	-9.838***	-0.030	-9.685***	-0.032	-11.556***	-0.032	-11.632***
PLUSAG	-0.471	-0.138	-0.543	-0.159	0.195	0.058		
EXPR$	0.177	5.429***	0.209	8.714***	0.182	5.666***	0.182	5.708***
DCPS_GD	-0.136	-1.003	-0.124	-0.906				
DBTTOT$	0.029	1.452			0.028	1.392	0.028	1.400
Adjusted R2	0.9885		0.9884		0.9885		0.9887	
F-statistic	410.5960		0.9884		432.1181		462.1054	
AIC	48.2280		48.2349		48.2205		48.1997	
D-W Statistic	2.5251		2.2823		2.4793		2.4786	

β = coefficient, AIC = Akaike information criterion, D-W = Durbin Watson, DBTTOT$ = total outstanding debt in billion US dollars, DCPS_GD = domestic credit to private sector as a percentage of GDP, EXPR$ = exports in billion US dollars, GDP$ = gross domestic product in billion US dollars, PLUSAG = dummy variable equal to 1 if country has been granted GSP+ status or special agreement by European Union, T = T-statistics.

*p < 0.1; **p < 0.05; ***p < 0.01.

Note: Periods: 6; cross-sections: 16; total observations: 96. Sample: 2011–2016.

Source: Author.

Table 7.5: Dependent Variable: Inflow of Portfolio Investment ($ billion) Panel Least Squares (Fixed Effect Model)

Explanatory Variable	Model: I		Model: II		Model: III		Model: IV	
	β	T	β	T	β	T	β	T
Constant	-3.510	-0.896	0.501	0.154	-3.960	-1.052	9.360	-2.286**
GDP$							-0.006	-3.237***
PLUSAG	-0.852	-0.436	-0.749	-0.378			-0.170	-0.092
EXPR$	0.031	1.770*			0.031	1.769**	0.050	2.856***
DCPS_GD	-0.162	-2.126**	-0.165	-2.130***	-0156	-2.094***	-0.029	-0.353
DBTTOT$	0.037	3.261***	0.053	7.920***	0.037	3.275***	0.044	4.068***
Adjusted R2	0.7989		0.7927		0.8013		0.8235	
F-statistic	19.9803		20.3420		21.3956		22.1194	
AIC	47.1212		47.1433		47.1010		46.9989	
D-W Statistic	2.2707		2.0648		2.2645		2.4757	

β = coefficient, AIC = Akaike information criterion, D-W = Durbin Watson, DBTTOT$ = total outstanding debt in billion US dollars, DCPS_GD = domestic credit to private sector as a percentage of GDP, EXPR$ = exports in billion US dollars, GDP$ = gross domestic product in billion US dollars, PLUSAG = dummy variable equal to 1 if country has been granted GSP+ status or special agreement by European Union, T = T-statistics.

*p < 0.1; **p < 0.05; ***p < 0.01

Note: Periods: 6; cross-sections: 15; total observations: 96. Sample: 2011–2016.

Source: Author.

Table 7.6: Dependent Variable: Exports (US$ billion), Panel Least Squares (Fixed Effect Model)

Explanatory Variable	Model: I		Model: II		Model: III		Model: IV	
	β	T	β	T	β	T	β	T
Constant	56.300	3.039***	40.600	2.107**	56.600	3.204***	50.600	5.248***
GDP$	0.121	7.988***	0.163	16.782***	0.121	8.052***	0.121	8.026***
PLUSAG	0.594	0.063	0.289	0.029			1.260	0.138
FDI$	-1.169	-7.054***	-1.540	-11.268***	-1.169	-7.100***	-1.181	-7.321***
DCPS_GD	-0.137	-0.363	-0.030	-0.075	-0.141	-0.385		
DBTTOT$	0.185	3.511***			0.185	3.534***	0.183	3.513***
Adjusted R2	0.9989		0.9988		0.9989		0.9989	
F-statistic	4434.0240		4061.4860		4729.3710		4721.3350	
AIC	50.2523		50.3836		50.2315		50.2332	
D-W Statistic	1.3460		1.4826		1.3458		1.3481	

β = coefficient, AIC = Akaike information criterion, D-W = Durbin Watson, DBTTOT$ = total outstanding debt in billion US dollars, DCPS_GD = domestic credit to private sector as a percentage of GDP, EXPR$ = exports in billion US dollars, GDP$ = gross domestic product in billion US dollars, PLUSAG = dummy variable equal to 1 if country has been granted GSP+ status or special agreement by European Union, T = T-statistics.

*p < 0.1; **p < 0.05; ***p < 0.01

Note: Periods: 6; cross-sections: 16; total observations: 96. Sample: 2011–2016.

Source: Author.

7.4 Impact of Environmental Conditions on Health Expenditures: Methodology

In the previous section, we analyzed the impact of ESG compliance on foreign investment in and exports from developing countries. No significant impact of ESG compliance was observed, which indicates that most international investors and importers do not pay much attention to ESG-related conditions in developing countries. Some industrialized countries (including the EU), however, have devised a mechanism to provide incentives to developing countries that are fulfilling their commitments to implement the international conventions on ESG standards. Compliance with these standards does not attract foreign investment or boost exports but may improve the domestic economy and its endogenous investment. Improvement in ESG conditions may improve labor productivity, organizational performance, educational standards, quality of life, health, average life expectancy, living standards, among others. Improvement in ESG conditions leads to economic growth. Because of this paper's limited scope, we cannot test the impacts of ESG-related conditions on endogenous economic factors, but we tested the impact of environmental conditions on the per capita health expenditures in South Asian countries, including Iran.

We tested the impacts of three environmental variables:

(i) Access to clean fuels and technologies for cooking as a percentage of the total population (CLEANFUEL). The greater the use of clean fuels and technologies for cooking, the fewer the environmental effects and, therefore, the lower the health expenditures.

(ii) CO_2 emissions in metric tons per capita (CO2TON). The higher the CO_2 emissions, the greater the health hazards and the higher the health expenditures.

(iii) Combustible renewables and waste as a percentage of total energy (WASTE). This may cause deterioration of public health.

The data on these three explanatory variables were extracted from World Development Indicators (World Bank, 2018). The primary source of World Bank data on energy-related variables is the World Health Organization (WHO) Global Household Energy database. The estimations are based on data from five South Asian countries (Bangladesh, India, Nepal, Pakistan, and Sri Lanka) and Iran from 2010 to 2014. The analysis includes only countries where data are available for 15 consecutive years. We used balanced panel data. Five alternative models were used to test the robustness of the parameters. We included per capita income as a control variable as it affects per capita health expenditures. To capture the country-specific policy and socioeconomic structure, we included four dummy variables, which reflect country-specific policies and structures in India, Iran, Pakistan, and Sri Lanka. The magnitude of these dummy variables is 1 for the country and 0 otherwise. We applied the panel least square method (Table 7.7).

Data for access to clean fuels and technologies for cooking are from the WHO Global Household Energy Database. Survey sources include Demographic and Health Surveys, Living Standards Measurement Surveys, Multi-Indicator Cluster Surveys, World Health Survey, other nationally developed and implemented surveys, and government agencies (for example, ministries of energy and utilities). To develop the historical evolution of clean fuels and technology-use rates, a multilevel nonparametrical mixed model, using both fixed and random effects, was used to derive polluting fuel use estimates for 150 countries. For a country with no data, estimates were derived by using regional trends or assumed to be universal access if a country was classified as developed by the United Nations.

Access to clean fuels and technologies for cooking is the proportion of total population primarily using them. Under the WHO guidelines, kerosene is not a clean cooking fuel.

The World Bank has arranged the data on CO_2 emissions through the US Department of Energy's Carbon Dioxide Information Analysis Center, which calculates annual anthropogenic emissions from data on fossil fuel consumption (from the United Nations Statistics Division's World Energy Data Set) and world cement manufacturing (from the US Department of Interior's Geological Survey [USGS, 2011]). Although estimates of global CO_2 emissions are probably accurate within 10%, country estimates may have larger error bounds. Estimates exclude fuels supplied to ships and aircraft in international transport because of the difficulty of apportioning fuel among benefiting countries.

CO_2 emissions are those from the burning of fossil fuels and the manufacture of cement. They include CO_2 produced during consumption of solid, liquid, and gas fuels, and from gas flaring. Emissions of CO_2 come from burning of oil, coal, and gas for energy; burning of wood and waste materials; and industrial processes such as cement production. In combustion, different fossil fuels release different amounts of CO_2 for the same level of energy: oil releases about 50% more CO_2 than natural gas, and coal releases about twice as much. Cement manufacturing releases about half a metric ton of CO_2 for each metric ton of cement produced. CO_2 emissions, which account for the largest share of greenhouse gases (GHGs), are largely produced from using energy and are associated with global warming. Environmentalists recommend switching from liquid

Table7.7: Dependent Variable:
Per Capita Health Expenditures, Panel Least Square

Explanatory Variables	Model: I		Model: II		Model: III		Model: IV		Model: V	
	β	T	β	T	β	T	β	T	β	T
Constant	-26.924	-3.446***	-44.158	-5.563***	-44.042	-5.610***	-38.860	-5.071***	-38.101	-5.051***
PCI	0.053	24.218***	0.0464	19.540***	0.0439	15.974***	0.048	16.254***	0.052	15.254***
CLEANFUEL	-1.589	-4.673***	-1.856	-5.976***	-1.859	-6.052***	-1.911	-6.522***	-2.617	-5.675***
CO2TON	30.220	6.609***	58.593	7.950***	66.330	7.716***	60.209	7.146***	55.357	6.404***
WASTE	0.583	5.210***	0.834	7.309***	0.826	7.309***	0.804	7.456***	0.943	7.389***
IRAN			-134.260	-4.635***	-178.215	-4.615***	-154.290	-4.105***	-68.978	-1.208
INDIA					-11.549	-1.697*	-11.002	-1.697*	8.967	0.746
SRILANKA							-16.692	-3.083***	-34.737	-3.268***
PAKISTAN									20.904	1.961*
Adjusted R2	0.9734		0.9786		0.9790		0.9810		0.9816	
F-statistic	815.3675***		813.8062***		693.8390***		656.9994***		595.3073***	
Akaike IC	8.7083		8.5028		8.4909		8.4034		8.3793	
D-W Stat	0.3029		0.4536		0.5055		0.5231		0.5229	

β = coefficient, Akaike IC = Akaike information criterion, CLEANFUEL = access to clean fuels and technologies for cooking as a percentage of the total, CO2TON = CO_2 emissions in metric tons per capita, D-W = Durbin Watson, PCI = per capita income in US dollars, T = T-statistics, WASTE = combustible renewables and waste as a percentage of total energy.

*$p < 0.1$; **$p < 0.05$; ***$p < 0.01$.

Note: Periods:15 years; cross-sections: 6; total observations: 9. Sample: 2000–2014.

Source: Author.

fuels to natural gas to protect the environment, because natural gas is lead-free, with no sulfur or particulate emissions. Emitting one-tenth the CO_2 that petrol does, natural gas is a highly environment-friendly motor fuel. It also produces lower CO_2 emissions than diesel oil, mitigating GHGs' global warming effect (Raza, 2009).

CO_2 is a naturally occurring gas fixed by photosynthesis into organic matter. A byproduct of fossil fuel combustion and biomass burning, CO_2 is emitted by land-use changes and other industrial processes. It is the principal anthropogenic GHG that affects the Earth's radiative balance. It is the reference gas against which other GHGs are measured. Burning of carbon-based fuels since the industrial revolution has rapidly increased concentrations of atmospheric CO_2, increasing the rate of global warming and causing anthropogenic climate change. CO_2 is also a major source of ocean acidification since it dissolves in water to form carbonic acid. This leads to an increase in the Earth's surface temperature and to related effects on climate, sea-level rise, and world agriculture.

Emissions intensity is the average emissions rate of a given pollutant from a given source relative to the intensity of a specific activity. Emissions intensity is used to compare the environmental impact of different fuels or activities. The related terms—emissions factor and carbon intensity—are often used interchangeably. The Kyoto Protocol, an environmental agreement adopted in 1997 by many parties to the United Nations Framework Convention on Climate Change (UNFCCC), is working to curb CO_2 emissions globally.

Energy data are compiled by the International Energy Agency, which makes these estimates in consultation with national statistical offices, oil companies, electric utilities, and national energy experts. The data for economies that are not members of the Organisation for Economic Co-operation and Development (OECD) are based on national energy data adjusted to conform to annual questionnaires completed by OECD member governments.

WASTE comprises solid biomass, liquid biomass, biogas, industrial waste, and municipal waste, measured as a percentage of total energy use. Total energy use refers to the use of primary energy before it is transformed into other end-use fuels (such as electricity and refined petroleum products). Renewable energy is derived from natural sources that are replenished at a higher rate than they are consumed. Solar, wind, geothermal, hydro, and biomass are common sources of renewable energy. Most renewable energy is from solid biofuels and hydroelectricity. Renewable sources of energy have been the driver of much of the growth in the global clean energy sector in the past few decades. Many governments are increasingly aware of the urgent need to make better use of the world's energy resources. Improved energy efficiency is often the most economical and readily available means of improving energy security and reducing GHG emissions.

7.5 Results and Conclusions

This study does not confirm that developing countries' compliance with international ESG-related conventions attracts foreign investment or boost exports. Industrialized countries giving developing countries trade and investment–related incentives or disincentives to ratify and implement ESG policies has not proved effective. But it does not mean that implementing ESG-related conventions does not affect developing countries' endogenous growth and competitiveness. For instance, Table 7.7 shows that improving environmental conditions can reduce per capita health expenditures.

The regression analysis shows that GDP and exports positively affect FDI$ (FDI) growth. The effects of GDP and exports on FDI are significant in all alternative scenarios, and the betas associated with these variables are robust. The positive impact of exports on net inflows of FDI is significant and robust, but a significant negative association between net inflow of FDI and GDP has been observed, which may indicate that after a saturation point of FDI$, net inflows start to decline. The effect of external outstanding debt (DBTTOT) is significantly positive on FDI$ but is not significant on net inflows of FDI$. Growth in domestic credit to the private sector (DCPS_GD) was not proved to be a significant determinant of FDI$ or net inflow of FDI$ (FDIINF).

The implementation of international ESG conventions by developing countries was assessed through GSP+ status. It has no significant role in determining FDI$ or net inflows of FDI$.

The effect of GDP on foreign portfolio investment in developing countries is negative, while that of exports and external debt is positive. Inflows of foreign exchange in developing countries are closely associated with their political relations with industrialized countries in the short to medium term. The explanation is that industrialized countries help developing countries by granting lending facilities, importing their products, and investing in their secondary capital markets. Domestic credit to the private sector was taken as a percentage of GDP. The conclusion is that expansion of domestic credit to the private sector negatively affects foreign portfolio investment. This is a phenomenon of enhancement in endogenous investment that replaces the foreign investment in stock markets. ESG compliance has no significant impact on foreign portfolio investment.

The size of the economy (in GDP) is positively associated with exports, which is highly significant. Betas are almost the same in all alternative scenarios, which show the robustness in the parameters. A similar relation between external outstanding debts and exports has been observed. The negative relation between exports and FDI is surprising. Mehar (2017) found the same results for Pakistan, which indicate that FDI supports endogenous utilization of raw material. Transnational corporations in developing countries convert endogenous raw material into finished goods for local consumption. The simultaneous decline in exports of primary and intermediate products and imports of finished goods is a consequence of foreign investment in manufacturing.

All the equations in the models are good fitted as confirmed by adjusted R-squares and F-statistics. The magnitudes of the Durbin-Watson test, Akaike information criterion, and other estimators show the results' statistical acceptance.

Table 7.7 shows a significant decline in the per capita health expenditures with the increase in the use of clean fuels and technologies for cooking (CLEANFUEL). Health expenditures increase as per capita income increases, which is an indicator of affordability. The higher the CO_2 emissions (CO2TON), the greater the health hazards, as confirmed by this study. The higher the CO_2 emissions (CO2TON), the higher per capita expenditures on health. WASTE has also been identified as a significant determinant of health expenditures.

In summary, implementation of ESG standards is important for endogenous economic growth, competitiveness, and productivity. International incentives or disincentives are not effective in implementing ESG standards.

References

Duffy-Deno, K. T., and R. W. Eberts. 1991. Public Infrastructure and Regional Economic Development: A Stimulation Equations Approach. *Journal of Urban Economics* 30: 329–343

European Commission. 2012. The Relevant GSP+ Conventions (Annex VIII of EU Regulations; No 978/2012.

European Commission. 2017. Mid-Term Evaluation of the EU's Generalized Scheme of Preferences (GSP)—Final Interim Report.

Hideo, N., N. Kotaro, H. Kazuaki, H. Atsushi, R. Seetha, J. K. Chul, and X. Kai. 2019. *Principles of Infrastructure: Case Studies and Best Practices.* Tokyo: Asian Development Bank Institute and Mitsubishi Research Institute.

Mehar, A. 2010. *Common Sense Economics: What Everyone Should Know About Wealth and Prosperity* (Special Pakistani Edition of James Gwartney, Richard Stroup and Dwight Lee). Islamabad: Economic Freedom Network.

Mehar, A. 2017. Infrastructure Development, CPEC and FDI in Pakistan: Is There Any Connection? *Transnational Corporation Review* September (Special Issue).

Raza, A. H. 2009. *Development of CNG Industry in Pakistan.* Islamabad: Hydrocarbon Development Institute of Pakistan.

United Nations Conference on Trade and Development (UNCTAD). 2014. *World Investment Report: Investment in the SDGs, An Action Plan.* New York: UNCTAD.

United Nations Conference on Trade and Development (UNCTAD). 2015. *World Investment Report: Reforming International Investment Governance.* New York: UNCTAD.

United Nations Environment Program (on behalf of PAGE). 2018. *International Investment Agreements & Sustainable Development: Safeguarding Policy Space & Mobilizing Investment for a Green Economy.* New York: United Nations.

World Bank. 2019. *World Development Indicators.* Washington: World Bank.

Yoshino, N., M. Helble, and U. Abidhadjaev. 2018. *Financing Infrastructure in Asia and the Pacific Capturing Impacts and New Sources.* Tokyo: Asian Development Bank Institute.

8

Environmental, Social, and Governance Investment in Green Energy Projects in Southeast Asia: Potential, Drivers, and Policy Options

Falendra Kumar Sudan

8.1 Introduction

Awareness of environmental, social, and governance (ESG) issues in green investment decisions in Asia has been growing, bolstered by the United Nations (UN)-supported Principles for Responsible Investment (PRI). Yet, investors and policy makers do not fully understand the significance of ESG investment and how to integrate ESG factors into green investment decisions. Demand for ESG investment is increasing because of its promising returns and because of calls to implement it, specifically in renewable energy in Southeast Asia. ESG factors help companies make socially responsible and sustainable investment decisions and, consequently, perform better financially and manage risk better, resulting in better efficiency and production. ESG investment has huge potential to realize the UN Sustainable Development Goals (SDGs), which are related to good business investment decisions, financial returns, and risk management. ESG investment and the SDGs, therefore, have common goals and reinforce each other.

Environmental factors are generally qualitative, subject to changing regulations and policies. Productive activities cause negative externalities, which are detrimental to ecosystems, the climate, and human health, pointing to the need to reduce emissions and comply with environmental regulations. Social factors are linked to maximizing social returns and implementing safe working practices and regulations. Governance factors are associated with robust, ethical management practices and conduct, including transparency and corporate governance. Widely used to mainstream long-term investment into green infrastructure projects globally, ESG investment can benefit business and society more than short-term high-risk investment can. More than financial returns alone, intangible assets such as investment in human capital and training, product standards, and safety regulations improve market value and companies' reputation for fair working practices. ESG investment, more than any other kind, can increase profit by reducing costs and increasing revenues, improving sustainability and competitiveness, reducing management risks, improving collective work performance, and increasing work satisfaction and retention of workers, leading to a win-win for companies, society, and government. ESG investment, therefore, should be integrated into core business strategies.

In 2014–2016, Asia, excluding Japan, recorded 16% growth in socially responsible investment (SRI), while Japan recorded 6,690% (GSIA, 2016). Malaysia, Singapore, and Indonesia have performed remarkably in sustainable investment. Asia, however, has a miniscule share of global ESG assets, reflecting the nascent state of its capital markets and its greater focus on growth and opportunities, which pose challenges to ESG investment and diminish the attractiveness of sustainable investment. It has increased rapidly worldwide, from $22.9 trillion in 2016 to $30.7 trillion in 2018, and sustainable assets ballooned by 300% in Japan during the same period (GSIA, 2018). ESG investing could skyrocket as markets and investors' needs change (ESL, 2019). ESG investment has received support from national and international organizations, including the UN. The PRI were launched in partnership with the UN in 2006 as an investor-sponsored initiative focusing on ESG issues, accumulating assets worth $60 trillion by 2016. The Global Reporting Initiative was founded in 1997 to focus on increasing awareness and understanding of sustainability and the initiative's Sustainability Reporting Standards, which uses more than 400 indicators of corporate sustainability performance. The Sustainable Stock Exchanges Initiative was launched in partnership with the UN Conference on Trade and Development (UNCTAD), the UN Global Compact, the UN Environment Programme Finance Initiative, and the PRI in 2009 to promote ESG and sustainable investment (ASEAN-Japan Centre, 2019).

Awareness of the ESG framework and the benefits of implementing it in green infrastructure projects have been increasing in Southeast Asia, resulting in improved ESG disclosure and transparency through public and private interventions. SRI has been expanding and the development and use of sustainability indexes increasing. Disclosure on governance is more frequent than on social and environmental aspects. SDG 7 envisages access to affordable, reliable, sustainable, and modern energy for all (UN, 2015), and the challenge is to meet not only current but also future energy needs (UNDESA, 2018) through ESG investment in renewable energy. Energy assets, mainly in coal mines, may be stranded in the transition to a low-carbon economy (GCEC, 2014). Fossil fuel energy sources must, therefore, be replaced and large-scale clean-energy systems built. Renewable energy capacity and energy efficiency must be increased and energy storage and smart grid infrastructure developed (IEA, 2015). Shifting ESG investment from fossil fuels and high-carbon technologies to clean energy and energy efficiency can lead to low-carbon and climate-resilient growth and a 2°C pathway. Development banks must scale up ESG investment in clean energy, including energy efficiency, to at least $1 trillion annually by 2030. Traditional finance fails to target decentralized energy access. This chapter analyzes the potential and drivers of ESG investment in green energy projects in Southeast Asian countries and recommends policy options to improve ESG investment in clean-energy development.

8.2 Objectives and Methodology

The study's main objectives are to evaluate the potential for ESG investment in green energy projects in Southeast Asia, the role of ESG investment in renewable energy and energy efficiency options, ESG investment for green energy projects, and barriers to ESG investment in clean-energy projects, and to draw up policy options to improve ESG investment in clean-energy development. Recent country-specific data related to ESG investment and green financing have not been sufficiently accessible to most Southeast Asian developing countries. This study, therefore, uses data sources and policy reports of the Asian Development Bank (ADB), World Bank, International Energy Agency (IEA), International Renewable Energy Agency (IRENA), national governments, and nongovernment organizations, including peer-reviewed research papers.

8.3 Literature Review

ESG investing differs from region to region, country to country, and even within countries. Green or sustainable investment has, therefore, been widely used in the development literature to reflect ESG strategies (Inderst and Stewart, 2018; Inderst, Kaminker, and Stewart, 2012).

Integration of ESG factors into investment decisions has increasingly
been gaining prominence in developed countries (Crifo, Forget, and
Teyssier, 2015) and more slowly in developing countries (Nair and
Ladha, 2014). ESG issues have largely been ignored by many companies
and investors (Ong, The, and Ang, 2014) and most empirical studies on
the effects of ESG disclosure on companies' market value have been
confined to developed countries (Klettner, Clarke, and Boersma, 2014;
Schadewitz and Niskala, 2010).

ESG investment incorporates nonfinancial criteria, including
impact on the environment, social issues, and governance practices,
into decisions (Wayne, 2019). Companies' environmental performance
is gaining importance because best management practices lessen air
emissions and wastes (Jasch, 2006), which improves firms' value and
attracts new stakeholders (Melnyk, Sroufe, and Calantone, 2003) and
boosts performance (Wagner and Schaltegger, 2004). Companies
have responsibilities to their employees, community, and economic
shareholders. High social performance attracts skilled employees
(Turban and Greening, 1997) and increases financial performance
(Wagner, 2010). Sound corporate governance optimizes business
performance, which is in the shareholders' best interests, reduces
costs, and favors firms' survival. Good corporate governance influences
corporate performance (Abidin, Kamal, and Jusoff, 2009) and robust
corporate environmental management practices lead to better economic
performance (Orlitzky, Schmidt, and Rynes, 2003).

Eccles, Ioannou, and Serafeim (2014) and Ferrell, Liang, and
Renneboog (2016) analyze the implications of corporate sustainability
activities for firms' performance. Corporate sustainability is not a function
only of investor sentiment but also of public sentiment (Stambaugh,
Yu, and Yuan, 2012). Firms are changing management practices to
handle reputational, legal, and regulatory risks, and their assets under
management in ESG funds have grown significantly and stand at about
one quarter of all professionally managed assets worldwide (GSIA,
2017). ESG investment differs across regions and is mainly concentrated
in Europe, followed by Australia, New Zealand, and the United States,
and not as much in Japan and other Asian countries. Pessimism about
ESG investment has disappeared, which allows firms to build their
reputations (Kitzmueller and Shimshack, 2012). Good corporate
governance has led to higher ESG performance, increased value of ESG
activities (Khan, Serafeim, and Yoon, 2016), and lower cost of capital (El
Ghoul, et al., 2011). Companies' high social performance leads to higher
employee satisfaction and improved financial performance (Edmans,
2011), while poor environmental outcome is linked to lower market
valuation (Prakash, Matsumura, and Vera-Muñoz, 2014).

ESG investment has received increasing attention since the 1990s and shifted from equity markets to other asset classes. Positive social and environmental impacts are among ESG investment's top objectives. ESG investment offers resilience in times of uncertainty and risk caused by political tensions, environmental threats, and cyber vulnerabilities. The number of ESG data and rating providers has grown to measure and track ESG investment's impacts. New and innovative ESG financial products such as climate and green bonds and the use of ESG criteria by leading financial institutions have resulted in more opportunities for ESG investment. Still, its adoption has been slower in Asian developing countries than in Australia, Europe, and North America because of limited knowledge and the skill resource gap of and lack of collective efforts by Asian regulators and governments to enforce ESG policies.

8.4 Potential for Environmental, Social, and Governance Investment in Green Energy Projects in Southeast Asia

Southeast Asia's gross domestic product (GDP) stood at $2.5 trillion in 2016 with annual growth of more than 4.0% (World Bank, 2017a), which increased to 5.1% in 2017 (IMF, 2017) and is estimated at 5.1% in 2018 (ADB, 2017a). Per capita incomes in Cambodia, the Lao People's Democratic Republic (Lao PDR), Myanmar, and Viet Nam stood at 20% of the regional average (ADB, 2017b). Southeast Asia's GDP is estimated at $3.5 trillion in 2020 and $5.4 trillion in 2030. Industrial energy use increased sharply by 70% in 2000–2016 because of the growth of large energy-intensive industries (IEA, 2017a). The urbanization rate is projected to reach 64% by 2050 compared with 48% by 2014 (UNDESA, 2014). Transport's share of energy use stood at 47% in Brunei Darussalam; 41% in Malaysia; 36% in the Philippines; 25% in Cambodia, Indonesia, and Thailand; and less than 20% in other Southeast Asian countries (IRENA and ACE, 2016). In the residential sector, 40% of the population uses traditional biomass for cooking, mainly in Indonesia, Myanmar, the Philippines, and Cambodia (IEA, 2017b). The use of electricity has increased five times because of universal access and rising incomes and consumption, and the use of traditional bioenergy has decreased (World Bank, 2017b). Energy consumption is likely to accelerate at 4% per annum until 2025. Regional coal demand is likely to build up to 128 million tons of oil equivalent by 2025, of which 90% will be used for power generation (IRENA and ACE, 2016). Fossil fuels are likely to dominate the regional energy mix but energy users are switching to clean energy because of growing demand (ACE, 2015). Per capita energy consumption is expected to increase by 140% by 2040 from the current level of below world average in most countries (ACE, 2017). Southeast Asia, therefore, offers immense potential for ESG investment in green energy projects with private participation.

Energy resources are unevenly distributed (ACE, 2015, 2017), accounting for 4.1% of global coal reserves, 3.4% of natural gas reserves, and 0.8% of oil reserves (IEA, 2017c). Hydropower potential is vast and the Lao PDR alone has 26 gigawatts (GW) of hydropower potential (OECD, 2017a). Bioenergy and solar and wind energy resources are substantial (IRENA and ACE, 2016). Singapore and Brunei Darussalam have massive potential for ESG investment in rooftop solar photovoltaic (OECD, 2017a) and Indonesia and the Philippines in geothermal resources. In Cambodia, a large part of hydropower resources is untapped, calling for substantial ESG investment in hydropower development (IRENA, 2013). Cambodia ambitiously targets universal village electrification by 2020, electrification of 70% households by 2030, and energy access increased and greenhouse gas (GHG) emissions reduced by 27% by 2030 through the use of renewable energy (IEA, 2017c), for which billions of dollars of ESG investment will be needed.

Energy demand for power generation is projected to increase by 95% by 2025 (IRENA and ACE, 2016), which is to be met mainly by coal, natural gas, and large hydropower, and a smaller portion by geothermal, bioenergy, wind, and solar photovoltaic (ACE, 2017). By 2030, ESG investment equivalent to 5.7% of regional GDP will be needed to generate, transmit, and distribute power (ADB, 2017c). Some countries aim for cross-border electricity trade. In 2015, exports of electricity from the Lao PDR to the People's Republic of China (PRC), Thailand, and Viet Nam stood at 11.5 terawatt-hours (IRENA, 2016a). Myanmar is a net exporter of hydroelectricity (IEA, 2017c), while Cambodia imports electricity from the Lao PDR, Thailand, and Viet Nam (ERIA, 2016). Nine cross-border power grids of 5.2 GW capacity and six projects of 3.3 GW capacity are under development and 16 projects of 23.2 GW capacity are being planned (APG, 2016), constituting a strategy to expand energy connectivity, energy market integration, and energy security.

8.5 Environmental, Social, and Governance Investment in Renewable Energy and Energy Efficiency

Renewable energy solutions include grid-based large-scale renewables to smaller-scale off-grid solar energy. The minigrids have

ESG investment potential of $300 billion until 2030, which is being exploited by some countries (IEA, 2017a). Off-grid solar markets have been rapidly expanding at about 60% per annum since 2010, and total market value stood at $3.9 billion in 2017. Solar home system-based rural electrification replaces kerosene or diesel use, generates financial savings for consumers, and reduces GHG emissions. Off-grid solar solutions offer great ESG investment and urban market opportunities and large financial and health benefits (IFC, 2018). The use of cleaner fuels and more efficient cook stoves helps curb deforestation. Universal access to clean cooking could reduce premature deaths by 1.8 million per annum by 2030 (IEA, 2017a). Many Southeast Asian countries, however, are still expanding low-cost coal capacity, focusing on-grid expansion and ignoring off-grid opportunities (REN21, 2016) because of the lack of ESG policies and market incentives to expand renewable off-grid and minigrid systems, limited ESG investment in renewable technologies, and public governance failure in the energy sector. Financing to support ESG investment in decentralized solutions is miniscule (less than 1% or about $200 million per annum) and available domestic investment focuses on grid expansion (World Bank, 2018). Awareness and capacity must be raised to boost ESG investment. The minigrids are not commercially viable in the least developing countries, which require more up-front ESG investment with a payback period of 10–20 years and need 50% public finance subsidy and public–private partnerships to attract ESG investment (Philips, 2018).

Development financial institutions and national governments can work with local financial institutions to raise awareness and develop local financial products to support low-cost ESG investment in decentralized solutions. Integrated energy and electrification plans for clean cooking and decentralized electricity should be implemented in a timebound manner by local stakeholders, who will monitor quantitative progress and qualitative universal electricity access before 2030 and provide subsidies to the poorest families. ESG investment and innovative business models should be supported to expand markets for distributed solar and clean cooking, import restrictions and tariffs on technology components should be lifted, and kerosene and diesel subsidies removed. Blended development finance should be extended to minigrid electrification, off-grid solar, and clean-cooking entrepreneurs (OECD, 2018). Development financial institutions, national governments, and the private sector should actively build and promote skills and leadership in clean-energy access supply chains (World Bank, 2017a).

Improving the supply of renewable energy will not be sufficient to meet growing energy needs. Energy efficiency must be improved through ESG investment. Improved renewable energy is targeted by reducing energy consumption in Brunei Darussalam, the Lao PDR, Myanmar, and Viet Nam; by reducing energy intensity in Malaysia, Singapore, and Thailand; and by reducing energy consumption and intensity in Indonesia and the Philippines (IEA, 2017a). The Association of Southeast Asian Nations (ASEAN) members target reducing energy intensity by 20% by 2020 and by 30% by 2025 compared with 2005 levels. Energy efficiency in buildings is essential to reduce energy demand and increase energy savings, and can be achieved by imposing energy standards, raising public awareness, and conducting energy audits. Energy benchmarking tools are being used in Viet Nam and the Philippines and building codes in Malaysia and Thailand. Implementing building codes, however, is hampered by the lack of local trained professionals. Energy efficiency labeling has been introduced for air conditioners, refrigerators, and motors, and systems have been introduced to reduce the increase in energy demand in Brunei Darussalam, Indonesia, the Lao PDR, Malaysia, Myanmar, the Philippines, and Thailand (ACE, 2017).

Energy efficiency in transport is essential to reduce energy demand and ensure energy security. Energy saving of up to 35% could be realized through mass transport, fuel switching, and transport management in Indonesia. Efficient vehicles and fuel-economy standards are used in Singapore and Thailand. Brunei Darussalam, Indonesia, and the Philippines plan to introduce fuel-economy standards. Liquid bio-fuels and electric vehicle technology are being used for transport. Rapid escalation of manufacturing is likely to increase energy demand. Industrial energy efficiency, therefore, needs to be greatly improved in high-energy–intensive industries (IEA, 2017a). Promoting recycling of iron and steel, paper and pulp, and chemicals and petrochemicals can improve energy efficiency. Other measures to increase industrial energy efficiency include energy audits, energy management, energy standards and labeling, and capability development programs. Energy efficiency measures need to be scaled up through policies, plans, and institutions; ESG investment and business models; robust regulations; and data and capacity building. Thailand is implementing integrated power sector development and energy efficiency programs (IRENA, 2017a). Government-guaranteed dedicated ESG investment in high-risk projects is essential to improve energy efficiency. A viability gap fund to reduce project investment costs in Indonesia, an energy performance contract fund in Malaysia, and an energy efficiency revolving fund in Thailand have been established to improve energy efficiency.

8.6 Environmental, Social, and Governance Investment for Green Energy Projects

A green project provides environmental benefits such as reduced GHG emissions and improved clean-energy access and energy efficiency. Globally, green finance stood at $437 billion in 2015 but declined by 12% in 2016 to $383 billion, while average green finance flows were 12% higher in 2015–2016 than in 2013–2014 (Buchner et al., 2017). Of total green finance, the share of clean-energy projects stood at 70% in 2015–2016 (REN21, 2017) but less than 1% of global bonds were labeled green. In 2016, the share of institutional investor allocation to green infrastructure projects was less than 1%, while total fossil fuel investments stood at $825 billion, compared with green finance at $330 billion (IEA, 2017a). Doubling the share of renewables in total energy supply by 2030 requires annual investment of $500 billion in 2015–2020 and $900 billion in 2021–2030, with cumulative investments in green infrastructure estimated at $2 trillion per annum by 2030 (IRENA, 2016b). ESG investment should be tapped to mobilize a significant share through banking and institutional investors. The high cost of investment is a major hurdle in clean-energy projects because of high capital costs up to 90% of total lifetime costs. Low-cost ESG investment can reduce clean-energy cost by 20% in developed countries and by 30% in developing countries. The focus should be on credit risk mitigation to enable banking investment and structured ESG investment through bond markets (IRENA, 2016c), including the use of risk sharing, credit enhancement, and guarantees through institutional financing for ESG investments.

Transitioning to renewable energy means switching from fossil fuels to more resource-efficient technologies through ESG investment, which comprises "all forms of investment or lending that consider environmental effect and enhance environmental sustainability" (Volz et al., 2015: 2). Many Southeast Asian countries are highly vulnerable to climate change. The Philippines and Thailand have been most affected by climate change in recent decades; they need to reduce carbon emissions through vast ESG investments in green and climate-resilient infrastructure. In developing Asia, the infrastructure gap stands at $26.2 trillion in 2016–2030 (ADB, 2017a); it needs to be bridged through ESG investment. In developing Asia, 66% electricity was generated from coal-fired power plants in 2013 compared with 14% in non-Asian developing countries and 32% in Organisation for Economic Co-operation and Development (OECD) countries (World Bank, 2014). Indonesia accounted for 51% and Malaysia for 39% (ADB, 2017b).

Renewable energy investment stood at $2.6 billion in 2016 in Southeast Asia, which constituted 1% of global renewable energy investment (BNEF, 2017). Renewable energy investment has fluctuated. Development of bioenergy in Thailand led to an increase in investment by more than 60% by 2007 in the region. Investment climbed steadily and reached its peak in 2011, when investments intensified in Thailand and Indonesia, and increased steadily thereafter, reaching $3.8 billion by 2015. Cumulative investment stood at $27 billion in 2006–2016; Thailand had the largest share at 40%, followed by Indonesia and the Philippines, both at 20% (REN21, 2017). Malaysia and Viet Nam saw renewable energy investment decline in 2001–2020. In the Philippines, investment in bioenergy stood at $920 million, followed by solar energy at $662 million and wind energy at $589 million (BNEF, 2017). Indonesia and the Philippines also invested significantly in geothermal energy. Development banks, including the World Bank, ADB, and the Japan Bank for International Cooperation invested $6 billion in renewable energy projects in the region in 2009–2016, of which loans constituted 73%, concessional loans 10%, and equity investments 3%. Concessional finance was greater than commercial loans. Indonesia's share accounted for 60% of regional cumulative renewable energy investments, mainly in geothermal energy. The Lao PDR, the Philippines, Thailand, and Viet Nam received funds from development banks to finance renewable energy deployment. Hydropower received 30% of cumulative investment from development banks in 2009–2016. Solar power received 12% and only in Thailand and Viet Nam. If primary renewable energy is to comprise 23% of all energy by 2025, Southeast Asia will need $290 billion in renewable energy investment (IRENA and ACE, 2016) from domestic and international and public and private ESG investors. Indonesia, Malaysia, the Philippines, Singapore, and Thailand have advanced capital markets, but Cambodia, the Lao PDR, Myanmar, and Viet Nam rely heavily on public institutions for ESG investments.

Few Southeast Asian financial institutions are involved in international sustainability initiatives. Financial centers in Singapore and Kuala Lumpur manage sustainable ESG assets. In 2016, sustainable investments stood at $52 billion or 0.8% of total managed assets in Asia (excluding Japan). Japan's sustainable investments alone stood at $473.6 billion or 3.4% of total assets under management. Asia's global share of SRI assets stood at 2.3% in 2016, with Japan's share alone accounting for 2.1% of global SRI assets (GSIA, 2017). Few institutional investors integrate ESG factors into their decision-making but Southeast Asian markets do have green financial innovations (Volz, 2015a), including the FTSE4Good Bursa Malaysia (F4GBM) Index and the Indonesian Stock Exchange (IDX) and KEHATI. Investors, however, prefer assets that maximize short-term risk-adjusted investment returns and are less concerned with ESG factors (ASrIA, 2014). Some local-currency bond markets have developed to meet the needs of long-term finance, but governments and enterprises have relied mainly on bank finance and forex lending, which poses macroeconomic and stability risks. Bond markets are affected by regulatory and corporate governance needed to expand local-currency bond markets to finance low-carbon and climate-resilient green infrastructure projects.

Bank Indonesia has boosted green lending, which increased from 1.2% of total lending in 2011 to 1.3% in 2012 and 1.4% in 2013. Indonesia's PT Ciputra Residence issued green bonds worth $44 million in 2014. In early 2017, the Monetary Authority of Singapore introduced the Green Bond Grant Scheme to develop the green bond market, with costs up to S$100,000 per issuance. The initiative followed the launch of the ASEAN Green Bond Standards by the ASEAN Capital Markets Forum in late 2017 and Indonesia's first sovereign green sukuk bond in early 2018. Public development banks and international financial institutions developed the green bond market and the Green Bond Principles. Institutional investors, including pension funds and insurance companies, were drawn to green projects (OECD, 2017b). Catastrophe bonds (cat bonds) were issued in Singapore to finance 100% of upfront issuance costs in early 2018. Financial systems are dominated by banking but green banking is rare because countries have little or no experience in environmental risk analysis.

8.7 Barriers to Clean-Energy Environmental, Social, and Governance Investment

The costs of renewable energy technology have declined significantly, lowering upfront capital. ESG investment in renewable energy projects, however, remains difficult because of barriers in institutional investor allocation, including the front-loaded cost structure, lack of experience, capacity gaps, insufficient investment, high transaction costs, financial regulations (IRENA, 2016b), and lower risk-adjusted rate of return (Yoshino and Taghizadeh-Hesary, 2017), suggesting that clean-energy investments could be catalyzed by enabling public policies and debt-based finance. Jones (2015) identified the barriers to clean-energy ESG investment; they are linked to policy, market, finance, clean energy, and physical risks and needs that should be tackled by robust public–private partnerships. Investors' risk perception leads to high cost of investment, which hampers clean-energy ESG investment and needs hedging solutions for risks, policy changes, regulatory interventions, and innovative finance.

Pension funds and insurance companies have long-term estimated investment potential of $2.80 trillion per annum in long-term clean-energy projects (IRENA, 2016b) compared with short-term sources of commercial banks (Yoshino and Taghizadeh-Hesary, 2018). Credit risk and policy risk are barriers to clean-energy ESG investment and need to be solved by enhancing credit to enable bond market investment. Technological obsolescence and commercial viability are barriers to clean-energy ESG investment. Clean-energy projects face volatile production because of uncertain ESG conditions, leading to excessive risk aversion and higher expected returns from ESG investments. Distributed clean-energy projects face problems of scale, insufficient ESG investment, and higher transaction costs, which discourage institutional investors. Clean-energy projects face maturity mismatch risk (Yoshino and Taghizadeh-Hesary, 2017, 2018), longevity risk (mismatch between long-term capital commitments and the short-term nature of regulations), technology risk, credit risk, and political risks (Yoshino and Taghizadeh-Hesary, 2014, 2015). Bond finance can be a viable option for clean-energy ESG investments, using credit enhancement and risk sharing. Lack of experience, capacity gaps, lack of transparency, inappropriate financial mechanisms, and unclear banking regulations discourage ESG investors from investing in clean-energy projects. Barriers related to ESG investment must, therefore, be overcome by reorienting institutions and planning the transition to sustainable energy.

8.8 Conclusion and Policy Options

Southeast Asia's strong growth has led to higher energy use in recent decades. Since 1995, regional energy consumption has doubled and energy demand is likely to increase by 4.7% annually until 2035 (ASEAN, 2015), mainly for electricity, industry, and transport. The energy mix is diverse: coal in Indonesia; coal and natural gas in Viet Nam; and hydro resources in Cambodia, the Lao PDR, and Viet Nam. Indonesia, Viet Nam, and the Philippines have significant fossil fuel resources to meet swelling electricity demand. Indonesia and the Philippines focus on developing efficient coal power generation; meeting ambitious clean-energy goals using wind, solar, hydro, and waste; and developing geothermal power. Energy access is uneven in the region: more than 65 million people have no access to electricity and 250 million depend on biomass for cooking, which requires decentralized options such as cost-effective renewable energy. Shifting to renewable energy offers socioeconomic benefits such as higher incomes, more jobs, better livelihoods, and improved welfare. The renewable energy sector is likely to increase GDP growth by 0.03%

by 2030, reduce the annual fossil fuel import bill by $40 billion by 2025 (IRENA and ACE, 2016), and potentially create 1.7 million jobs by 2030. Accelerated deployment of renewables, which needs strong technical, marketing, and administrative skills, could create 2.2 million direct and indirect jobs by 2030 (IRENA, 2017b).

Carbon dioxide emissions from fossil fuels and industry have increased significantly with oil production. Indonesia, Myanmar, and the lower Mekong basin, however, have immense untapped potential to produce renewable energy. The potential for solar and wind energy is strong in Indonesia, the Philippines, Thailand, and Viet Nam. Geothermal potential is significant in Indonesia and the Philippines. Indonesia, the Philippines, and Singapore have substantial ocean energy potential. The region has high bioenergy potential. Economies must diversify and transition from fossil fuels to low-carbon clean energy to achieve robust, equitable, and environmentally sound development. Well-crafted ESG strategies will be needed to phase out coal power generation and create alternative sources of revenue for affected people and regions. Renewable energy involves higher capital cost than other infrastructure because of limited investments and political risks related to future prices and capital scarcity. Future electricity prices must be certain and a system of blended finance (strategic use of public or philanthropic development capital to mobilize additional external private commercial finance) must reduce risk for private ESG investors. Countries have set medium- and long-term goals for renewable energy development to reduce GHG emissions. The region, however, is unlikely to achieve ASEAN's renewable energy target of 23% by 2025 (IRENA and ACE, 2016). Strong government interventions are needed to unlock the full potential of modern renewables through ESG investment, specifically to increase access to clean energy for electricity, heating, and cooling. Renewables remain underutilized in end-use sectors because of the patchwork of ESG policies and incentives.

Tapping substantial renewables needs financial incentives, tax exemptions, purchase guarantees, awareness raising, bioenergy and land policies, fuel-efficiency policies, data and information, and synergies between renewable energy and energy efficiency. Increasing the share of renewable energy in primary energy requires concerted efforts to improve project readiness, increase blended finance, raise capital from domestic banks, lend in local currency, mitigate risk, establish green investment banks, and sell green bonds. Such efforts need the active participation of governments, national public finance institutions, development finance institutions, and the private sector. Renewable energy and energy efficiency projects require new financial instruments such as green banks, green bonds, and regulatory frameworks. The financial system must be aligned with sustainability goals by using climate-proofing and climate resilience measures and by safeguarding the stability of financial systems.

Multilateral development banks such as the World Bank and ADB could finance the transition to renewable energy by raising huge long-term debt from capital markets at low interest rates for lending to governments and public–private investment entities. Carbon taxes must be levied to raise revenue to finance the transition. More savings and investments have recently been channeled into environmentally harmful projects, more so in high-income than in low-income countries. The investment landscape must be reshaped to support long-term ESG investment to secure a sustainable future. The financial sector needs to focus on future market prices and on policies to shift to green and renewable sources in line with the SDGs and the Paris Agreement.

New ESG investment mechanisms, improved credit assessment, and policy prescriptions are needed. Despite existing regulations, taxes, and subsidies, capital mobilization remains insufficient. Enabling policies, risk mitigation, and structured ESG investment are needed. Public finance institutions can be critical in catalyzing private ESG investments (IRENA, 2016b), mitigating risks of investors, smoothing cash flow, securing an investible grade rating, and offering credit guarantees on behalf of the borrower (Yoshino and Taghizadeh-Hesary, 2016). Public finance institutions have high credit ratings and can facilitate green bond financing to unlock large-scale and long-term non-bank ESG investment (IRENA, 2016c). ESG investment guidelines and regulations to promote green lending, including green insurance and environmental risk analysis, have been framed in many Asian countries, including Bangladesh (Barkawi and Monin, 2015) and the PRC (UNEP, 2017), which doubtless cannot be directly compared with other Asian countries. Country-specific policy options should, therefore, take into account differences in financial market structures to avoid adverse effects (Volz, 2015b). Corporate governance should be strengthened through strict internal and external audit, including robust accounting practices and risk management, along with regular review of green investment policies.

The enforcement of environmental regulations to reduce production and consumption externalities has gaps, which need to be bridged through binding environmental regulations and emission-trading schemes (ADB, 2016). Fossil fuel subsidies and post-tax energy subsidies cause enormous price distortions, which call for phasing out energy subsidies. ESG investments in renewable energy are hampered by non-conducive regulatory and legal environments (Volz, 2015a). More transparent and credible policies are needed to reduce emissions faster and more efficiently. The financial system is constrained from dealing with ESG investment risks and opportunities because awareness of environmental and climate risks is lacking. The financial industry lacks staff trained to assess environmental and climate risks or experienced in financing renewable energy projects. The result is high transaction costs. Bankable and investable renewable energy projects are scarce. Mandatory environmental risk analysis and ESG disclosure are nonexistent. Sustainability must be mainstreamed into ESG investment using a coordinated and systematic approach involving all stakeholders. Robust sustainable investment governance should focus on raising awareness among regulators and market participants. ESG mechanisms should be equipped to carry out environmental risk analysis.

Community-based funds such as the Hometown Investment Trust Fund are a potent way of investing in small and medium-sized green energy projects (Yoshino and Kaji, 2013; Yoshino and Taghizadeh-Hesary, 2014) and will help risky sectors grow. New financial technologies such as blockchain, the Internet of Things, and big data could unlock green finance (Nassiry, 2018). Green bonds and climate funds are new ESG investment instruments in Southeast Asia. They are fixed-income securities and include qualifying debt securities. In 2017, Singapore launched a green bond grant scheme (Climate Bonds Initiative, 2017) and Malaysia issued the first climate bond in Asia to finance renewables. However, the renewable energy market is not sufficiently developed for the issuance of large-scale green bonds. In 2017, global energy investment stood at $1.8 trillion, down 2% from 2016. After rising in the previous few years, global investment in renewables and energy efficiency declined by 3% in 2017, which could curb the expansion of green energy.

ESG investment must, therefore, be steered toward renewable energy projects and transit to a low-carbon economy. However, financial institutions and banks consider most renewable energy projects to be risky and are reluctant to finance them. Banks face maturity mismatch because they have short- and medium-term deposits but renewable energy projects need long-term ESG investment. New channels of ESG investment must, therefore, be found. Non-bank financial institutions, including pension funds and insurance companies, hold long-term financial resources and could be tapped to invest in green projects (Gianfrate and Lorenzato, 2018). Green central banking could be steered to fill the gap in ESG investment through robust governance policies to mitigate environmental risk and promote sustainable investment (Dikau and Volz, 2018). Fiscal policy could be used to increase returns from green projects by using tax relief or tax credits for renewable energy development (Azhgaliyeva, Kapsaplyamova, and Low, 2018) and to refund the increase in tax revenue from the spillover effect of privately funded green energy projects (Yoshino and Taghizadeh-Hesary, 2018). In sum, enabling policies and regulatory frameworks are essential to support market participants, reduce uncertainty, provide adequate incentives, mitigate long-term risks, catalyze private sector interest, reduce technology costs, attract foreign capital and technology, and provide education and training and research and development for long-term ESG investments in renewable energy development in Southeast Asia.

References

Abidin, Z. Z., N. M. Kamal, and K. Jusoff. 2009. Board Structure and Corporate Performance in Malaysia. *International Journal of Economic and Finance* 1(1): 150–164.

ASEAN Centre for Energy (ACE). 2015. The 4th ASEAN Energy Outlook 2013–2035. Jakarta: ACE.

———. 2017. *The 5th ASEAN Energy Outlook 2015–2040*. Jakarta: ACE.

Asian Development Bank (ADB). 2016. *Emissions Trading Schemes and Their Linking: Challenges and Opportunities in Asia and the Pacific*. Manila: ADB.

———. 2017a. *Asian Development Outlook 2017, Update: Sustaining Development through Public–Private Partnership: Highlights*. Manila: ADB.

———. 2017b. *Basic Statistics 2017*. Manila: ADB.

———. 2017c. *Meeting Asia's Infrastructure Needs*. Manila: ADB.

ASEAN-Japan Centre. 2019. *ESG Investment: Towards Sustainable Investment in ASEAN and Japan*. Tokyo: ASEAN-Japan Centre.

ASEAN Power Grid (APG). 2016. *ASEAN Power Grid: Route to Multilateral Electricity Trade*. Manila: APG.

Association of Southeast Asian Nations (ASEAN). 2015. ASEAN Energy Development. In *ASEAN Plan of Action for Energy Cooperation (APAEC) 2025*. Jakarta: ASEAN.

Association for Sustainable and Responsible Investment in Asia (ASrIA). 2014. *2014 Asia Sustainable Investment Review*. Hong Kong, China: ASrIA.

Azhgaliyeva, D., Z. Kapsaplyamova, and L. Low. 2018. Implications of Fiscal and Financial Policies for Unlocking Green Finance and Green Investment. ADBI Working Paper 861. Tokyo: Asian Development Bank Institute.

Barkawi, A., and P. Monin. 2015. Monetary Policy and Sustainability: The Case of Bangladesh. UNEP Inquiry Working Paper No. 15/02. Geneva: UNEP Inquiry into the Design of a Sustainable Financial System.

Bloomberg New Energy Finance (BNEF). 2017. *New Energy Outlook 2017*. New York: BNEF.

Buchner, B. K., P. Oliver, X. Wang, C. Carswell, C. Meattle, and F. Mazza. 2017. *Global Landscape of Climate Finance 2017*. London: Climate Policy Initiative..

Climate Bonds Initiative. 2017. *Hot Off the Press: Singapore's Central Bank Announces Green Bond Grant Scheme to Cover Any Additional Issuance Costs of Going Green*. London: Climate Bonds Initiative.

Crifo, P., V. D. Forget, and S. Teyssier. 2015. The Price of Environmental, Social and Governance Practice Disclosure: An Experiment with Professional Private Equity Investors. *Journal of Corporate Finance* 30: 168–194.

Dikau, S., and U. Volz. 2018. Central Banking, Climate Change and Green Finance. ADBI Working Paper 867. Tokyo: Asian Development Bank Institute.

Eccles, R. G., I. Ioannou, and G. Serafeim. 2014. The Impact of Corporate Sustainability on Organizational Processes and Performance. *Management Science* 60(11): 2835–2857.

Economic Research Institute for ASEAN and East Asia (ERIA). 2016. *Primary Energy Data.* General Department of Energy and General Department of Petroleum, in Cambodia National Energy Statistics 2016, ERIA Research Project Report 2015-8. Jakarta: ERIA.

Edelweiss Securities Limited (ESL). 2019. *Seeking Growth: The ESG Way.* Mumbai: ESL.

Edmans, A. 2011. Does the Stock Market Fully Value Intangibles? Employee Satisfaction and Equity Prices. *Journal of Financial Economics* 101(3): 621–640.

El Ghoul, S., O. Guedhami, C. C. Kwok, and D. R. Mishra. 2011. Does Corporate Social Responsibility Affect the Cost of Capital? *Journal of Banking & Finance* 35(9): 2388–2406.

Ferrell, A., H. Liang, and L. Renneboog. 2016. Socially Responsible Firms. *Journal of Financial Economics* 122(3): 585–606.

GCEC. 2014. *Better Growth, Better Climate.* London and Washington, DC: New Climate Economy.

Gianfrate, G., and G. Lorenzato. 2018. Stimulating Non-Bank Financial Institutions' Participation in Green Investments. ADBI Working Paper 860. Tokyo: Asian Development Bank Institute.

Global Sustainable Investment Alliance (GSIA). 2016. *Global Sustainable Investment Review.* London: GSIA.

____. 2017. 2016 *Global Sustainable Investment Review.* London: GSIA.

____. 2018. *Global Sustainable Investment Review.* London: GSIA.

Inderst, G., Ch. Kaminker, and F. Stewart. 2012. Defining and Measuring Green Investments. OECD Working Papers on Finance, Insurance and Private Pensions, No. 24. Paris: Organisation for Economic Co-operation and Development.

Inderst, G., and F. Stewart. 2018. *Incorporating Environmental, Social and Governance (ESG) Factors into Fixed Income Investment.* Washington, DC: World Bank Group.

International Energy Agency (IEA). 2015. *Special Report on Energy and Climate Change.* Paris: IEA.

____. 2017a. *Southeast Asia Energy Outlook 2017.* Paris: IEA.

____. 2017b. *Electricity Information: Overview 2017 edition.* Paris: IEA.

____. 2017c. *World Energy Outlook 2017.* Paris: IEA.

International Finance Corporation (IFC). 2018. *Off-Grid Solar Market Trends Report 2018.* Washington, DC: IFC.

International Monetary Fund (IMF). 2017. *World Economic Outlook: Seeking Sustainable Growth*. Washington, DC: IMF.

International Renewable Energy Agency (IRENA). 2013. *Renewable Energy Country Profiles: Asia*. Abu Dhabi: IRENA.

_____. 2016a. *Renewable Energy Data in Lao PDR*. EAST and Southeast Asia Renewable Energy Statistic Training Workshop. Institute of Renewable Energy Promotion, Ministry of Energy and Mines, 12–14 December. Bangkok and Abu Dhabi: IRENA.

_____. 2016b. *The True Cost of Fossil Fuels: Saving on the Externalities of Air Pollution and Climate Change*. Abu Dhabi: IRENA.

_____. 2016c. *Unlocking Renewable Energy Investment: Role of Risk Mitigation and Structured Finance*. Abu Dhabi: IRENA.

_____. 2017a. *Renewable Energy Outlook: Thailand*. Abu Dhabi: IRENA.

_____. 2017b. *Renewable Energy Benefits: Leveraging Local Capacity for Solar PV*. Abu Dhabi: IRENA.

IRENA and ACE. 2016. *Renewable Energy Outlook for ASEAN: A Remap Analysis*. Abu Dhabi: IRENA, and Jakarta: ACE.

Jasch, C. 2006. Environmental Management Accounting (EMA) as the Next Step in the Evolution of Management Accounting. *Journal of Cleaner Production* 14(14): 1190–1193.

Jones, A. W. 2015. Perceived Barriers and Policy Solutions in Clean Energy Infrastructure Investment. *Journal of Cleaner Production* 104: 297–304.

Khan, M., G. Serafeim, and A. Yoon. 2016. Corporate Sustainability: First Evidence on Materiality. *The Accounting Review* 91(6): 1697–1724.

Kitzmueller, M., and J. Shimshack. 2012. Economic Perspectives on Corporate Social Responsibility. *Journal of Economic Literature* 50(1): 51–84.

Klettner, A., T. Clarke, and M. Boersma. 2014. The Governance of Corporate Sustainability: Empirical Insights into the Development, Leadership and Implementation of Responsible Business Strategy. *Journal of Business Ethics* 122(1): 145–165.

Melnyk, S. A., R. P. Sroufe, and R. Calantone. 2003. Assessing the Impact of Environmental Management Systems on Corporate and Environmental Performance. *Journal of Operations Management* 21: 329–351.

Nassiry, D. 2018. The Role of Fintech in Unlocking Green Finance: Policy Insights for Developing Countries. ADBI Working Paper 883. Tokyo: Asian Development Bank Institute.

Nair, A. S., and R. Ladha. 2014. Determinants of Non-Economic Investment Goals Among Indian Investors. *Corporate Governance: The International Journal of Business in Society* 14(5): 714–727.

Ong, T. S., B. H. The, and Y. W. Ang. 2014. The Impact of Environmental Improvements on the Financial Performance of Leading Companies

Listed in Bursa Malaysia. *International Journal of Trade, Economics and Finance* 5(5): 386–391.

Organisation for Economic Co-operation and Development (OECD). 2017a. *Economic Outlook for Southeast Asia, China and India 2017: Addressing Energy Challenges*. Paris: OECD.

_____. 2017b. *Green Bonds—Mobilizing the Debt Capital Markets for a Low-Carbon Transition*. Paris: OECD.

_____. 2018. *Making Blended Finance Work for the Sustainable Development Goals*. Paris: OECD.

Orlitzky, M., F. L. Schmidt, and S. L. Rynes. 2003. Corporate Social and Financial Performance: A Meta-Analysis. *Organization Studies* 24: 403–441.

Philips, J. 2018. *7 Takeaways from the Energy Access Project Launch*. Durham, NC: Duke University.

Prakash, M., E. M. Matsumura, and S. C. Vera-Muñoz. 2014. Firm-Value Effects of Carbon Emissions and Carbon Disclosures. *The Accounting Review* 89(2): 695–724.

Renewable Energy Policy Network for the 21st Century (REN21). 2016. *Renewables 2016 Global Status Report*. Paris: REN21, REN21 Secretariat.

_____. 2017. *Renewables 2017 Global Status Report*. Paris: REN21, REN21 Secretariat.

Schadewitz, H. and M. Niskala. 2010. Communication via Responsibility Reporting and Its Effect on Firm Value in Finland. *Corporate Social Responsibility and Environmental Management* 17(2): 96–106.

Stambaugh, R. F., J. Yu, and Y. Yuan. 2012. The Short of It: Investor Sentiment and Anomalies. *Journal of Financial Economics* 104(2): 288–302.

Turban, D. B., and D. W. Greening. 1997. Corporate Social Performance and Organizational Attractiveness to Prospective Employees. *The Academy of Management Journal* 40(3): 658–672.

United Nations (UN). 2015. *Transforming Our World: The 2030 Agenda for Sustainable Development*. New York: UN.

United Nations, Department of Economic and Social Affairs (UNDESA). 2014. *World Urbanization Prospects: The 2014 Revision: Highlights*. New York: UNDESA, Population Division.

_____. 2018. *World Population Prospects 2018*. New York: UNDESA, Population Division.

United Nations Environment Programme (UNEP). 2017. *Establishing China's Green Financial System: Progress Report 2017*. Geneva: UNEP Inquiry into the Design of a Sustainable Financial System.

Volz, U. 2015a. *Towards a Sustainable Financial System in Indonesia*. Geneva and Washington, DC: UNEP Inquiry into the Design of a Sustainable Financial System and IFC.

_____. 2015b. *Effects of Financial System Size and Structure on the Real Economy. What Do We Know and What Do We Not Know?* Geneva: UNEP Inquiry into the Design of a Sustainable Financial System.

Volz, U., J. Böhnke, V. Eidt, L. Knierim, K. Richert, and G.-M. Roeber. 2015. *Financing the Green Transformation – How to Make Green Finance Work in Indonesia.* Houndmills, Basingstoke: Palgrave Macmillan.

Wagner, M. 2010. The Role of Corporate Sustainability Performance for Economic Performance: A Firm-Level Analysis of Moderation Effects. *Ecological Economics* 69(7): 1553–1560.

Wagner, M., and S. Schaltegger. 2004. The Effect of Corporate Environmental Strategy Choice and Environmental Performance on Competitiveness and Economic Performance. *European Management Journal* 22(5): 557–572.

Wayne, W. 2019. *Environmental, Social, and Governance (ESG) Investing: An Evaluation of the Evidence.* San Francisco: Pacific Research Institute.

World Bank. 2014. *World Development Indicators, 2014.* Washington, DC: World Bank.

_____. 2017a. *Putting Clean Cooking on the Front Burner.* Washington, DC: World Bank.

_____. 2017b. *World Development Indicators Database.* Washington, DC: World Bank.

_____. 2018. *Tracking SDG7: The Energy Progress Report 2018.* Washington, DC: World Bank.

Yoshino, N., and S. Kaji, eds. 2013. *Hometown Investment Trust Funds.* Tokyo: Springer.

Yoshino, N., and F. Taghizadeh-Hesary. 2014. Analytical Framework on Credit Risks for Financing SMEs in Asia. *Asia-Pacific Development Journal* 21(2): 1-21.

_____. 2015. Analysis of Credit Risk for Small and Medium-Sized Enterprises: Evidence from Asia. *Asian Development Review* 32(2): 18–37.

_____. 2016. Optimal Credit Guarantee Scheme Ratio for Asia. ADBI Working Paper No. 586. Tokyo: Asian Development Bank Institute.

_____. 2017. Alternatives of Bank Finance: Role of Carbon Tax and Hometown Trust Funds in Developing Green Energy Projects in Asia. ADBI Working Paper No. 761. Tokyo: Asian Development Bank Institute.

_____. 2018. Alternatives to Private Finance: Role of Fiscal Policy Reforms and Energy Taxation in Development of Renewable Energy Projects. In Financing for Low-carbon Energy Transition, edited by V. Anbumozhi, K. Kalirajan, and F. Kimura. Tokyo: Springer.

Zainal Abidin, Z., N. Mustafa Kamal, and K. Jusoff. 2009. Board Structure and Corporate Performance in Malaysia. *International Journal of Economic and Finance* 1(1): 150–164.

9

Corporate Social Responsibility and Financial Performance in Microfinance Institutions

Mahinda Wijesiri and Diane-Gabrielle Tremblay

9.1 Introduction

An examination of textbook definitions of corporate social responsibility (CSR) provides the most general guide to theoretical content. CSR is a complex, multifaceted, and dynamic concept. It can be described simply as a voluntary action that business can take to achieve social objectives such as sustainable development and improved quality of life (Carroll, 1979). Because microfinance institutions (MFIs) are community based, they have social responsibility at the core of their raison-d'être and actions (Allet, 2014). As MFIs have commercialized and scaled up, however, some have drifted from their social objectives to pursue profit by devoting fewer resources to socially beneficial purposes (Shahriar, Schwarz, and Newman, 2015). Drifting from social responsibility often leads to serious moral, ethical, and environmental issues that distort MFIs' social reputation.

CSR in MFIs is important for two reasons. First, commitment to socially responsible practices enables MFIs to broaden the sources of capital from which they would otherwise be disqualified. While a large number of MFIs receive funds as subsidized loans or grants, some others use clients' deposits to form a significant part of their capital base. Since investments in socially responsible practices can improve the reputation of MFIs, implementing CSR practices can help foster stakeholder trust and expectations and improve the long-term viability of the MFIs. Second, following the 2010 microfinance crisis in Andhra Pradesh, India, client protection policies have received heightened attention from MFI stakeholders and society (Taylor, 2011). The serious outcomes of the crisis emphasize the importance of adherence to transparent and ethical practices in interest rate disclosure, transparent information on pricing, terms and conditions, collection methods, client complaint resolution mechanisms, as well as to client protection principles to ensure that operations of MFIs have no negative influence on their numerous stakeholders.

Diverse studies examine the link between the social benefits of microfinance and MFI financial performance. But these studies overlook other important dimensions of social responsibility, particularly environmental and ethical standards. This is surprising given that the concept of microfinance is not necessarily limited to providing financial services to the poor who are excluded from traditional financial institutions.

This chapter investigates the relationship between MFIs' socially responsible practices and their financial performance. Using a sample of 388 MFIs in 2011–2014, we examine whether MFIs' socially responsible strategies lead to more efficient financial performance. To obtain more insight into how socially responsible practices affect MFIs' performance, we consider MFIs' strategic orientation toward the environment, clients, and employees, which are among the most widely measured dimensions of corporate social performance (Cavaco and Crifo, 2014). Our empirical analysis consists of two steps. First, we use a network data envelopment analysis (DEA) model to measure the efficiency of each MFI over the sampled period. Second, we estimate the effect of socially responsible practices by regressing MFIs' performance in three social responsibility elements and several control variables.

9.2 Data and Variables

9.2.1 Data Collection

We use annual datasets collected from the Microfinance Information Exchange (MIX) Market, a global web-based microfinance platform that provides high-quality standardized information about a large number of MFIs operating in different geographic regions and has become the premier source of information on microfinance (Servin, Lensink, and Van den Berg, 2012; Bauchet and Morduch, 2010). We do not include MFIs with insufficient key variables for consecutive years as we need to build a balanced panel data set. We also exclude MFIs for which the data are not annual to ensure comparability with annual data. A total of 388 MFI–year observations for 2011–2014 remain in the sample after missing variables are eliminated.

9.2.2 Variables

Dependent Variable: Measure of Microfinance Institutions' Financial Performance

We use financial performance measured by efficiency as the dependent variable, which is defined as the optimal level of inputs used to meet for-profit goals. We use a network DEA approach to calculate the efficiency score of each MFI in our sample. The network DEA model distinguishes the divisional efficiencies as well as the overall efficiency in a unified framework, which was introduced by Färe (1991) and expanded by several authors (e.g., Kao [2009], Tone and Tsutsui [2009]).

To assess MFIs' financial performance, this study uses the non-radial network DEA model based on network slacks-based measures (NSBM) of Tone and Tsutsui (2009). We assume that there are n MFIs ($j = 1, ..., n$) consisting of K divisions ($k = 1, ..., K$). We also consider that there are m_k and r_k inputs and outputs to division k, respectively. We note the link leading from division k to division h by (k, h) and the set of links by L. The observed measurements of inputs to MFI_j at the division k are $\{x_j^k \in R_+^{m_k}\}$ ($j = 1, ..., n; k = 1, ..., K$) and the observed measurements of outputs from MFI_j at the division k are $\{y_j^k \in R_+^{r_k}\}$ ($j = 1, ..., n; k = 1, ..., K$) and linking intermediate products from division k to division h are $\left\{z_j^{(k,h)} \in R_+^{t_{(k,h)}}\right\}$ ($j = 1, ..., n; (k, h \in L)$ where $t_{(k,h)}$ is the number of items in link (k, h).

The production possibility set $\{(x^k, y^k, z^{(k,h)})\}$ is given by

$$x^k \geq \sum_{j=1}^n x_j^k \lambda_j^k \quad (k = 1, ..., K),$$

$$y^k \leq \sum_{j=1}^n y_j^k \lambda_j^k \quad (k = 1, ..., K),$$

$$z^{(k,h)} = \sum_{j=1}^n z_j^{(k,h)} \lambda_j^k \quad (\forall(k, h)(as\ output\ from\ k), \qquad (1)$$

$$z^{(k,h)} = \sum_{j=1}^n z_j^{(k,h)} \lambda_j^h \quad (\forall(k, h)(as\ input\ to\ h),$$

$$\sum_{j=1}^n \lambda_j^k = 1(\forall k), \quad \lambda_j^k \geq 0(\forall j, k),$$

where $\lambda^k \in R_+^n$ is the intensity vector corresponding to Division $k(k = 1, ..., K)$.

$MFI_o(o = 1, ..., n)$ can be represented by

$$x_o^k = X^k \lambda^k + s^{k-} \quad (k = 1, ..., K),$$

$$y_o^k = Y^k \lambda^k - s^{k+} \quad (k = 1, ..., K), \qquad (2)$$

$$e\lambda^k = 1 \ (k = 1, ..., K),$$

$$\lambda^k \geq o, \ s^{k-} \geq o, \ s^{k+} \geq o, \ (\forall k),$$

where

$$X^k = \left(x_1^k, ..., x_n^k\right) \in R^{m_k \times n},$$

$$Y^k = \left(y_1^k, ..., y_n^k\right) \in R^{r_k \times n}, \tag{3}$$

and $s^{k-}(s^{k+})$ (are the input (output) slacks vectors.

For the linking constraints, we use the "fixed" link value case in which the linking activities are kept unchanged (nondiscretionary):

$$z_o^{k,h} = Z^{(k,h)} \lambda^h \ \left(\forall (k, h)\right), \tag{4}$$

$$z_o^{(k,h)} = Z^{(k,h)} \lambda^k \ \left(\forall (k, h)\right).$$

Assuming an input-oriented NSBM model with the variable return to scale (VRS) assumption, the overall efficiency for an MFI (θ_0^*) can be defined as:

$$\theta_0^* = \min_{\lambda^k, s^{k-}} \sum_{k=1}^K w^k \left[1 + \frac{1}{m_k} \left(\sum_{i=1}^{m_k} \frac{s_i^{k-}}{x_{io}^k} \right) \right] \tag{5}$$

where $\sum_{k=1}^k w^k = 1$, $w^k \geq o \ (\forall k)$, and w^k is the relative weight of division k.

The k divisional efficiency θ_k can be defined as

$$\theta_k = 1 - \frac{1}{m_k} \left(\sum_{i=1}^{m_k} \frac{s_i^{k-*}}{x_{io}^k} \right) (k = 1, ..., K) \tag{6}$$

where s^{k-*} is the optimal input slacks of (5).

A detailed presentation of NSBM and more information are in Tone and Tsutsui (2009).

We select input and output variables according to earlier studies (e.g., Gutiérrez-Nieto, Serrano-Cinca, and Molinera [2007, 2009]; Servin, Lensink, and Van den Berg, [2012]) and based on data availability. Table 9.1 presents the main descriptive statistics for all input and output variables.

Table 9.1: Summary Statistics of Inputs, Outputs, and Intermediate Variables Included in the Data Envelopment Analysis Model, and Their Units of Measurement

	2011		2012		2013		2014	
Variables	Mean	Std. dev.	Mean	Std. dev.	Mean	Std. dev.	Mean	Std. dev.
Assets ($ thousands)	154,435	304,174	191,937	371,356	227,115	449,055	241,942	448,764
Labor (number)	823	2009	918	1958	1003	1964	1075	2021
Raised Funds ($ thousands)	91,196	225,389	113,272	260,493	131,255	295,913	136,692	284,677
Gross Loan Portfolio ($ thousands)	120,842	234,319	149,347	288,607	168,464	308,121	185,801	326,717
Financial Revenue ($ thousands)	29,183	54,180	34,409	60,524	40,854	69,427	42,881	68,724

Std. dev. = standard deviation.
Note: Assets, raised funds, gross loan portfolio, and financial revenue are in thousands of United States dollars.
Source: Authors.

Input Variables
Assets. Total value of resources controlled by the MFI as a result of past events and from which future economic benefits are expected to flow to the MFI. For calculation purposes, assets are the sum of each individual asset account listed.

Labor. The number of individuals who are actively employed by an MFI, including contract employees or advisors who dedicate a substantial portion of their time to the entity, even if they are not on the entity's employees roster.

Output Variables
Gross loan portfolio. All outstanding principals due for all outstanding client loans, including current, delinquent, and renegotiated loans (but not loans that have been written off), and off-balance sheet portfolio.

Financial revenue. Revenue generated from the gross loan portfolio and from investments plus other operating revenue.

Intermediate Variable
Raised funds. Includes the sum of deposits and donations.

The two-stage DEA model for microfinance efficiency evaluation and the inputs, outputs, and intermediate measure selections are depicted in Figure 9.1.

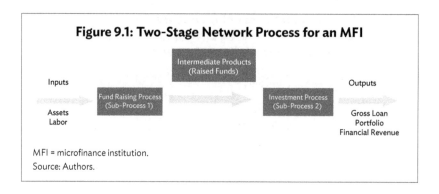

Figure 9.1: Two-Stage Network Process for an MFI

Inputs

Intermediate Products
(Raised Funds)

Outputs

Fund Raising Process
(Sub-Process 1)

Investment Process
(Sub-Process 2)

Assets
Labor

Gross Loan
Portfolio
Financial Revenue

MFI = microfinance institution.
Source: Authors.

Corporate Social Responsibility Index

The CSR index is the primary focus independent variable in our study. This study measures CSR of MFIs by constructing a score that indicates the extent of their involvement in socially responsible practices. We designed this metric based on the MIX database, which reports 17 individual activity items and groups them according to three social responsibility attributes: environment, clients, and employees. The environmental dimension of CSR consists of activities carried out by MFIs related to raising awareness of environmental impacts. CSR in the environment is evaluated on four items, client protection on eight, and employee relations (how an MFI treats its employees) on five.

Following earlier studies (e.g., Lanis and Richardson [2012], Aribi and Arun [2015]), we construct aggregate CSR measures in MFIs related to the three stakeholder groups. Consistent with earlier studies, we obtain dichotomic responses from MFIs on a fraction basis, which is the ratio of the number of items adopted by an MFI and the sum of the items that make up the CSR category:

$$CSR_i = \frac{\sum_{t=1}^{n} X_i}{n_i} \qquad (7)$$

Where CSR_i is an aggregate measure of corporate social responsibility in i^{th}MFI ($0 \leq CSR_i \leq 1$), X_i is the number of items that have been disclosed by i^{th}MFI ($X_i = 1$ if the item is disclosed, 0 otherwise), and n_i is the sum of the items that make up the CSR index of i^{th}MFI.

Control Variables

The choice of control variables is guided by the extant literature. Age (AGE), return on assets (ROA), size (SIZE), debt-to-equity ratio (DEQ), and ownership type (OWNSIP) have been suggested in earlier research

Table 9.2: Descriptive Statistics, 2011–2014

Variable	Mean	Std. Dev.
FP	0.5078	0.3302
CSR	0.4579	0.1443
AGE	0.9046	0.2941
SIZE	7.6698	0.8077
ROA	0.0209	0.0770
DEQ	4.5705	4.9222
BANK	0.2474	0.4321
CU	0.2165	0.4124
NBFI	0.2887	0.4537

AGE = age, CSR = corporate social responsibility, FP = financial performance, SIZE = size, ROA = return on assets, DEQ = debt-to-equity ratio, CU = credit union, NBFI = nonbank financial institution, Std. Dev. = standard deviation.

Source: Authors.

as factors that affect MFIs' overall performance (e.g., Gutiérrez-Nieto, Serrano-Cinca, and Molinera [2009], Galema et al. [2012], Thrikawala, Locke, and Reddy [2016]). Each variable is operationalized as a control variable. AGE is a dummy variable that takes the value of 1 if an MFI is mature, 0 otherwise. SIZE, measured as logarithm of total assets, accounts for MFI scale economies. ROA, measured by MFI net income divided by total assets, is an indicator of profitability. DEQ, measured by total liabilities divided by total equity, is a proxy for financial leverage. OWNSIP accounts for the effect of governance and regulatory models on MFI performance. Table 9.2 presents the descriptive statistics of these variables.

9.3 Regression Analysis

The financial performance measures for each MFI are regressed upon the CSR index and control variable to determine the impact of CSR on financial performance. We use ordinary least square (OLS) regression analysis:

$$FP_{it} = \alpha_0 + \alpha_1 CSR_{it} + \alpha_2 AGE_{it} + \alpha_3 SIZE_{it} + \alpha_4 ROA_{it} \qquad (8)$$
$$+ \alpha_5 DEQ_{it} + \alpha_6 OWNSIP_{it} + \varepsilon_{it}$$

where FP is the financial performance of ith MFI in year t, CSR_{it} is the corporate social responsibility index for i^{th} MFI in year t. AGE indicates the operation years of an MFI since its inception. It is a dummy variable that takes the value of 1 if an MFI is mature, and 0 otherwise. SIZE is the size of an MFI, measured as the natural logarithm of total assets; MFI profitability, ROA, is the ratio of net income to total assets; debt-to-equity ratio (DER) is a proxy for an MFI's leverage intensity and is measured by total liabilities divided by total equity; OWNSIP is a dummy variable (equal to 1 if an MFI is a bank and 0 otherwise; equal to 1 if an MFI is a cooperative and 0 otherwise; equal to 1 if an MFI is a nonbank financial institution (NBFI) and 0 otherwise). $\in$ is the error term.

9.4 Regression Results

The OLS estimation results are in Table 9.3. Financial performance as the dependent variable is seen as negative and strongly related to CSR at $p < .01$, suggesting that MFIs' CSR engagement with the community, employees, and environment is not necessarily in harmony with improving financial performance. The finding is in line with the trade-off hypothesis, which suggests that meeting the needs of key stakeholders results in additional costs that reduce financial return and shareholder wealth. The finding confirms that achieving financial sustainability while maintaining improved CSR performance is not easy, especially in the context of commercialization (Abate et al., 2014).

Regarding control variables, the results in Table 9.3 show a positive impact of AGE on financial performance. However, the impact is not statistically significant. The coefficient concerning the relationship between SIZE and financial performance is positive and significant at $p < .001$. This finding confirms the earlier findings (e.g., Cull, Demirgüç-Kunt, and Morduch [2007], Caudill, Gropper, and Hartarska [2009]) and is consistent with the view that economies of scale and scope allow larger MFIs to be more efficient and perform better financially. Larger MFIs may use sophisticated technologies and be better equipped to diversify their products and services, leading to improved financial performance. ROA exhibits a negative and statistically significant relationship with efficiency. DEQ shows a positive and statistically significant relationship with financial performance, which may indicate that MFIs with better financial performance use more debt financing. Concerning the control variables for legal status, credit union (CU) is positively correlated with financial performance. Coefficients for banks, NBFIs, and nongovernment organizations are not statistically significant.

Table 9.3: Ordinary Least Square Estimation Results

Variable	
CSR measure	–.362209*
	(–3.69)
AGE	–.018102
	(0.37)
SIZE	.07547*
	(3.3)
ROA	–1.1666*
	(–6.23)
DEQ	.02333*
	(7.94)
BANK	–.03961
	(–0.81)
CU	.2372*
	(5.5)
NBFI	–.06429
	(–1.51)

AGE = age, CSR = corporate social responsibility, FP = financial performance, SIZE = size, ROA = return on assets, DEQ = debt-to-equity ratio, CU = credit union, NBFI = nonbank financial institution.

Notes: Numbers in parenthesis are t-statistics. * stands for $p < .001$.

Source: Authors.

9.5 Summary and Conclusion

Our study provides an initial contribution to the literature on the relationship between CSR and financial performance in microfinance. Using a sample of 388 MFIs in 2011–2014, we examined whether MFIs' socially responsible strategies improve financial performance. We measured MFIs' financial performance in terms of efficiency by using an innovative DEA model. We created a CSR index of each MFI in our sample by aggregating three social responsibility constituents.

Our results show that integrating the interests of different stakeholders into business models leads to MFIs' poor financial performance. We explain this finding by using the trade-off hypothesis, which predicts that meeting the needs of key stakeholders results in additional costs that can reduce financial return and shareholder wealth. Our study adds value to an emerging research paradigm on socially responsible practices of social enterprises and their impact on financial performance. The findings of this study have several implications for investors, donors, practitioners, and policy makers, and could be useful for investors and donors who adopt social investment criteria to decide on funding.

References

Allet, M. 2014. Why Do Microfinance Institutions Go Green? An Exploratory Study. *Journal of Business Ethics* 122(3): 405–424.

Aribi, Z. A., and T. Arun. 2015. Corporate Social Responsibility and Islamic Financial Institutions (IFIs): Management Perceptions from IFIs in Bahrain. *Journal of Business Ethics* 129(4): 785–794.

Bauchet, J., and J. Morduch. 2010. Selective Knowledge: Reporting Biases in Microfinance Data. *Perspectives on Global Development and Technology* 3(4): 240–269.

Carroll, A. B. 1979. A Three-Dimensional Conceptual Model of Corporate Performance. *Academy of Management Review* 4(4): 497–505.

Caudill, S. B., D. M. Gropper, and V. Hartarska. 2009. Which Microfinance Institutions Are Becoming More Cost Effective with Time? Evidence from a Mixture Model. *Journal of Money, Credit and Banking* 41(4): 651–672.

Cavaco, S., and P. Crifo. 2014. CSR and Financial Performance: Complementarity between Environmental, Social and Business Behaviours. *Applied Economics* 46(27): 3323–3338.

Cull, R., A. Demirgüç-Kunt, and J. Morduch. 2007. Financial Performance and Outreach: A Global Analysis of Leading Microbanks. *Economic Journal* 117(517): F107–F133.

Färe, R. 1991. Measuring Farrell Efficiency for a Firm with Intermediate Inputs. *Academia Economic Papers* 19(2): 329–340.

Galema, R., R. Lensink, and R. Mersland. 2012. Do Powerful CEOs Determine Microfinance Performance? *Journal of Management Studies* 49(4): 718–742.

Gutiérrez-Nieto, B., C. Serrano-Cinca, and M. Molinero. 2007. Microfinance Institutions and Efficiency. *Omega* 35(2): 131–142.

————. 2009. Social Efficiency in Microfinance Institutions. *Journal of the Operational Research Society* 60(1): 104–119.

Kao, C. 2009. Efficiency Decomposition in Network Data Envelopment Analysis: A Relational Model. *European Journal of Operational Research* 192(3): 949–962.

Lanis, R., and G. Richardson. 2012. Corporate Social Responsibility and Tax Aggressiveness: An Empirical Analysis. *Journal of Accounting and Public Policy* 31(1): 86–108.

Servin, R., R. Lensink, and M. Van den Berg. 2012. Ownership and Technical Efficiency of Microfinance Institutions: Empirical Evidence from Latin America. *Journal of Banking & Finance* 36(7): 2136–2144.

Shahriar, A. Z. M., S. Schwarz, and A. Newman. 2015. Profit Orientation of Microfinance Institutions and Provision of Financial Capital to

Business Start-Ups. *International Small Business Journal* 34(4): 532–552.

Taylor, M. 2011. Freedom from Poverty is Not for Free: Rural Development and the Microfinance Crisis in Andhra Pradesh, India. *Journal of Agrarian Change* 11(4): 484–504.

Thrikawala, S., S. Locke, and K. Reddy. 2016. Board Structure-Performance Relationship in Microfinance Institutions (MFIs) in an Emerging Economy. *Corporate Governance: The International Journal of Business in Society* 16(5): 815–830.

Tone, K., and M. Tsutsui. 2009. Network DEA: A Slacks-Based Measure Approach. *European Journal of Operational Research* 197(1): 243–252.

Lightning Source UK Ltd.
Milton Keynes UK
UKHW022207061220
374718UK00007B/205